A Photo History of the Secret Wars

A Photo History of the Secret Wars

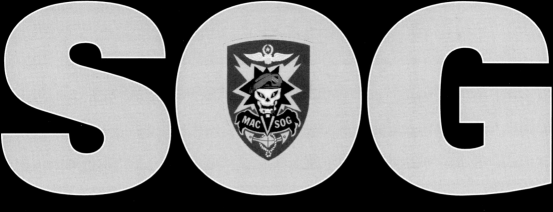

SOG

A Photo History of the Secret Wars

John L. Plaster

Paladin Press • Boulder, Colorado

SOG: *A Photo History of the Secret Wars*
by John L. Plaster

ISBN 10: 1-58160-058-5
ISBN 13: 978-1-58160-058-2
Printed in the United States of America

Published by Paladin Press, a division of
Paladin Enterprises, Inc.
Gunbarrel Tech Center
7077 Winchester Circle
Boulder, Colorado 80301 USA
+1.303.443.7250

Direct inquiries and/or orders to the above address.

Visit our Web site at www.paladin-press.com

Contents

This book is dedicated to all of SOG's Medal of Honor recipients and especially to Robert Howard, the most highly decorated American of this or any previous war. May America always find such courageous spirits when she needs them.

Acknowledgments

This book would not exist but for the generous assistance of hundreds of men and women who understood the need to tell the story of SOG and its remarkable warriors. They include everyone from families of lost SOG men to former Chiefs SOG, from young Green Berets to general officers, from fighter pilots to helicopter doorgunners—their irreplaceable pictures became the stunning mosaic captured in these pages. Each contributor's name is cited beside his photos.

Some people lent considerable time and resources to help this project, particularly the Special Operations Association's archivist, Steve Sherman, who helped identify men and piece together events of 30 years ago. Professor Richard Shultz of the Fletcher School of Law and Diplomacy shared his extensive library of declassified SOG documents. Robert Fisch, weapons curator at the West Point Military Museum, along with Z. Frank Hanner, director of the National Infantry Museum at Ft. Benning, Georgia, and Roxanne Merritt, director of Ft. Bragg's JFK Special Warfare Museum, contributed pictures and valuable information. Author Shelby Stanton provided liberal access to his collection of Special Forces wartime photographs. Veteran Huey pilots Mike Sloniker and Fred Norris went all out to find helicopter photos and aircrew and unit identities. Lee Hess, president of the

"Stray Goose" Blackbird crewmen's association, gathered outstanding pictures from among his MC-130 veterans. Complete photo collections were loaned or even donated by Eldon Bargewell, Dale Boswell, Frank Greco, Mary Ann Harrison, Richard Jalloway, George Gaspard, Eugene McCarley, and Ted Wicorek.

All these photographs and slides were processed by a crew of excellent photo technicians, including Douglas Black, Roger Kennedy, Charles Farrow, and Holly Hatch. The superb maps were designed by graphic artist Joy Benson, while original art flowed from the pen of Tami Odegard.

And, finally, I thank my publisher, former Green Beret Peder Lund, who understood the historical importance of this project and allowed me the time to do it right.

Introduction

Piecing together a photo history of the Studies and Observations Group (SOG) should have been an impossible task. As a top-secret, covert operations unit, SOG had no photo archive, and its ranks included neither public information officers nor staff historians. Press photographers never visited SOG units. But SOG's intelligence-gathering mission required that each recon team and Hatchet Force carry a special-issue Pen EE camera, and—though it was forbidden—empathetic darkroom technicians often slipped SOG men a few "souvenir" photos.

The official intelligence photographs were ordered burned in 1972, but the unclassified personal copies sat for three decades in dusty trunks and old shoe boxes, each SOG veteran having saved a few pictures. Add to these photos those shot by helicopter crews, fighter pilots, and FACs, and we have this book. It is not a novel, yet you'll see it's a true "techno-thriller" containing quite possibly the most spectacular collection of special operations combat photos ever published, a mosaic of amazing images that tell the story of the largest U.S. covert operations unit of the last half of the 20th century.

In a few cases, photographs of important subjects simply did not exist, so I've substituted artist's drawings. I also built a replica of a Nightingale firefight simulator and replicas of our wiretap devices. Otherwise, *everything* you see here is real, photographed in wartime by the very men who performed SOG's amazing missions.

And it is these men, not their hardware, who are the core of this book. I've sought to humanize and make real these phenomenally courageous men, to help readers understand in our image-conscious era that it's what's inside such extraordinary warriors that makes them special. Were a Roy Benavidez or Fred Zabitosky to stand behind you in a supermarket checkout line, you probably wouldn't look twice at him—yet each was an incredible hero. Equally, today's youths need to see that a highly respected Green Beret like David "Babysan" Davidson was not big or tough looking—but he was one of the best.

My purpose, too, is to rebut the oft-repeated media claim that "there are no heroes anymore." SOG operatives displayed the purest kind of selfless courage—not some form of abstract moral or political courage, but *physical* courage in the face of death, terrible injuries, or vanishing forever, an all too real fate for too many SOG men. Day after day, mission after mission, they put on their rucksacks and voluntarily descended into the most dangerous haunts of Southeast Asia, for which they seldom received any recognition and, like other Vietnam veterans, returned to find a nation largely ungrateful.

I hope, too, that readers will better understand the camaraderie that bound SOG men together. Shortly before he was killed in action, posthumous Medal of Honor recipient George "Ken" Sisler explained this comradeship in a letter to his wife, Jane:

Many of us form friendships with people who play our game of cards, share our like of flowers, or attend our church. These kinds of friendships are many, lasting, and wonderful. I find that there is a step above these—it is the feeling you have for a man who puts his life on the line for you. It is a sight to behold to see two men who have fought side-by-side in a hard battle, each knowing the other saved his life. It is reflected in the unspoken word, the boyish and sometimes rough expressions passed between men who have faced such things and won. To me it evokes feelings that aren't often stirred in more casual relationships. I think it is beyond description. How much broader it makes our horizons is immeasurable—the depths of feelings are endless. I shall always prize those feelings, for they are not tarnished in any way. I don't regret one bit being here. I've learned what is important and what isn't.

By sharing the sentiments of great soldiers like Ken Sisler, I have done my best to tell an important story accurately and completely; for any shortcomings, I alone bear responsibility. So that 100 years from now historians can draw upon these dramatic photos to continue to tell SOG's story, I am providing one set of these images to the JFK Special Warfare Center at Ft. Bragg, North Carolina, and a second set to the U.S. Army Center of Military History at Carlisle, Pennsylvania.

As well, a portion of the proceeds of this book is being donated to the Special Operations Association's (SOA's) George C. Morton Scholarship Fund to assist the college education of orphans and children of

U.S. special operations veterans. To send donations or to inquire about joining the SOA, please write Special Operations Association, 5130 E. Charleston Boulevard, Suite 5-583F, Las Vegas, NV 89122. We're always looking for a few more SOG veterans and welcome combat veterans of all wartime covert activities, from World War II to today.

—John Plaster, Major, USAR (Ret.)
U.S. Army Special Forces
January 2000

PART ONE

THE
SECRET
WAR
BEGINS

Chapter One

Colby's Covert War

When CIA Station Chief William Colby arrived in Saigon in 1960, the French had been gone barely five years, the same number of years as had passed since a Geneva Convention had split Indochina into a communist north and noncommunist south. Although fighting officially had ended, Colby soon saw that the war was continuing.

Beginning in 1959, old communist Vietminh fighters who had emigrated to the North after the French-Indochina War started to reappear in South Vietnam's most remote provinces to organize a guerrilla force, the Vietcong (VC), which falsely insisted that it had no connection to Hanoi. The new CIA station chief was neither naive nor inexperienced in the ways of secret wars. Sixteen years earlier, Office of Strategic Services (OSS) Lt. William Colby had parachuted into Nazi-occupied France to lead French resistance fighters against the Germans. A year later he'd parachuted into Norway to demolish Nazi rail lines. Colby could see through Hanoi's subterfuge.

Troubled by reports of North Vietnamese infiltration, the new Kennedy administration immediately approved a CIA proposal to increase its Vietnam programs. National Security Adviser McGeorge Bundy signed National Security Action Memorandum 52 (NSAM-52), which expanded the CIA efforts to detect infiltration and to insinuate a network of CIA operatives in North Vietnam. NSAM-52 also authorized Colby to employ U.S. Army

Special Forces and Navy SEALs to train and advise the operatives for the CIA's covert missions.

THE CIA'S JUNK FLEET

Colby had inherited a small infiltration program begun by his predecessor that used cleverly disguised junks to deliver agents and supplies to the coast of North Vietnam. In February 1961, only weeks after the Kennedy inauguration, a CIA junk landed Colby's first agent, Agent Ares, in North Vietnam, near Cam Pha, some 40 miles south of China. Over the next eight years, Agent Ares would prove the most prolific U.S. operative in the North. But Colby was looking for more than agents.

In Danang, Colby's assistant, Tucker Gougleman, and a SEAL detachment were preparing Vietnamese Sea Commandos to raid North Vietnam's coast. Despite his odd-sounding name, Gougleman was a man to be taken seriously. As a U.S. Marine Raider on Guadalcanal in 1942, Gougleman had been severely wounded, then fought in Korea, but had left the Corps on a medical discharge and established himself as one of the CIA's top paramilitary officers. "He had that unappointed leadership quality," said SEAL Barry Enoch. "It didn't matter what he wore on his shoulder or arm; status-wise, he'd become a leader in any group. I thought he was a Marine, a hardcore Marine, and we loved him. We just absolutely loved him."

Beginning in 1962, Gougleman's SEAL-trained Sea Commandos ran harassment and sabotage raids on the coast of North Vietnam. For these quick across-the-beach attacks, SEAL Gunners Mate Enoch rigged a packboard with four cardboard tubes, each containing a 3.5-inch rocket and an electrical delay mechanism. Using Enoch's rig, a Vietnamese raider could slip ashore, aim the packboard toward a target, and be long gone by the time the rockets fired.

When an 84-foot North Vietnamese Swatow patrol boat captured a CIA junk, Gunners Mate Enoch modified the rest of the boats so they could better defend themselves yet did not display any visible weapons. It wasn't long before one of Enoch's modified CIA junks found itself hailed by a Swatow and ordered to stand to. As the Swatow came alongside, the captain waved and the mate lifted his hand but instead of waving, his fingers found a toggle switch, whose wires ran to six canvas-covered troughs atop the wheelhouse, each holding a 3.5-inch rocket, with the whole of them arranged to hit a pattern the size of a Swatow. Lashed to each mast where a crewman stood was an innocent-looking 55-gallon drum containing a hidden .50-caliber machine gun on a custom, pop-up mount. And below the gunwhale lay the final two crewmen, cradling cocked Swedish K 9mm submachine guns and awaiting their captain's signal.

Just as the Swatow cut its engines, six rockets crashed into her, two crewmen raised their Swedish Ks to riddle the boarding party, and both .50 calibers raked the Swatow's deck. Before they'd finished firing, the captain started a powerful diesel engine, another feature Enoch had hidden in the junk. Then the junk was gone.

Inevitably the North Vietnamese got smart, and Swatows patrolled in pairs, with one covering while the other cautiously approached. Finally, two North Vietnamese Swatows cornered a CIA junk and ripped it in two with gunfire.

COVERT AGENTS AND AIRDROPS

With his junks now too vulnerable for agent landings, Bill Colby switched to airdrops from specially modified C-46s and C-47s and called upon the expertise of U.S. Air Force Col. Harry "Heinie" Aderholt to assist him. At this point, Aderholt, based at Takhli, Thailand, was wrapping up the CIA's top-secret Tibet airlift, in which hundreds of pro-Dalai Lama guerrillas and thousands of tons of supplies had been parachuted into Chinese-occupied Tibet. During the 5-year Tibet airlift not one of Aderholt's unmarked C-130s had been lost.

Colby asked Aderholt to provide instructor pilots to train Vietnamese in infiltration flying and to select routes for penetrating North Vietnam. U.S. Air Force Maj. Larry Ropka, who'd planned the Tibet flights, found that the smartest way into North Vietnam was its mountainous Laotian "backdoor" and laid out routes to exploit hundreds of mountains for terrain masking and electronic confusion.

Meanwhile in Saigon, Colby recruited a flamboyant Vietnamese air force pilot to head a special squadron of unmarked C-47s outfitted with long-range fuel tanks to fly the secret missions. The squadron commander, Nguyen Cao Ky, later would command his country's air force and eventually serve as president of South Vietnam.

LONG-TERM AGENT TEAMS

The small teams Ky and his pilots would parachute into the North were mostly northerners who'd come south in 1954, such as Catholics and tribal minorities who'd fought along-

CIA Saigon Station Chief William Colby in traditional Vietcong black pajamas. (Photo provided by the Colby family)

side the French. But unlike the Vietminh infiltrating the South, U.S. policy forbade Colby's long-term agents from building a resistance, or even having contact with civilians. The teams were neither short-term raiders, who could hit a target and be extracted, nor guerrillas, who blended with the populace from whom they might draw strength, support, and sustenance. The agent teams were operational orphans, totally dependent on airdropped supplies, hiding in the jungle to survive. It was a concept begging for disaster.

The long-term agent teams trained behind the tarp-covered cyclone fences at Camp Long Thanh, a secret CIA training center 25 miles northeast of Saigon where Green Berets and CIA officers taught them fieldcraft, weapons skills, small-unit tactics, demolitions, and survival. Team radio operators studied Morse code, encryption, and secret duress codes to let the CIA know that they'd been captured and were transmitting under enemy control.

The top-secret CIA (and later SOG) base at Camp Long Thanh. Note the covered fences on the inner compound. (Photo provided by Dale Boswell)

Especially important was the team members' specialized parachute training. Unlike conventional paratroops, the agents would jump in inky darkness into mountainous, triple-canopy jungle and then rappel to the ground. To survive such hazardous landings, they wore heavily padded U.S. Forest Service smoke-jumper suits and crash helmets.

By late spring 1961, dozens of new agents were ready to join Ares in North Vietnam. However, the first team to deploy—Team Atlas—never sent a single message, and its insertion aircraft did not return. Eventually Hanoi prosecuted the team's three survivors in a much-publicized show trial, though little heed was paid in the Western press.

Because of this ominous loss, Nguyen Cao Ky personally flew the next mission to drop Team Castor. This mission came off without incident: Team Castor landed safely but soon went off the air. Then CIA handlers realized that Teams Dido and Echo were under enemy control so the teams were played as "doubles." The last team parachuted into North Vietnam in 1961, Team Tarzan, was lost and presumed captured.

Over the next 29 months, the CIA airdropped 22 teams into North Vietnam. Fourteen teams were lost almost as soon as they landed, with 109 men captured or killed. Airdrops in June and July 1963 proved particularly costly, losing eight complete teams, one right after another— Dauphine, Becassine, Bart, Tellus, Midas, Nike, Giant, and Packer— scooped up as quickly as they arrived. The last three teams inserted in

Top: At Camp Long Thanh, agent trainees studied raid tactics on this model of an oil tank farm. (Photo provided by Bill Kendall)

Middle: Bridge demolition was instructed on this tabletop model. (Photo provided by Bill Kendall)

Bottom: Agents who sabotaged light manufacturing facilities used this model for study. (Photo provided by Bill Kendall)

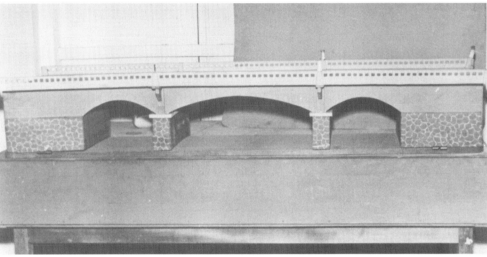

1963—Swan, Bull, and Ruby—also were captured, with a further 21 men lost. Only four teams—Bell, Remus, Easy, and Tourbillon—plus Ares—remained intact by late 1963.

RECONNAISSANCE IN LAOS

While the long-term agent teams roamed North Vietnam, U.S. Green Berets in Nha Trang were training South Vietnamese 1st Observation Group commandos to penetrate the expanding Ho Chi Minh Trail. Led by the sons of Vietnam's most prominent political families, the paracommandos proved more a ceremonial guard beholden to President Diem than kill-or-be-killed operators. The 1st Group mounted 41 recon operations into the Laotian infiltration corridor during 1961 and 1962, but the uninspired officers who led these teams so effectively eluded contact that they avoided finding anything of consequence.

Green Berets of the Okinawa-based 1st Special Forces Group (SFG) trained Mountain Scouts at Dak To in the Central Highlands, but when the illiterate Montagnards walked into Laos they lacked the sophistication to grasp, record, and report what they saw. Likewise, although the Green Berets trained tough Montagnard tribesmen for several Vietnamese-led raider companies, the Montagnards could do no more than their cautious Vietnamese officers allowed.

Amid this intelligence vacuum, North Vietnam was steadily boosting its infiltration rate, while whole shiploads of weapons were arriving on the coast of South Vietnam and the Ho Chi Minh Trail grew and grew. The CIA effort expanded to keep apace, but soon the covert programs had more military special operations advisers than CIA officers. This growing imbalance soon would change the complexion of the secret war.

Above: Initially, Colby's operatives infiltrated North Vietnam aboard CIA junks disguised as communist fishing boats. (Photo provided by U.S. Navy)

Right: North Vietnamese Swatow patrol boat. (Photo provided by DRV)

Above left: Long-term agents of Teams Easy and Bull with their American trainer. The Bull agents were captured immediately upon landing in North Vietnam, while Team Easy members were captured, "doubled," and played back by Hanoi. (Photo provided by Bill Kendall)

Above: An agent team radio operator practices Morse code. After capture, radiomen were the focus of enemy duress because they alone could signal their predicament to Saigon. (Photo provided by Bill Kendall)

Left: Initial recon in Laos was led by South Vietnamese 1st Observation Group Commandos, who accomplished little. Note their French-style fatigues and French wings on helmets. (Photo provided by William Ewald)

Top: An unmarked C-46 makes a practice agent resupply drop. Note the bundle below the cargo door. (Photo provided by Bill Kendall)

Above: Arriving in dark of night, agent teams found resupply bundles like this by the electronic transponder they carried. (Photo provided by Bill Kendall)

Right: Long-term agents were taught "rough terrain" parachuting and wore U.S. Forest Service canvas "smokejumper" suits and caged visor helmets. (Photo provided by U.S. Forest Service)

Left: Colby personally recruited Nguyen Cao Ky (left), the future president of South Vietnam, to fly dangerous agent airdrops over North Vietnam. (Photo provided by U.S. Air Force)

Above right: Col. Harry Aderholt helped Colby plan the North Vietnam airdrops. Colonel Aderholt directed the CIA's Tibet airlift and later would found SOG's "Bright Light" POW rescue program. (Photo provided by U.S. Air Force)

Above: Some CIA raider teams hit their targets by emplacing 3.5-inch rockets fired by time delay. (Photo provided by U.S. Army)

Team	Date	# Pers.	Remarks

CIA AGENT TEAM INSERTIONS IN NORTH VIETNAM (FEBRUARY 1961 – DECEMBER 1963)

Team	Date	# Pers.	Remarks
Ares	Feb. '61	1	Intact, transferred to MACV*-SOG Jan. 64
Atlas	Mar. '61	4	2 killed, 2 captured upon landing
Castor	May '61	4	Ceased radio contact, July 6
Dido	June '61	4	Captured, then played as double agents
Echo	June '61	3	Captured, played as double agents until Aug. '62
Tarzan	Mid-'61	6	Ceased radio contact, June '63
Europa	Feb. '62	5	Ceased radio contact, Jan. '64
Remus	Apr. '62	8	Intact, team transferred to MACV-SOG Jan. '64
Tourbillon	May '62	8	Intact, team transferred to MACV-SOG Jan. '64
Eros	June '62	5	Captured, then played as double agents
Pegasus	Apr. '63	6	Captured soon after landing
Jason	May '63	5	Captured soon after landing
Dauphine	June '63	5	Captured soon after landing
Bell	June '63	7	Intact, team transferred to MACV-SOG Jan. '64
Becassine	June '63	6	Captured soon after landing
Bart	June '63	5	Captured soon after landing
Tellus	June '63	4	Captured soon after landing
Midas	June '63	8	Captured soon after landing
Nike	June '63	6	Captured soon after landing
Giant	July '63	6	Captured soon after landing
Packer	July '63	6	Captured soon after landing
Easy	Aug. '63	8	Intact, team transferred to MACV-SOG Jan. '64
Swan	Sept. '63	6	Captured soon after landing
Bull	Oct. '63	7	Captured soon after landing
Ruby	Dec. '63	8	Captured soon after landing

* Military Assistance Command Vietnam

BETWEEN FEBRUARY 1962 AND DECEMBER 1963, the CIA landed 25 long-term agent teams in North Vietnam, with all but the first, Ares, being inserted by parachute. As the statistics show, Hanoi's Ministry of Security did an incredible job of rolling up the CIA network, seizing some 14 teams almost as quickly as they landed.

Three more teams simply went off the air, while the CIA soon concluded that another three teams—Dido, Echo, and Eros—were double agents under enemy control that the CIA played back as double double agents to feed disinformation to Hanoi.

By the time of SOG's creation, only five CIA agent teams were still intact: Ares, Remus, Tourbillon, Bell, and Easy.

Chapter Two

Switching Back—SOG Is Born

At the very moment that William Colby was beginning his secret war in Southeast Asia, half a world away a CIA-trained force of nearly 2,000 Cuban exiles landed in southern Cuba at the Bay of Pigs to overthrow Fidel Castro. Instead, they were defeated and captured by Castro's army. President Kennedy appointed Gen. Maxwell Taylor to investigate the debacle to learn what had gone wrong.

The Taylor Commission concluded that the Cuba project had escalated beyond a size manageable by the CIA and recommended a worldwide review to learn whether other CIA enterprises had grown beyond purely intelligence operations and, if so, recommended switching them to military control. Therefore, President Kennedy ordered that Colby's covert Vietnam programs be transferred to the military on 1 November 1963. The CIA code-named the transfer Operation Parasol, while the military dubbed it Operation Switchback.

CREATION OF SOG

The November 1963 overthrow of South Vietnamese President Diem delayed Operation Parasol/Switchback; then three weeks later President Kennedy's assassination further postponed it. Although Defense Secretary Robert McNamara approved a plan issued on 15 December 1963 for the new covert unit's first operations, Military Assistance Command Vietnam (MACV) didn't even get around to founding the organization until 24 January 1964—seven days before its first scheduled seaborne raid on North Vietnam.

Commanded by an army colonel, the new unit was called the Special Operations Group (SOG)—then someone realized this made a mockery of security so it was renamed the Studies and Observations Group, with a cover story that SOG existed to study the combat lessons of Vietnam. In actuality, SOG would include elements of all services, including U.S. Army Green Berets, Air Force Air Commandos, and Navy SEALs. Due to its great secrecy and the sensitivity of its missions, SOG would answer directly to the Joint Chiefs of Staff in the Pentagon via a special liaison, the special assistant for counterinsurgency and special activities (SACSA). In Saigon, only Gen. William Westmoreland and four non-SOG officers were even briefed on SOG. With its budget buried in U.S. Navy appropriations, SOG could receive any money it requested— South Vietnamese piastres to pay mercenaries, old French colonial silver for long-term agents in North Vietnam, U.S. greenbacks to bribe enemy officers for POW information, or even British gold sovereigns for SOG pilot survival kits.

CHIEF SOG

SOG's first commander—with the title Chief SOG—was Col. Clyde Russell, a World War II paratrooper who'd come into Special Forces in the 1950s. A veteran of combat parachute jumps in France and Holland with the 82nd Airborne Division's 505th Airborne Infantry Regiment,

Colonel Russell had been secretary of the Infantry School at Ft. Benning, Georgia, and then commanded the Europe-based 10th SFG and the 7th SFG at Ft. Bragg, North Carolina.

But what would SOG be? With Secretary of Defense McNamara impatiently demanding covert attacks on North Vietnam, there was little time for contemplation, so Russell's staff shaped SOG like the old OSS into air and maritime sections, plus a psychological operations (psyops) division.

COUNTERINSURGENCY SUPPORT OFFICE

SOG could not possibly have conducted its covert operations without extraordinary logistical support and the authority to go outside military channels to meet its unique needs. The vehicle for this critical support was the Okinawa-based Counterinsurgency Support Office (CISO), created at the same time as Operation Switchback. CISO would grow to keep pace with SOG's growing needs, eventually operating its own fleet of landing ships (LST) to carry supplies to Vietnam.

The CIA, too, offered SOG logistic support via the agency's Far East support base at Camp Chinen, Okinawa. Such exotic CIA hardware as silenced weapons and wiretap devices were transferred to CISO's Okinawa property books until they were shipped to SOG, and then— poof!—they went off the books.

The need for sterility—concealing the origin of each item so it couldn't be traced back to the United States—created some special challenges for CISO's civilian deputy, Conrad "Ben" Baker. Everything issued to a SOG operative—from weapons and uniforms to rucksacks and rations—had to be untraceable. In the latter case, Baker personally developed SOG's foil-wrapped rations, called "project indigenous rations" (PIRs), a variety of rice-based meals. Contents were described symbolically; for example, a teacup represented powdered tea, and a pepper showed that a packet contained ground red peppers. Not one word of English or any language was used.

A self-taught engineer, Baker also developed SOG's impressive family of knives, which he manufactured clandestinely in Japan. Like the V-42 stiletto issued to the 1st Special Service Force in World War II, Baker's SOG knives—especially the 6-inch recon knife—have become valuable artifacts of America's secret wars, much prized by collectors.

SOG AND THE TONKIN GULF INCIDENT

From its January 1964 founding until the August 1964 air strikes that followed the Tonkin Gulf Incident, SOG was the sole U.S. instrument for military action against North Vietnam, which the Johnson administration preferred to keep as covert as Hanoi's role in the southern fighting. The purpose of SOG's covert raids, a McNamara memo said, was to "make it clear to the leaders of the North that they would suffer serious reprisals for their continuing support of the insurgency in South Vietnam."

At this time, SOG was of such strategic interest that each mission plan had to weave its way among the Defense Department, State Department, and the White House for approval, with each stop liable to change, restrict, or delay SOG's proposal. Ironically, one young foreign service officer who hand-car-

ried the SOG target proposals from the State Department to the White House was Daniel Ellsberg, later famous as an antiwar activist who leaked the Pentagon Papers to the *New York Times*.

Although SOG had inherited five CIA long-term agent teams in North Vietnam, this tiny handful of operatives was preoccupied just trying to avoid the Communist security service. The only other means for McNamara's covert strikes was SOG's five newly arrived high-speed gunboats, which had replaced the obsolete CIA junks. SOG's Norwegian-built Nasty class Patrol Type, Fast (PTF) boats were light, heavily armed, and, at 47 knots, the fastest such boats in the world.

To oversee the Nastys and train the boat crews and Sea Commandos, SOG created Naval Advisory Detachment, Danang, which included Detachment Echo, Seal Team One, plus a few trainers from Boat Support Unit One at Coronado, California, and a handful of U.S. Marine Force Recon advisors.

McNamara's impatience and deniability requirements led to the strangest episode of Vietnam's covert war. Unaccustomed to any motorized boat, the small-statured Vietnamese helmsmen were slow to master the Nasty's tricky high-speed maneuvers. The CIA even brought in a half-dozen former Norwegian Nasty boat captains to help train the Vietnamese, but, still, they weren't ready. SOG's SEALs volunteered to crew the Nastys, but this was unacceptable; no

Col. Clyde Russell, the first "Chief SOG," 1964–65, oversaw SOG's frantic startup and covert role in the Gulf of Tonkin incident. (Photo provided by U.S. Army)

19

American SEALs ever would be allowed north of the 17th Parallel.

But what about the Norwegian boat captains? *They weren't Americans!* It seemed a twisted interpretation of "deniability," but in the rush to get McNamara's raids underway the Norwegian skippers were pressed into service.

On the night of 16 February 1964, the Norwegians attempted to land Sea Commandos to demolish a bridge on Highway One, but they came under fire before any charges had been emplaced and aborted the mission. A few days later, a swimmer demolition was attempted, and it, too, failed, with eight Sea Commandos lost. Finally, after a three-month break for more training and planning, on the night of 12 June the Nasty boats raced 100 miles north of the demilitarized zone (DMZ) to bombard a storage area and barracks, leaving several buildings afire. By July SOG's Nastys and Sea Commandos were raiding with some regularity. Then on 30 July, SOG

Above: SOG headquarters in Saigon, 137 Pasteur Street. (Photo provided by U.S. Army)

Right: SOG's Saigon safehouse, "House Ten," offered comfortable, air-conditioned rooms and its own bar for visiting field operatives between missions. (Photo provided by Bill Kendall)

launched its biggest night raid yet, employing all five Nastys to bombard radar sites on Hon Me and Hon Ngu Islands, so far north they were closer to Haiphong than their base at Danang.

Two days later, North Vietnamese PT boats attacked the U.S. destroyer *Maddox* near Hon Me Island in what the U.S. press called the "Gulf of Tonkin Incident." Although he made no reference to the SOG raids, of which he was well apprized, President Lyndon Johnson warned Hanoi that another high seas attack would have dire consequences, and ordered the destroyer *Turner Joy* to reinforce the *Maddox*.

On the night of 3 August, SOG Nastys pounded a radar at Vinhsan and threw a few shells at an enemy base on the Rhon River. The next night the *Maddox* and *Turner Joy* reported themselves under attack, leading to the first U.S. retaliatory bombing and the Congressional Gulf of Tonkin Resolution. After the second incident, the Johnson administration further tightened controls on SOG, with each raid painstakingly

reviewed by Deputy Defense Secretary Cyrus Vance. And no matter how important their temporary duty, the Norwegians went home, their historic role unrevealed for a quarter century.

Chief SOG Russell prophetically observed, "If we were trying to convince the North Vietnamese that they could not operate from a sanctuary because the South Vietnamese were capable of hitting their beaches and their coastline, we were successful. But there is a limit to how much success you can have in that type of operation."

LEAPING LENA

During that summer of 1964, a senior Special Forces officer found himself pulled into a Saigon meeting with visiting Defense Secretary McNamara. "Out of a clear blue sky I was asked how soon I could launch operations into Laos," he recalled. "I tried to pin them down as to what kind of operations and what the mission would be since nobody had

Although impressive in heavy camouflage for training, South Vietnamese Special Forces did not measure up to the demands of Leaping Lena. Of 40 men parachuted into Laos, only four survived their first—and only—mission. (Photo provided by William Ewald)

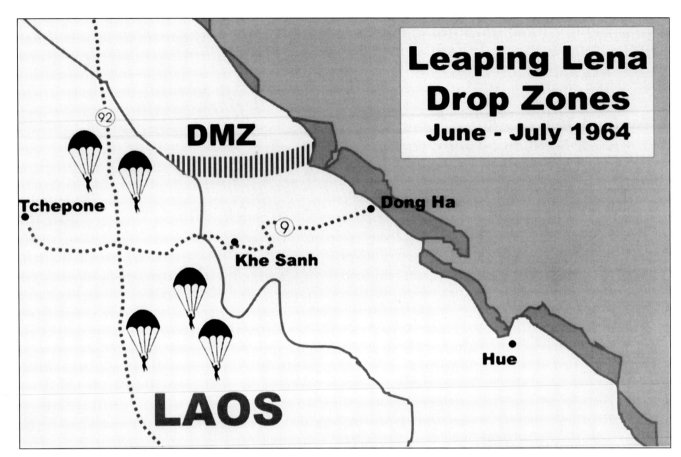

Leaping Lena Drop Zones
June - July 1964

DMZ

(92)

Tchepone

Dong Ha

(9)

Khe Sanh

Hue

LAOS

Top: Leaping Lena drop zones, June–July 1964

Above: U.S. Secretary of Defense Robert McNamara (middle) interceded repeatedly in SOG's early operations. His impatience caused the premature launch of Nasty boat raids and the failure of "Leaping Lena" recon in Laos. (Photo provided by Shelby Stanton)

enlightened me or tied it into our planning that we had already submitted."

McNamara wanted the Army of the Republic of Vietnam (ARVN, pronounced Arvin) to recon Laos, west of Khe Sanh, along the Ho Chi Minh Trail. The Special Forces officer warned that he could not ensure success unless American Green Berets accompanied the teams. McNamara wouldn't allow that and insisted that the recon missions begin immediately. The resulting effort, called Project Leaping Lena, came under the newly arrived 5th Special Forces Group, whose Project Delta was created to train and advise the Vietnamese recon unit.

Five Leaping Lena teams, each with eight Vietnamese, were parachuted into Laos between 24 June and 1 July, with two teams dropped north of Tchepone astride Highway 92 near where a new road came

out of North Vietnam's Mu Ghia Pass, while three teams landed 20 miles southeast of Tchepone. It was a disaster.

Presidential adviser McGeorge Bundy was told, "All of the teams were located by the enemy, and only four survivors returned." The survivors reported encountering company-size elements of the North Vietnamese Army (NVA) and finding the bridges along Route 9 heavily defended by communist Pathet Lao. While fleeing eastward, they'd crossed a network of roads and trails invisible from the air, some carrying truck convoys.

Leaping Lena was finished. Soon afterward, the 5th Special Forces converted Project Delta into the first U.S. long-range recon unit in Vietnam. But what was happening in southern Laos? Now it would be up to SOG to find out.

Top: CISO's Okinawa office staff and secretaries ham it up in sterile uniforms and Chinese weapons. Some of SOG's most clever psyop "gift kit" ideas originated in their fertile minds. (Photo provided by Ben Barker)

Below: SOG's answer to James Bond's "Q," Ben Baker was a self-educated engineer whose CISO office developed everything from electronic booby traps and fighting knives to the sterile "PIR" rations shown here. (Photo provided by Ben Baker)

Above: SOG family of knives designed by Ben Baker included (top) "banana knife" for chopping and three fighting knives. These are (left to right) Naval Commando knife with serrated upper blade, along with recon knives with 7- and 6-inch blades. All were untraceable. (Photo provided by Ben Baker)

Short of boats, SOG's clandestine squadron initially included Korean War-era PT810 (redesignated PTF 1). Obsolete, she was sunk in 1965 as a gunnery target. (Photo provided by W.T. "Red" Cannon)

Top: Although war critics later alleged that there was no Tonkin Gulf clash, the first incident documentably occurred. Shown here, a Communist PT boat runs past USS *Maddox* as a shell bursts to her rear. (Photo provided by U.S. Navy)

Bottom: Flying no colors, PTF 2 (left) and PTF 3 practice high-speed maneuvers. PTF 2 and its sister craft, obsolete Korean War boats, soon were replaced by the 47-knot Norwegian Nastys, like PTF 3. (Photo provided by Batservice Holding A/S)

Illustration: NAD's unofficial emblem featured a mask behind whose eyes lurked the U.S. Navy and Marine Corps, symbolizing that they were behind the Vietnamese raids on North Vietnam.

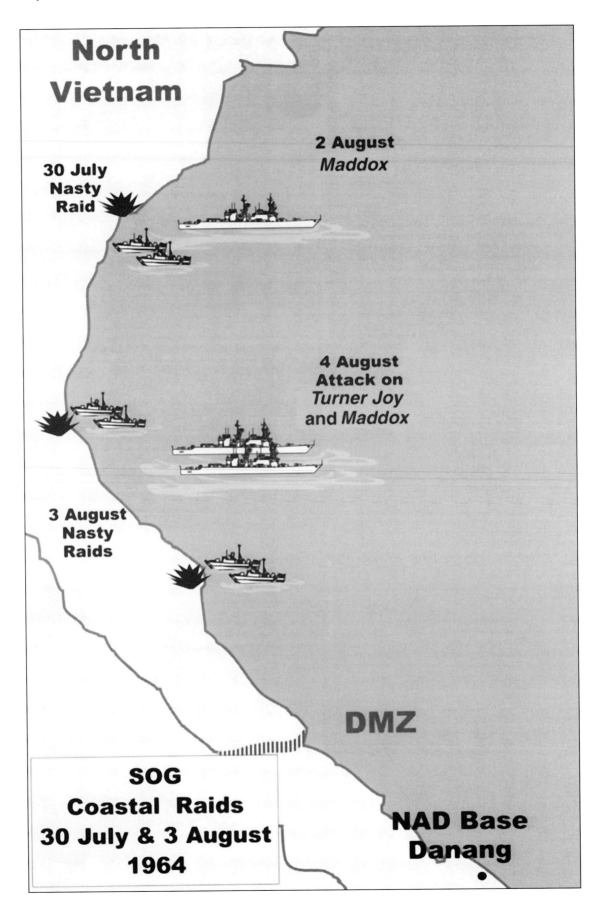

North
Vietnam

30 July Nasty Raid

2 August *Maddox*

4 August Attack on *Turner Joy* **and** *Maddox*

3 August Nasty Raids

DMZ

SOG Coastal Raids 30 July & 3 August 1964

NAD Base Danang

GET OUT OF JAIL FREE CARD

TO PREVENT INQUISITIVE military police (MPs) or curious officers from disrupting clandestine activities, SOG's American operatives were issued the Vietnam War's most unique credential, nicknamed the "Get Out of Jail Free Card." Officially MACV Form 4569, the SOG card authorized its bearer civilian clothes, entry into off-limits areas, concealed weapons, no curfews, and the authority to commandeer soldiers, weapons, and vehicles without need for explanation. Early on, the card was carried by all SOG troopers, but after a few inebriated Green Berets commandeered MP jeeps for barhopping in Saigon, the good deal came to a halt. After that the card was issued to the select few who absolutely needed it.

MILITARY ASSISTANCE COMMAND VIETNAM STUDIES AND OBSERVATION GROUP
APO SAN FRANCISCO 96307

NAME _____

GRADE _____ BLOOD TYPE _____

SERVICE NO. _____

SPECIAL IDENTIFICATION AND PASS
THE PERSON WHO IS IDENTIFIED BY THIS DOCUMENT IS ACTING UNDER THE DIRECT ORDERS OF THE PRESIDENT OF THE UNITED STATES!

DO NOT DETAIN OR QUESTION HIM!
HE IS AUTHORIZED TO WEAR CIVILIAN CLOTHING, CARRY UNUSUAL PERSONAL WEAPONS, TRANSPORT AND POSSESS PROHIBITED ITEMS INCLUDING U. S. CURRENCY, PASS INTO RESTRICTED AREAS AND REQUISITION EQUIPMENT OF ALL TYPES INCLUDING WEAPONS AND VEHICLES.

IF HE IS KILLED OR INJURED, DO NOT REMOVE THIS DOCUMENT FROM HIM. ALERT YOUR COMMANDING OFFICER IMMEDIATELY.
JPC · JAPAN

"Get Out of Jail Free" card.

Along with PTFs 1 and 6, these Nasty boats raided North Vietnam's coast on 30 July and 3 August 1964. The Norwegian-led raids probably instigated the Gulf of Tonkin incident. (Photo provided by W.T. "Red" Cannon)

SOG'S AMAZING NASTY BOATS

WILLIAM COLBY HAD IDENTIFIED THE NEED for high-speed foreign gunboats for covert operations in Southeast Asia when he headed these operations. Due to its great speed and deniability, the Norwegian Tjeld class PT boat was selected, with the contractor, Batservice A/S, delivering the first of 14 boats to the United States in December 1962. SOG received five boats in early 1964.

The fastest craft of their type in the world, the 88-footers were called Nasty class and understandably designated Patrol Type, Fast (PTFs). Propelled by two powerful 6,200-horsepower, 36-cylinder, British Deltic Napier turbo-diesel engines, the plywood-hulled Nastys skimmed the water at 47 knots, while rattling away with one 40mm and two 20mm cannons plus a .50-caliber machine gun. Some boats even added an 81mm mortar. The Norwegian torpedo tubes had been removed to lighten the Nastys and allow space for its considerable other armaments. Given this combination of speed and firepower, a Nasty could outrun North Vietnam's sluggish, Chinese-supplied Swatows or outshoot Hanoi's 45-knot, Soviet P-4 PT boats.

With a cruising range of 860 nautical miles, the Danang-based boats could raid the entire coast of North Vietnam, all the way up to southern China. To replace lost Nastys and expand SOG's flotilla, six more were built from 1967 to 1968, on license by John Trumpy & Sons of Annapolis, Maryland, and finally an additional four by the Stewart Seacraft Division of Teledyne in Berwick, Louisiana.

Despite efforts to conceal the location and purpose of SOG's top-secret raiding boats, the 1969–1970 edition of *Jane's Fighting Ships* listed the Nastys and observed, "These craft are used on clandestine missions in Southeast Asia."

Chapter Three

Shining Brass

W   With the arrival of U.S. combat troops in 1965, there grew a parallel need for detailed, reliable intelligence about enemy activities beyond the borders of South Vietnam. Thus, on 7 March 1965, one day before the first U.S. Marine Corps ground units waded ashore at Danang, SOG was assigned the responsibility for cross-border intelligence gathering.

Inside SOG, this new strategic reconnaissance project was code-named Shining Brass, under which small teams of six or eight indigenous soldiers led by U.S. Green Berets would infiltrate Laos to unravel the mysteries of the Ho Chi Minh Trail.

Overseeing SOG would be a new chief, a truly legendary Special Forces officer, Col. Donald "Headhunter" Blackburn, famous as a Philippine guerrilla leader in World War II. When the Japanese overran the Philippines in 1942, 25-year-old Capt. Don Blackburn refused to surrender, evading deep into the jungle, where he recruited and trained a force of Igarote tribesmen—former headhunters who soon were nicknamed "Blackburn's Headhunters." By the time Douglas McArthur returned in 1944, Blackburn commanded 20,000 guerrillas and wore the eagles of a full colonel—the youngest one in the U.S. Army. Blackburn's World War II exploits were lionized in a 1955 book, *Blackburn's Headhunters*, which Hollywood later turned into a motion picture.

RECON IN LAOS

Colonel Blackburn could think of but one Special Forces officer to head Project Shining Brass, the stout-shouldered Col. Arthur D. "Bull" Simons. "He was all business," recalls Colonel Blackburn. "He wasn't one who showed much frivolity in anything. A real disciplinarian, but he showed good judgment and common sense." During World War II, Bull Simons' 6th Ranger battalion was the eyes and ears of the 11th Airborne Division and led the way ashore at Leyte. Simons spent the Korean War as an instructor at the Ranger Training Center, where he taught hand-to-hand combat and close-quarters shooting.

Providing the men for Shining Brass was the 1st SFG on Okinawa, whose Green Beret recon volunteers began intense training that summer of 1965 in Okinawa's Northern Training Area. By late summer, 16 volunteers were left, exactly the

number required to man five U.S.-led recon teams, with one man to spare. Arriving in Vietnam, they were mated with their native teammates. At the start, SOG's indigenous troops were all Nungs, who'd emigrated from southern China, but as SOG grew and casualties mounted, indigenous ranks would include Vietnamese civilians, Montagnard hill tribesmen, and even former NVA soldiers.

As quickly as President Johnson approved Shining Brass, the U.S. ambassador to Laos added his own rules of engagement, limiting Blackburn's recon area to just two "boxes" 6 miles deep and 12 miles long. Combined, they covered only 24 miles of the 200-mile Laotian border.

To support its cross-border activities, Shining Brass needed a forward operating base (FOB) near the Laotian frontier, where recon teams would live and helicopters could refuel and rearm. Colonel Simons decided to put the FOB at the Kham Duc Special Forces Camp, 60 miles southwest of Danang, an isolated, lonely outpost unvisited by nosy reporters. Although this made for good security, chronically bad weather and poor living conditions left much to desire. "It was miserable," recalls a Special Forces non-commissioned officer (NCO) who served there.

To direct the SOG missions launched from Kham Duc, Bull Simons recruited one of the most remarkable officers in Special Forces, a Finnish-American captain, Larry Thorne.

ONE-ZERO

By early fall of 1965, SOG's first five U.S.-led recon teams (RTs)—named for the states Iowa, Alaska, Idaho, Kansas, and Dakota—were at

Chief SOG, 1956–66, Col. Don Blackburn displays the elephant tusk presented to him by the recon man who killed one to prove that the NVA were using them as beasts of burden. (See story on p. 52.) (Photo provided by John Plaster)

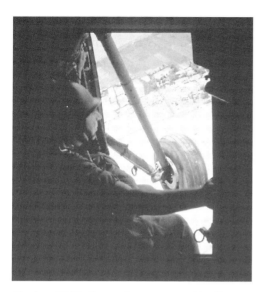

Heading SOG's Shining Brass recon on Ho Chi Minh Trail, Col. Arthur "Bull" Simons prepares for a practice parachute jump from a SOG H-34 "Kingbee." (Photo provided by the George K. Sisler family)

Kham Duc finishing training under the guidance of their Green Beret team leaders, whose command position was code-numbered "One-Zero."

The One-Zero recon team leader became SOG's most prestigious title. Any man appointed a One-Zero had proven his judgment under life-and-death stress, displayed personal bravery, and acquired hazardously gained tactical expertise. Each One-Zero recruited and trained his own indigenous soldiers, chose however he thought best to arm and equip them, and possessed amazing latitude in planning operations. Throughout SOG, One-Zeros would be held in a respect that verged on awe, because once on the ground, this was the lone commander who must outwit everything the enemy could throw at his team—from trackers and ambushers to pursuers by the hundreds or even thousands.

The One-Zero's other two Green Berets also received code numbers, the assistant team leader becoming the "One-One," and the radio operator the team "One-Two."

One-Zero for SOG's first cross-border operation was M. Sgt. Charles "Slats" Petry, whose team, RT Iowa, included seven Nungs, one ARVN lieutenant, and a One-One, Sfc. Willie Card. For deniability, RT Iowa was "sterile"—they wore no rank or unit insignia, and even their uniforms and rucksacks were untraceably Asian made. For weapons, they carried Carl Gustav Model 1945 9mm submachine guns—Swedish Ks—and Belgian-made Browning 9mm pistols. If captured, the men were to claim that they'd stumbled into Laos while looking for a missing C-123 and had no idea they'd crossed the border.

Petry and RT Iowa were briefed extensively. Although Hanoi denied having a single soldier in Laos, by October 1965 its security, engineer, and logistics troops numbered at least 30,000, plus an additional 4,500 men passing through each month en route to South Vietnam. About 200 truckloads of supplies rolled down the Trail monthly, and by late 1965, the U.S. Air Force already knew the enemy had spun its 900-mile road system the length of Laos to Vietnam's Central Highlands.

THE FIRST MISSION

RT Iowa's objective was designated Target D-1, about 20 miles northwest of Kham Duc, where Laotian Highway 165 almost reached the South Vietnamese border. U.S. intelligence believed the NVA were infiltrating troops and carrying supplies through D-1 for attacks on Danang and Chu Lai. Far beyond the range of any U.S. artillery, if Petry and his men got into trouble they'd depend upon Thai-based F-105 fighter-bombers for fire support.

On Monday, 18 October, while

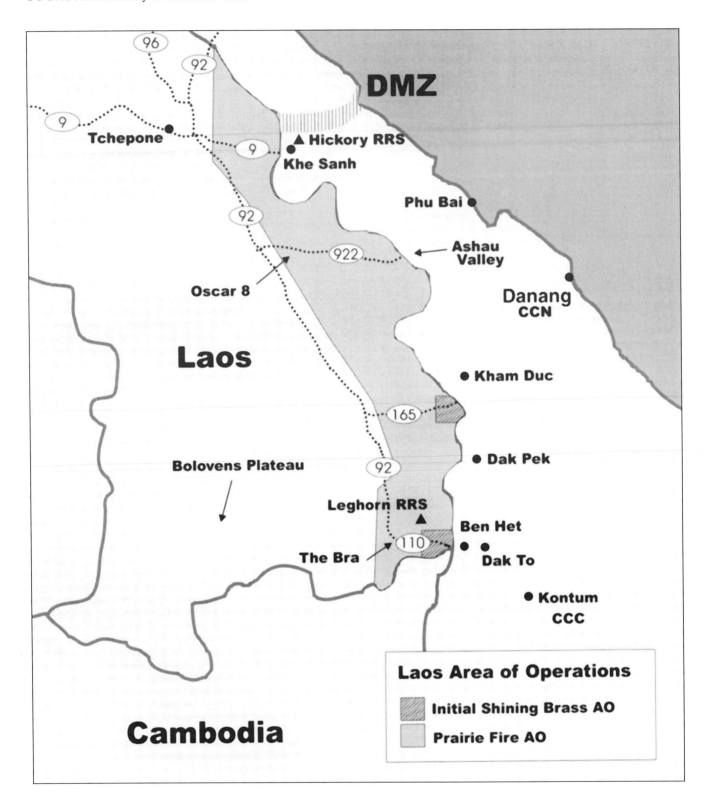

the 1st Air Cavalry Division fought the war's first major U.S. engagement in the Ia Drang Valley, RT Iowa's men stood beside the airstrip at Kham Duc, opened their rucksacks, and emptied their pockets for a final inspection to ensure they carried nothing attributable to the United States. The two Americans turned in their dogtags, military ID cards, and Geneva Convention cards and wallets. If their bodies were put on display, there was no way to prove they were Americans.

They planned to land at last light so it would be dark before the NVA could send a reaction force or trackers after them, giving Petry's men at least a full night's head start. At 6:00 P.M. Captain Thorne wished Petry good luck and waved RT Iowa to three unmarked H-34 "Kingbee" helicopters, which cranked engines and then lifted away. RT Iowa rode the first bird, while Captain Thorne rode aboard the second of three Kingbees. Over Laos the weather proved especially hazardous, and they began taking .50-caliber machine gun fire, but the Kingbees took no hits.

Soon they met the forward air controller (FAC), a tiny O-1 spotter plane flown by U.S. Air Force Maj. Harley Pyles, with a SOG air liaison officer, U.S. Marine Corps Capt. Winfield Sisson, in the backseat. Minutes later, the H-34s went in a downward spiral and then roared away, and it was done: SOG's first American-led team had landed in Laos. In case Petry's team ran into trouble, Captain Thorne kept his Kingbee overhead, sending the other helicopters back to Kham Duc. Soon, Petry radioed an "OK," and then Thorne radioed Kham Duc that he, too, was headed back.

The Finnish-American's H-34 did not return, and Larry Thorne was never

seen again. Then the FAC's O-1 Bird Dog lifted off for Danang airbase with U.S. Air Force Major Pyles and U.S. Marine Corps Captain Sisson aboard. They, too, disappeared. In its first day, Shining Brass had generated three people missing in action (MIA).

Meanwhile, beneath heavy overcast and drizzle, RT Iowa found Target D-1 crawling with NVA, but the enemy was preoccupied with his own labors and at first Petry had an easy go of it.

On the third day, Petry heard truck engines so he maneuvered RT Iowa to investigate—and they bumped head-on into an NVA patrol. In the quick exchange of fire RT Iowa's Nung point man collapsed, mortally wounded, and the chase was on. The North Vietnamese fanned out, searching high and low for them.

Two days later the weather broke, and RT Iowa struck back with 37 sorties of F-105 fighter-bombers before the Kingbees lifted them out. Then Petry went back with a FAC and called in an additional 51 sorties on targets he'd discovered, touching off "numerous" secondary explosions.

MORE MISSIONS

SOG's second Shining Brass operation proved as hazardous and productive as the first one.

Inserted on 2 November 1965 about 10 miles south from the first operation, RT Alaska searched for a hidden highway terminus just inside Laos. Led by M. Sgt. Dick Warren, One-Zero, with Sfc. David Kauhaahaa as his assistant, or One-One, and Sfc. Wilbur "Doc" Donaldson as One-Two packing the radio, RT Alaska found pretty much what the Saigon intelligence people had expected—a network of 5-foot-wide bicycle and foot trails coming in

Patches of CCN, CCC, and CCS.

Top: When SOG's original recon men began rotating out, Chief SOG Blackburn phoned Mrs. Billy Alexander at the Department of the Army personnel office to obtain top-quality Green Beret replacements. She enthusiastically supported Special Forces. (Photo provided by Steve Sherman)

Above: U.S. Ambassador to Laos William Sullivan often impeded or limited SOG operations. (Photo provided by Richard Shultz)

from nearby Laotian Highway 165, and patrols—lots of patrols—sweeping and searching for them.

For three days, One-Zero Warren managed to bypass or hide from the enemy, but by the fourth day there were so many enemy that contact was inevitable. It came in a fast exchange of fire in which Alaska bettered the NVA, hitting several without any recon men being hit—then it was a footchase.

The gunfire drew dozens of NVA determined to run Warren's men into the ground. When they paused on a hilltop for "Doc" Donaldson to radio a FAC, the North Vietnamese streamed up and spread out around them, trapping them in head-high elephant grass. The enemy hesitated to come into the grass, so they set it afire to push RT Alaska into the open.

Then a set of F-105s arrived and turned loose 20mm Vulcan cannons, but the NVA stood their ground. Without warning, a lone Kingbee roared right over the shooting NVA, and in 30 seconds RT Alaska was up and gone, with not one man wounded.

One-Zero Warren went back with the FAC to direct 82 fighter-bomber sorties against targets RT Alaska had located, destroying a bridge and 36 buildings. By early December, RTs Kansas and Idaho, too, had run missions out of Kham Duc, and Shining Brass chief Bull Simons decided it was time to shift southward to the other "box" the ambassador had approved.

Relocating to the airstrip at Dak To in Vietnam's Central Highlands, the SOG men began exploring areas along Highway 110 in far southern Laos. NVA soldiers were here in considerable strength, they found, and didn't appreciate SOG's intrusions into their heretofore sanctuaries.

RT Kansas was hit so forcefully

that the team split, and two Nungs disappeared. During the second operation, RT Idaho suffered the first U.S. recon casualty when one Green Beret was slightly wounded. But the teams were producing results.

After each mission, the recon men were flown to SOG's Saigon headquarters to debrief. It was during these Saigon debriefs that at last U.S. intelligence began to unravel the secrets of the Ho Chi Minh Trail.

By the end of 1965, there had been eight Shining Brass penetrations of Laos, uncovering major North Vietnamese base camps, roads, and supply dumps. The cost? Two Nungs were missing, two more dead, several Nungs wounded, an H-34 Kingbee lost with its Vietnamese crew, one USAF O-1 Bird Dog missing with two U.S. aviators, and SOG's first Special Forces MIA, Capt. Larry Thorne.

Having proven the value of its Shining Brass reconnaissance, Chief SOG Blackburn persuaded the ambassador in Laos to open the entire 200-mile frontier to the SOG recon teams but limited penetrations to 12 miles.

Meanwhile Blackburn found that his first generation of SOG recon volunteers were beginning to rotate to Okinawa and the States. Desperate to replace them with pick-of-the-litter Green Berets, Colonel Blackburn phoned the woman at the Pentagon who oversaw Special Forces overseas assignments, Mrs. Billy Alexander, and set up his own replacement pipeline. Thanks to Mrs. Alexander's patriotic and unacknowledged support, throughout the war more than a few of the "cream" of the Green Berets reached SOG's ranks, ensuring a qualitative edge for these most dangerous operations.

LOST LEGEND: LARRY THORNE

SOG'S FIRST MISSING IN ACTION (MIA) in Laos, Larry Thorne, was lost on its initial Shining Brass cross-border operation and is missed to this day. To every man who ever worked with him, Capt. Larry Thorne was one of the most remarkable officers in Special Forces. Before Americanization, the legendary Finnish-American's name was Lauri Torni, and it took only a few heavily accented words and one look at his lean, leathery face to see his Scandinavian roots. An unabashed smoker and drinker who disciplined himself into iron-hard physical condition, Thorne took delight in running into the ground soldiers half his age and displayed an infectious zest for life as a scuba diver, skydiver, boxer, skier, and first-class mountain climber.

Thorne had first seen combat in 1940, when the Russians invaded his tiny Finnish homeland. At the hands of nimble Finnish ski troops who hit without warning and disappeared into the snowy landscape, the Soviets suffered astronomical casualties. Moscow forced a peace on the Finns, but a year later, when Germany invaded Russia, the Finns went back to war to recapture territory wrested away by Stalin. Thorne spent four years leading special reconnaissance and raiding parties behind Russian lines, inserting by parachute or boat or on skis. By 1945, Thorne's expansive chest displayed every award his country could bestow, including three wound medals and Finland's highest decora-

MOMENTOUS DAY—18 OCTOBER 1965. RT Iowa One, Zero Charles "Slats" Petry on Kham Duc airfield, for the launch of SOG's first cross-border recon. Capt. Larry Thorne (left), who would disappear by nightfall, walks with Maj. Earl Emmons and is watched by Kingbee pilot "Cowboy" (right). (Photo provided by Ray Call)

Larry Thorne began his military career as Lauri Torni, a Finnish commando whose exploits behind Russian lines resulted in the award of the Mannerheim Cross, Finland's highest honor. (Photo provided by the Lindholm-Ventola family)

tion, the Mannerheim Cross, awarded to him for an amazing convoy ambush that cost the Russians 300 dead with not one of Thorne's men lost. Not only had the Germans awarded Thorne an Iron Cross, but selected him for advanced special operations training at an SS school. After Finland's surrender, the Soviet-appointed occupation government twice arrested Thorne as an "enemy of the people," but he escaped and made his way to the West.

Aware of Thorne's impressive wartime record, former OSS chief "Wild Bill" Donovan personally interceded to get him U.S. residency and permission to enlist in the U.S. Army. Soon Thorne was commissioned a second lieutenant at Ft. Bragg and then sent to Europe with the 10th SFG.

Maj. Robert Rheault, the 10th SFG's S-3 operations officer, found Thorne "the finest soldier I've ever known." He tapped his Finnish friend's vast winter expertise to replace the U.S. Army's outdated skis and ski doctrine. "We brought modern skiing into the United States Army despite the United States Army," Rheault recalls.

It was Rheault who dispatched Thorne and the 10th SFG's Ski Committee to Iran's highest glacier in 1963 to recover bodies from a crashed U.S. military transport. A European mountain rescue unit already had failed to reach the Zagros Mountains' most formidable slope. Thorne and his men did the job so quickly that it seemed easy.

By 1965, Rheault was in Vietnam as the 5th SFG's executive officer and tried to give the 46-year-old Finn a desk job. "You've done enough fighting," Rheault said. "You've got so much skill; we need you to train these young guys." But the next thing Rheault knew, Thorne was back in the thick of it, as Bull Simons' Shining Brass launch officer at Kham Duc.

Unwilling to stay safely behind at Kham Duc, Thorne overflew the first Laos insertion aboard a Kingbee helicopter and then stayed above RT Iowa until they radioed they were safe. Then Thorne radioed that he, too, was headed back. He was never seen again.

SOG aircraft overflew the valley for 30 days with negative results. Two years later a SOG team located the crash site and recovered the dead helicopter crewmen, but the Finn's body was not in the wreckage. After Thorne's status was switched from missing to likely dead, his stateside friends filled Ft. Bragg's JFK Center Chapel for a memorial service, prominent among them his fellow Finnish-American Green Berets. After the eulogy and a poetry reading, the service closed with a delicate, emotional rendition of Sibelius' "Finlandia," chords that would touch the soul of a Finnish warrior like Thorne, no matter where he was.

Left: Thorne in 1941 in a Waffen-SS uniform. Desperate for help in fighting the Russians, Finland sent 650 men to Germany for advanced training, not realizing that these honorable soldiers could later be depicted as Nazis. (Photo provided by H.A. Gill III)

Below: A winter operations expert, Thorne led a 1963 Special Forces mission to recover bodies from an aircraft crash high on an Iranian glacier. (Photo provided by Robert Rheault)

Above: SOG's first recon patch symbolized the dual missions of first finding intelligence and then, if the situation allowed, striking the enemy a mighty blow. (Photo provided by Jason Woodworth)

Top right: Chinese Nung Recon Team. Note their "eyeball" recon patches. (Photo provided by Mecky Schuler)

Bottom: Kham Duc, the remote launch site for SOG's first cross-border recons into Laos. (Photo provided by U.S. Air Force)

Left: ALL SMILES. RT Alaska is all smiles after being snatched to safety by SOG H-34 during the second Shining Brass mission. One-Zero Dick Warren (left), One-One David Kauhaahaa (behind Warren), and One-Two Wilbur "Doc" Donaldson had been surrounded by NVA. (Photo provided by Charlie Norton)

Top: Displaying the High Morale of SOG recon. Leonard Tilley poses outside the RT Iowa team room he shared with One-Zero Jerry Wareing and Danny Jenkins, one of the few SEALs ever to run recon in SOG. (Photo provided by Leonard Tilley)

Bottom: Leonard Tilley, RT Iowa, in a Montagnard Village. Recon men recruited their own indigenous soldiers, whether they were Nungs, 'Yards, or Vietnamese. (Photo provided by Leonard Tilley)

Far left inset: Tension showing in their faces, Sfc. David Kauhaahaa (in doorway) and Sfc. Jason Woodworth (left) aboard Kingbee, ready for Laos insertion, February 1966. (Photo provided by Jason Woodworth)

Far left: For purposes of deniability, SOG teams initially carried untraceable Swedish K submachine guns. (Photo provided by Leonard Tilley)

PART TWO

THE HO CHI MINH TRAIL

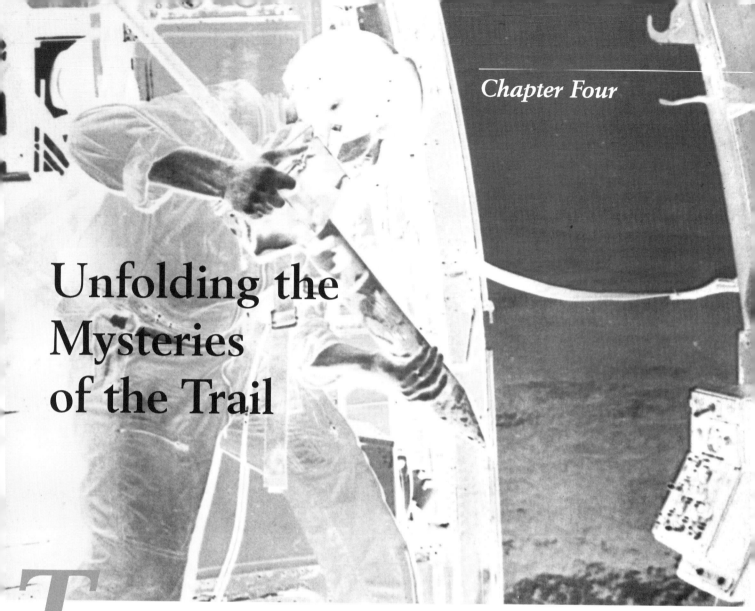

Chapter Four

Unfolding the Mysteries of the Trail

The North Vietnamese didn't use the term "Ho Chi Minh Trail," preferring to call their mysterious Laotian infiltration network the Truong Son Route because it wound through a mountain chain of the same name. The Trail was hidden in a jungled, misty area the size of Massachusetts, where SOG RTs discovered an entire infrastructure of units, installations, services, and equipment to infiltrate and sustain a half-million-man North Vietnamese field army, with everything from supply depots and hospitals to barracks and classrooms. At its height, the Ho Chi Minh Trail nightly carried 10,000 heavily camouflaged trucks along 2,000 miles of hidden roads watched over by some 10,000 antiaircraft guns, while 20,000 to 30,000 support soldiers serviced the network, defended by another 40,000 to 60,000 security troops.

SHADOWY ORIGINS

Although its existence had been scarcely mentioned until 1966, the Trail by then was some seven years old. It had been created by the April 1959 15th plenum of the North Vietnamese Communist Party Central Committee, which had voted in secret session to return covertly to South Vietnam thousands of communist veterans of the French-Indochina War. These former Vietminh would join cadres who'd remained in South Vietnam to execute a

Ho Chi Minh Trail architect and commander, NVA General Vo Bam, photographed on his 80th birthday in 1995. (Photo provided by Edward Emering)

Minh Trail commander, Brig. Gen. Vo Bam, cautioned, "This route must be kept absolutely secret."

The first Communists headed south three months later in August 1959, wearing untraceable peasant garb, armed with untraceable French-made weapons. By early 1961, the 559th Group had delivered 26 parties of infiltrators numbering some 4,500 cadre members into South Vietnam.

THE *BINH TRAM* SYSTEM

Essential to the Ho Chi Minh Trail was a network of logistical sub-headquarters called *binh trams*, which translate literally to "communication-liaison sites." Commanded by a full colonel, each *binh tram* was a specially tailored regiment assigned a specific length of road—usually 15 to 20 miles—to defend it from ground and air attack, quickly repair it when damaged by weather or bombing, and keep the trucks rolling and supplies moving. *Binh tram* personnel also built and maintained temporary shelters for troops passing through and base camps to house NVA units when they rested in Laos after fighting in South Vietnam.

conquest intended from inception to be deniable as an operation originating in the North. If the North's role was deniable, Hanoi believed, it would undercut the moral case for U.S. intervention.

To infiltrate on so vast a scale, the Central Committee created a special army unit, the 559th Support Group—the numbers commemorating its May 1959 founding—which, in tandem with North Vietnam's Trinh Sat secret intelligence service, would train and move people and supplies southward and operate the Ho Chi Minh Trail. The Ho Chi

Most *binh trams* included a 500-man infantry battalion to defend that length of road from SOG recon teams and Hatchet Forces; an antiair-

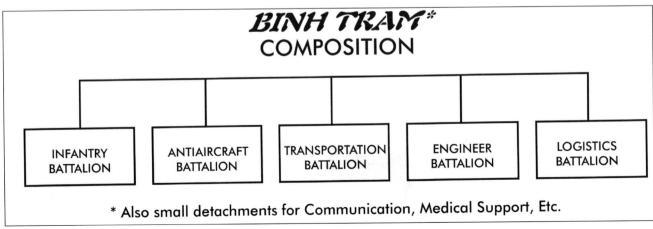

craft artillery battalion to engage attacking U.S. fighters or SOG helicopters; a transportation battalion whose trucks moved supplies from one *binh tram* to the next; an engineer battalion to repair road damage; and a logistics battalion to unload trucks, maintain stockpiles of supplies and ammunition, and manage logistical movement toward South Vietnam. U.S. intelligence estimated that 12 to 15 *binh trams* operated the Trail, with each one typically overseeing a major east-west road that led to the border of South Vietnam.

BASE CAMPS AND BASE AREAS

In a sense, each *binh tram* commander was a motel manager—a new flock of travelers arrived daily needing overnight accommodations and meals. Thus each *binh tram* included a number of "way stations" where NVA soldiers could rest overnight on their way to South Vietnam. In addition to *binh trams*, the other sizable enemy presence in Laos was the many base camps inhabited by NVA combat units resting after fighting in South Vietnam. Safely beyond the reach of U.S. artillery or ground attack, NVA regiments and divisions laid low in Laos for months at a time to retrain and receive replacements and then would recross into South Vietnam only at the start of a new offensive. A major SOG intelligence mission was to locate and monitor these unit base camps and then track their troops as they infiltrated back into South Vietnam.

The NVA displayed great care in concealing its bivouacs hewn from dense mountain forests. For SOG recon men it was always startling to step from dense jungle into a clearing beneath a ceiling of treetops—almost a domed stadium—and find hundreds

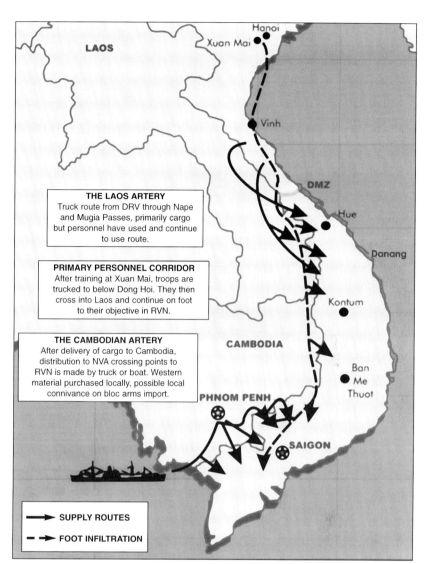

THE LAOS ARTERY
Truck route from DRV through Nape and Mugia Passes, primarily cargo but personnel have used and continue to use route.

PRIMARY PERSONNEL CORRIDOR
After training at Xuan Mai, troops are trucked to below Dong Hoi. They then cross into Laos and continue on foot to their objective in RVN.

THE CAMBODIAN ARTERY
After delivery of cargo to Cambodia, distribution to NVA crossing points to RVN is made by truck or boat. Western material purchased locally, possible local connivance on bloc arms import.

→ SUPPLY ROUTES

- -► FOOT INFILTRATION

of NVA inhabitants. NVA division and regiment headquarters were very carefully positioned for concealment and defense, with some located in immense limestone caves that pockmarked central Laos.

Because of U.S. B-52 strikes, the NVA had widely dispersed its units. For instance, a 2,000-man NVA regiment might be spread across a 5-mile-long valley, with a company dug in on each hilltop. This helps explain why some SOG teams just vanished—unwittingly landing amid such an overlapping concentration of NVA forces. No matter which way a team went, every half-mile it could bump

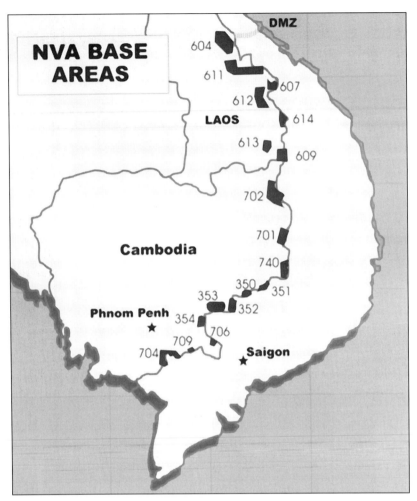

SOG intelligence was assembled and collated into "base area" concentrations in Laos and Cambodia.

roads were functional and simple, but most impressive was the meticulous camouflage that made highways all but invisible from the air. Instead of just bulldozing trees as most armies would have done, NVA engineers wound the roads round and round to retain as many trees as possible. And where overhead gaps did appear, they had soldiers climb trees to tie adjacent branches together or construct bamboo trellises on which they would place fresh-cut greenery. In some places the NVA went so far as to transplant whole trees. They were especially careful to conceal side road turnoffs to keep keen-eyed U.S. Air Force FACs from following them to base camps, truck parks, and cache sites. Because of this astounding camouflage, had it not been for B-52 strikes, many roads would never have been visible from the air. Meanwhile, new roads often went undiscovered until SOG RTs crossed them.

The North Vietnamese took pride in their roads and paths, laying them out as flat as though aligned with a mason's level. When a road was in active use, not a twig nor a leaf was to be found on its hard surface, so closely did NVA maintenance personnel monitor its condition. The same was true of footpaths. And where an NVA trail climbed a hill, there were dugout steps and bamboo handrails so well made that they were marvels of handicraft.

TRUCKS AND CONVOYS

To visualize the Ho Chi Minh Trail highway network, one must imagine it as a circulatory system. Its heart was near Vinh, North Vietnam, from which flowed major arteries through three mountain passes into Laos and then southward parallel to South Vietnam's border, safely

head-on into enemy platoons or companies—even 500-man battalions.

As SOG analysts debriefed returning teams and plotted NVA troop concentrations, these reports eventually began to indicate areas where the enemy was almost always found in strength. These consistent concentrations became "base areas," and it was here that most cross-border B-52 strikes were targeted.

CONSTRUCTING AND HIDING THE ROADS

From the French-Indochina War, the North Vietnamese had acquired extensive experience at building hidden jungle roads from China that had supported that war's great Vietminh victory at Dien Bien Phu. Enemy

beyond U.S. artillery range. Through these arteries truck convoys flowed southward and then eastward along major roads that formed infiltration corridors toward the South Vietnamese frontier. As the roads neared the border, they splintered into a maze of high-speed bicycle tracks and trails that, like capillaries, carried supplies and troops invisibly to the surface, to the battlefields of South Vietnam.

Just before dark each night the NVA would post sentries every 200 or 300 yards along a road. Once it was dark and no aircraft engines could be heard, the sentries relayed signal shots to announce that the road was clear. Then trucks that looked like leaf piles appeared from nowhere and began rolling as convoys. To disappear, they had only to pull under overhanging jungle cover; along the most frequently bombed sections of road, the NVA dug protective shelters into hillsides. On overcast nights when there was little chance of U.S. air attacks, the NVA might run 100 trucks in a convoy; on clear nights they broke them up into smaller convoys. These convoys usually made one trip each night, about 20 miles from one way station to the next and then back. Drivers drove the same route each night, so they could drive with blackout lights or no lights at all. The most experienced drivers led their convoys. The daily truck convoys ended just before dawn each morning, with thousands of NVA trucks leaving the Laotian highways to spend the day hidden in truck parks containing anywhere from five to 25 trucks.

Since the priority truck cargo was ammunition, NVA soldiers heading south usually traveled by foot. To further reduce its overtaxed logistics pipeline, Hanoi required southward-

SOG recon men found the Trail a marvel of ingenuity and handicraft in which enemy engineers took pride. (Photo provided by Shelby Stanton)

bound troops to be self-sustaining, which meant that they carried several weeks of provisions when they left North Vietnam. Likewise, troops stationed along the Trail grew their own vegetables and hunted for fresh meat to reduce the need for food shipments and increase truck space for ammunition.

But these belt-tightening efforts could not make up for the mounting losses of trucks to U.S. Air Force bombing, losses that rose dramatically after AC-130 Spectre gunships began prowling the Laotian night sky. To replace these lost trucks, Gen. Vo Bam implemented an ingeniously simple system: when a U.S. air attack destroyed one *binh tram*'s truck, the next *binh tram* closer to North Vietnam was to give it one truck, which in turn was to be replaced by the next *binh tram* up the line until, at the end of the line in North Vietnam, a new truck was off-loaded from a Soviet ship onto a Haiphong

Top: NVA supply road in Laos viewed from a SOG helicopter. (Photo provided by Mecky Schuler)

Above: NVA bamboo bridge crosses a gorge just 100 yards inside "neutral" Cambodia, Base Area 609. (Photo provided by Mike Buckland)

bulldozers. Should one be destroyed, it would be replaced by shifting a replacement dozer from units farther up the Trail.

Although the Ho Chi Minh Trail had been a bombing target from the war's earliest days, by 1969—with a bombing halt on North Vietnam— aerial interdiction of the Laotian highways had become a strategic priority, attracting thousands of strikes. U.S. Air Force intelligence analysts had identified dozens of places that lent themselves to cuts by repeated bombing. Particularly inviting were steep ridges where bombing could bury a road with a landslide, mountain passes that could be blocked, and river fords where bomb craters might render crossing impossible. Known as interdiction points (IDPs), these targets became the focus of air attacks and a protracted side fight of the Vietnam War—a contest between the U.S. Air Force's ability to close roads and the NVA's ability to keep them open. Often, the NVA simply built camouflaged bypasses around the most critical IDPs, so even if these points were closed by bombing, the trucks still got through.

Near the most frequently bombed IDPs, the NVA stockpiled timbers, matting, and fill for quick repair plus stationed engineers and equipment nearby. Working at night by torchlight, or in daytime between air strikes, hundreds of NVA soliders with shovels and wheelbarrows would scurry to fill bomb craters, move aside rubble, and smooth the road's surface. It was astonishing for U.S. Air Force FACs to watch a B-52 strike slide a mountainside across a highway one afternoon and then return the next morning to find the same road open again. But the enemy's amazing ability to repair roads overnight also was an indicator of the war's greatest

dock. Thus, no matter how high the Laotian area losses, the trucks could be replaced, at the latest, a day or two after by having every unit along the Trail shift the required number of trucks southward.

REPAIRING THE HIGHWAYS

As the single most critical piece of machinery for road repair, each *binh tram* was assigned two or three

untold crime: the forced impressment of thousands of illiterate hill tribesmen as coolie labor to work on the Trail. Virtual slaves, these men, women, and children were "expendable" to Hanoi, thus exposing them to U.S. bombs, disease, and malnourishment meant nothing.

Nature took its toll too. During the annual three-month monsoon, much of the Laotian road system would be washed out in a cycle of such regularity that it determined the timing and scale of enemy "dry season" offensives in South Vietnam. Aware of this, the CIA conducted Project Popeye to increase monsoon rainfall by seeding clouds and air-dropping a detergent-like emulsifier to cause some passable roads to become too mushy to support truck traffic. SOG supported this CIA effort by having its RTs gather soil samples all across southern Laos.

One major NVA effort to reduce U.S. interdiction of precious truck fuel was the 1969 installation of a 6-inch pipeline from Vinh through the Mu Ghia Pass into Laos. Soon multiple pipelines reached another 25 miles to the NVA 559th Group's forward headquarters in Target Oscar-Eight southwest of Khe Sanh and then began to snake eastward toward the Ashau Valley. Because these pipelines were so heavily patrolled, it was extremely dangerous for SOG teams even to approach suspected pipeline routes.

Complementing the pipelines was an ingenious exploitation of nature by the NVA, floating half-filled oil drums on south-flowing Laotian rivers. This old trick, used by the Japanese during World War II to resupply their troops cut off on South Pacific islands, used buoyant drums to deliver supplies. In the NVA's case, the drums bounced along monsoon-swollen rivers until

reaching a cable that the NVA had strung over the stream so the current would push the barrels to shore. This was no small-scale effort: SOG and U.S. 7th Air Force FACs spotted 10,000 barrels floating in Laotian rivers from the short period of 1 April to 10 June 1970.

BICYCLES, PORTERS, AND BEASTS OF BURDEN

U.S. journalists illustrated the enemy's supply efforts with images of bicycles and human porters because—unaware of what was happening in Laos—the journalists saw only the delivery means employed when supplies were finally crossing the border into South Vietnam. Incredibly, many reporters assumed that the entire Ho Chi Minh Trail was nothing but a series of bicycle paths!

But the bicycles, human porters, and beasts of burden should not be minimized, because in areas where NVA trucks simply could not operate the communist war effort depended entirely upon these primitive delivery systems. When SOG teams brought

North Vietnamese bicycle porters on a trail in Laos. Each bike could carry up to 500 pounds of cargo. (Captured enemy photo)

back captured NVA pack bikes, they were found to be heavy-framed two- or three-wheelers, using wide "balloon" tires, somewhat like today's mountain bike tires. Saigon analysts learned that a single NVA bicycle carried up to 220 pounds of cargo on each side, for nearly 500 pounds of total capacity, far more than a man could carry and much more than they had previously estimated. By watching NVA supply paths, SOG men learned that a bicycle porter didn't ride his loaded bicycle, but walked it from one way station to the next and then rode it back for the next load. A short piece of bamboo was lashed to one side of the handlebar to be extended, so that the rider could steer it while walking alongside. Like his truck driver counterpart, a bicycle porter was assigned a fixed stretch of road or path and came to know it so well that he could maneuver even on dark nights.

Beasts of burden—elephants and water buffalo—were encountered infrequently, but SOG teams found both in use at various crossing paths from Laos into South Vietnam. In one well-known incident, several recon

teams reported that they'd observed NVA elephant convoys near Kham Duc—only to be scoffed at by know-it-all analysts in Saigon. Incensed, several recon men went back to the area, shot and killed an NVA elephant with an M79 grenade launcher, sawed off a tusk, and then presented it to Chief SOG Blackburn. Today that tusk is displayed in General Blackburn's living room, one of his proudest possessions. (See p. 30 for photo.)

ANTIAIRCRAFT DEFENSES

President Johnson's November 1968 halt to bombing North Vietnam freed thousands of enemy antiaircraft guns, allowing them to be shifted into Laos for a greater concentration of fire than that faced by Allied bombers over Nazi Germany in World War II. By 1970, the U.S. Air Force estimated that 10,000 antiaircraft guns were along the Ho Chi Minh Trail with the heaviest antiaircraft belts around Tchepone, Laos—Base Area 604—and in SOG Target Oscar-8 at the junction of Highways 92 and 922—Base Area 611. The Air Force lost more aircraft and more aircrews at these two spots than at any other place in Laos. Despite such heavy antiaircraft fire, SOG operations were not seriously impeded because SOG helicopters flew above 5,000 feet to cross or bypass them, or, if helicopters had to fly into the area, employed "nap of the Earth" tactics, flying virtually at treetop level.

The largest antiaircraft gun SOG usually encountered in Laos was the optically controlled 37mm, agile enough to be towed on the worst roads and manhandled into position. Thirty-sevens were usually encountered in three-gun platoons, positioned separately but with roughly interlocking fire on the aerial approaches to an important target, such as a road junc-

NVA 37mm antiaircraft gun, the heaviest normally found in Laos. Note the salami-sized shells (left) loaded in 5-round clips. (Photo provided by National Archives)

tion or mountain pass. They didn't aim directly at U.S. aircraft—which could fly past faster than they could swivel—but fired planned patterns in hopes that an aircraft would fly into an airburst. A direct hit by a 37mm round usually meant an instant fireball and catastrophic destruction. Even a near-miss caused considerable damage from shell fragments—or the loss of an aircraft.

The 23mm antiaircraft gun, spewing point-detonating slugs the size of cigars at a faster rate than many machine guns, was found throughout Laos. The NVA preferred dual-barreled 23s, which could be dragged up hillsides that seemed too steep to hold antiaircraft guns. The 23's great volume of fire, flat trajectory, and agility made it particularly deadly against helicopters.

But the antiaircraft gun most often encountered was the 12.7mm heavy machine gun, a Soviet weapon firing a round similar to the Browning .50-caliber. Because they could be disassembled and carried by three men, the NVA often repositioned its 12.7s while a SOG team was being pursued, with NVA commanders moving the 12.7s like chess pieces in anticipation of where the team's exfiltration landing zone (LZ) might be. Many a recon team thought it was home free only to come under intense 12.7mm fire when the extraction helicopter arrived.

Enemy AK fire, too, was directed at aircraft, particularly helicopters, but intervening jungle usually disrupted aiming. Although AK bursts often wounded passengers and aircrews, it was rare that an aircraft went down purely from AK hits. The NVA's deadliest shoulder-fired, antihelicopter weapon was the RPG (rocket-propelled grenade) rocket launcher, whose bazooka-like rocket could

transform a Huey helicopter into a fireball. In addition to detonating upon impact, the newer RPG-7 round self-detonated at 920 meters, which caused the enemy to lob rockets skyward in hopes that an airburst might damage or down an aircraft. And, indeed, that sometimes happened.

All of these insights on the Ho Chi Minh Trail were discovered at great cost, paid for with the blood of Special Forces recon men and their native teammates, a toll that would rise because the NVA continually added dynamic layers to its defenses. As we shall see, in addition to all these antiaircraft guns, road sentries, and security forces stationed on the Trail, the North Vietnamese developed special counterreconnaissance LZ watchers, trackers, and hunter-killer units in the quest to pursue and kill SOG men.

From 10 miles away, Ho Chi Minh Trail's location could be discerned by a pattern of B-52 craters. (Photo provided by Frank Greco)

Top right: Exploiting natural protection from B-52 strikes, the NVA placed some major headquarters in Laotian caves. (Photo provided by National Archives)

Bottom right: This NVA base camp in Laos was located by a single visible roof. This was an unusual error by the NVA and resulted in a U.S. air attack. (Photo provided by Mike Buckland)

Below: This North Vietnamese "way station," photographed by a SOG recon team, offered overnight lodging for troops en route to South Vietnam. (Photo provided by John Plaster)

Left: Communist troops construct a bridge along the Ho Chi Minh Trail. (Photo provided by DRV)

Below: A clever trick to mislead U.S. intelligence: the NVA radio antenna (left) in Virochey, Cambodia, was connected by wire to the transmitter at regimental headquarters miles away. (Photo provided by Ted Wicorek)

Top right: Virtual rolling brush piles, camouflaged NVA trucks roll along this Laotian road in daylight, probably during a U.S. bombing halt. (Photo provided by National Archives)

Bottom right: This truck park in southern Laos, its camouflage stripped away by bombs, became a truck graveyard. (Photo provided by U.S. Air Force)

Below: The NVA motto "Keep the trucks rolling" meant that convoys had to make it through even if soldiers had to push trucks by hand. (Photo provided by National Archives)

Left: NVA engineers fill marshy bomb craters and cover with bamboo mats. Instead of being cut for several days, the road is again passable in a few hours. (Photo provided by National Archives)

Below: Repeatedly bombed, this river ford on Laotian Highway 92, 34 miles northwest of Khe Sanh, shows traces of fresh truck tracks. (Photo provided by Mecky Schuler)

Top left: Bomb-pocked river ford on Highway 92, Laos. (Photo provided by Jim Martin)

Top right: Abandoned antiaircraft gun position overlooking Highway 92. (Photo provided by Jim Martin)

Above: Closed by U.S. bombs, this road cut on Highway 96 in Laos was filled and leveled overnight by an NVA bulldozer. (Photo provided by Ted Wicorek)

Above: Virtual slaves, these Montagnards escaped the NVA in 1968 after years of forced labor. (Photo provided by Steve Sherman)

Top left: Where terrain was too rough for bicycles the NVA employed human porters. (Photo provided by National Archives)

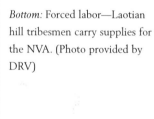

Bottom: Forced labor—Laotian hill tribesmen carry supplies for the NVA. (Photo provided by DRV)

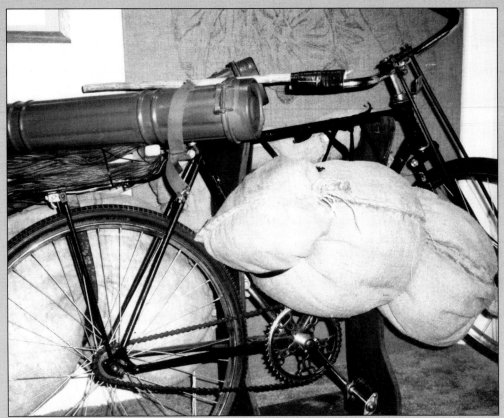

Top: NVA bike at the Infantry Museum, Ft. Benning, Georgia, shows the bamboo handlebar extension that allowed the porter to walk beside it. (Photo provided by John Plaster)

Bottom right: Proudly posing with an enemy transport bicycle they brought out of Cambodia is CCS RT Pick, with Sgt. Dale Kerr (left) and Sfc. Atley Sharp. (Photo provided by Atley Sharp)

Below: NVA ammo bunkers were dug in to protect them from bombing and covered to protect them from the elements. (Photo provided by Jim Hudson)

Above: FLAK TRAP? This disabled NVA truck on a Laotian road seems an inviting target—but it may be a burned-out hulk, dragged there to lure U.S. aircraft into enemy gunners' sights. (Photo provided by Mecky Schuler)

Top left: NVA gunner's view through a 12.7mm antiaircraft gun's sights. Note the miniature airplane (left) for holding a proper lead. (Photo provided by Frank Greco)

Bottom: Shrapnel damage to a Cobra gunship from a 37mm hit absorbed by outboard rocket pod. Had the round hit the fuselage, these 361st Attack Helicopter Company pilots probably would have died. (Photo provided by Ted Wicorek)

Above: The deadliest low-level antiaircraft gun in Laos was the twin-barreled 23mm. It was fast firing and highly portable, and its projectiles exploded upon impact. (Photo provided by John Plaster)

Top right: RT Moccasin members found the following inscription on a tree in Laos: "It's a duck-fucking world." Evidence that the NVA morale sometimes faltered. (Photo provided by Robert Masterjoseph)

Bottom: NVA engineers build a contour road on a Laotian hillside. (Photo provided by DRV)

Top: This NVA truck passes a bulldozer repairing a Laotian highway. (Photo provided by DRV)

Middle: NVA engineers clear a road after a B-52-instigated mountainslide. (Photo provided by DRV)

Bottom: Trucks roll through an area showing combined effects of defoliants and B-52s. (Photo provided by DRV)

Top: Heavily camouflaged NVA trucks look like rolling brush piles. (Photo provided by DRV)

Middle: NVA trucks cross an underwater bridge that is invisible from the air. (Photo provided by DRV)

Bottom: While marching on the Ho Chi Minh Trail, disciplined NVA soldiers changed camouflage several times per day. (Photo provided by DRV)

NVA HAVEN: LAOTIAN NO-BOMB LINES

NVA FORCES REALIZED THAT U.S. AIRCRAFT WOULD NOT ATTACK them when they were on "neutral" Cambodian territory. In most of Laos, however, the opposite was true, so they stayed as invisible as possible. But there were also a few critical havens in Laos that were free of U.S. bombing.

These were "no-bomb lines" (NBLs), carefully drawn around any sizable Laotian town to prevent inadvertent casualties among Laotian civilians. It didn't take long for the NVA forces to determine where these "lines" were, after which they'd seize the town and then operate there openly, immune from U.S. attack. The great irony is that in trying to protect such towns from inadvertently dropped U.S. bombs, the United States practically ensured the villages' intentional capture by the NVA.

Attopeu, Laos, was occupied by the NVA. Behind the protection of a "no-bomb line," the NVA boldly drove military vehicles in daylight. (Photo provided by John Plaster)

PROJECT IGLOO WHITE

Below: Igloo White sensor is burrowed into the ground; its sensor is almost indistinguishable from the jungle foliage. (Photo provided by U.S. Air Force)

Bottom: Igloo White sensor is hand-dropped along the Ho Chi Minh Trail to signal intelligence data back to Thailand. (Photo provided by U.S. Air Force)

IN 1967, U.S. SECRETARY OF DEFENSE McNAMARA ordered the building of a barrier along the demilitarized zone (DMZ), quickly dubbed the "McNamara Line." Deluded by unrealistic visions of interlocking fences, mine fields, and barbed wire barricades, Washington-based techno-experts thought the barrier would end NVA infiltration into South Vietnam. Of course, that failed.

A McNamara Line byproduct was a family of human and vehicular sensors that soon were being emplaced by aircraft and SOG teams to detect enemy movements around the besieged U.S. Marines at Khe Sanh. During the siege, sensor-generated information provided considerable intelligence for B-52 strikes, a success that led to Project Igloo White, in which hundreds of sensors were sprinkled along the Ho Chi Minh Trail system in Laos to detect trucks and troops.

SOG recon teams hand-emplaced dozens of sensors, disguised as tropical plants. Others were airdropped from U.S. Navy Neptunes, and still more were delivered by U.S. Air Force helicopters of the Thailand-based 21st Special Operations Squadron. Along with SOG recon teams, Igloo White became the primary source for intelligence along the Trail. Each night in a top-secret building at Nakhon Phanom Air Force Base (AFB), Thailand, a wall-sized map would light up as sensors signaled the passage of trucks and troops from the Mu Ghia Pass all the way down. Unfortunately, this information was not shared in real time with U.S. Air Force bombers so little combat effect resulted from the multimillion-dollar program.

And because the Igloo White sensors were proving modestly effective, NVA countermeasures soon followed. To confuse "people sniffers" that detected ammonia in human urine—indicating NVA troop concentrations—the NVA hung buckets of urine in trees in unoccupied areas. To deceive magnetic truck counters (and magnetically tripped mine fuses), the NVA herded water buffalo along, dragging heavy chains behind them. The most sophisticated countermeasure was a modified Soviet-designed BTR-50 armored car carrying a powerful diesel-electric generator with a heavy cable wrapped around it; by transmitting a strong electromagnetic force, it confused sensors and detonated U.S. Air Force magnetic fuse antitruck mines.

Of questionable effectiveness in Southeast Asia, these first-generation sensors eventually evolved into today's sophisticated remote-sensing systems and self-initiated mines.

ARC LIGHTS ON THE FALLS

ONE OF THE MOST PROMINENT U.S. AIR FORCE B-52 TARGETS in southern Laos was a narrow pass where Highway 96/92 wove its way between jungled hills not far from a waterfall. It was thus nicknamed "the Falls."

The Falls site was so well known that during Christmas 1970, the repeated B-52 Arc Light strikes inspired a SOG recon rendition of *Deck the Halls*:

> *Deck the Falls*
> *With Bombs for Charlie*
> *Fa-la-la-la-la, la-la, la la.*
> *Tis the season*
> *To nuke him hardy,*
> *Fa-la-la-la-la, la-la, la la.*

No clearer chronology of B-52 strikes gradually blasting away the jungle to lay bare major NVA supply roads exists than the three-photo sequence, 1967, 1969, and 1970, shot by three different SOG recon men.

And as the final photo discloses, despite thousands of bombs, overlapping craters, and nothing left but pulverized soil, fresh vehicle tracks weave their way through toward South Vietnam.

Left: 1967: The Falls interdiction point shows initial damage from B-52 strikes. (Photo provided by Mecky Schuler)

Below left: 1969: Although B-52s have thinned out trees, the road remains open and passable. (Photo provided by Frank Greco)

Below right: 1970: Despite the years of B-52 strikes pulverizing the Falls, fresh truck tracks wind through it. (Photo provided by Ted Wicorek)

PART THREE
SOG's
AIR
ARM

Chapter Five

Blackbirds and Night Skies

SOG needed its own air arm to penetrate the night skies of North Vietnam to insert agents, drop supplies, and support deception programs. Initially SOG used C-46s and C-47s inherited from the CIA, but SOG planners found that these obsolete Vietnamese-flown transport planes lacked the speed, range, sophistication, and cargo capacity that SOG's expanding mission demanded.

The twin-engine C-123 was a suitable replacement. Its cargo compartment was almost twice as large as a C-47's, but, even more important, it offered better arrangement for airdrops with a tailgate, as well as two side doors. On paper the C-123 was only 20 mph faster than the C-47, but when burdened with long-range fuel tanks the older plane chugged along at 190 mph, about 60 miles slower than the C-123. In early 1964, six U.S. Air Force C-123s were stripped of serial numbers, outfitted with removable U.S. insignia, beefed up with advanced navigational aids and electronic counter-measures, and then delivered to SOG as the First Flight Detachment.

FIRST FLIGHT DETACHMENT

Assigned to fly these "off-the-books" C-123s was perhaps the most unique flying outfit of the Vietnam War, some 38 Nationalist Chinese civilians who also were reserve pilots in the Republic of China's air force.

Although officially the First Flight Detachment claimed no lineage, it had evolved from Asia's most highly classified Allied air unit, the Republic of China's 34th Squadron, which had a long history of penetrating Communist China to insert and resupply agent teams for the CIA, much as SOG was now doing in North Vietnam. Many First Flight pilots were old hands from the 34th, and by the time they arrived in 1964 they had accumulated more than 200 missions over Red China, most of them flown at treetop level beneath a 30-percent moon—flying techniques they had so mastered that while with SOG they would never lose a plane to a SAM or a MiG. Their low-level evasive tactics had been perfected during infiltration exercises across Cape Cod in the late 1950s against U.S. Air Force

fighters playing the role of MiGs.

First Flight's existence overlapped the Civil Air Transport Service (CATS), a CIA-owned airline founded in 1949 to evacuate Chiang Kai-Shek and his defeated Nationalist Chinese army from the mainland to Taiwan. During its colorful history, CATS resupplied encircled French paratroopers at Dien Bien Phu, then clandestinely assisted a 1958 coup attempt against Indonesia's strongman, President Sukarno. In 1959 CATS was transformed into the well-known Air America, while its deep-cover element became the Nationalist Chinese 34th Squadron.

While serving with SOG, each First Flight plane also had a U.S. Air Force crew that manned it for flights in-country or over Laos; the Chinese piloted most flights into North Vietnam and Cambodia. Early on,

An unmarked SOG C-46 flown by Nationalist Chinese pilots. (Photo provided by Ken Bowra)

An unmarked SOG First Flight Detachment C-123. Note the unusual camouflage pattern. (Photo provided by Rick Jalloway)

SOG attempted to qualify its Vietnamese C-47 pilots in C-123s, but a Vietnamese trainee crew plowed its plane into Monkey Mountain near Danang, killing all aboard, including SOG's long-term agent, Team Centaur. The 1964 crash ended any Vietnamese air force involvement with First Flight.

U.S. Air Force Col. Don Radike, who worked with the Chinese, admired their guts and experience and recalled, "We had one navigator, for example, who had been shot down on the Chinese Mainland seven times and walked out every time. What could I possibly tell him about survival?"

Air Force Lt. Col. Bill Rose spent two tours with First Flight Detachment, eventually serving as its U.S. commander, and found the Chinese crews professional. While their U.S. crew chiefs showed a pref-

erence for Hawaiian shirts, blue jeans, and cowboy boots, the pilots opted for tan pants, white shirts, ordinary street shoes, and aviator sunglasses, looking to all the world like middle-aged office workers.

Every other month, members of each Chinese crew would spend a week at their home base on Taiwan; during these welcome respites their C-123s displayed slide-on Nationalist Chinese insignia. While in Vietnam these Chinese crews carried Vietnamese ID cards, although they spoke scarcely one word of the language. "I don't think anyone in MACV knew we had them," Chief SOG Steve Cavanaugh believes. Securely behind the walls of their Nha Trang villa, the Chinese pilots proved themselves the city's finest clandestine hosts—each evening saw a party with Harvey Wallbangers by

Top: SOG jump school graduate stands before "pull-off" insignia of a 1st Flight C-123. (Photo provided by Dave Boswell)

Above: Unofficial Blackbird "Stray Goose" patch; "S/D" means "secret/dangerous." (Photo provided by Scott Kilpatrick)

the pitcher and exquisite Chinese meals that built toward a monthly gourmet Chinese dinner with—Air Force Col. Bill Page recalls—each course preceded by a toast of 150-proof Chinese cognac. At their monthly banquet, every 15 minutes another pilot would emerge from the kitchen to present a heaping platter of some Mandarin delicacy, causing the whole gathering to stand, call, "*Gom-bay!*" [Drink up], empty their cognac, and set the glasses upside down to prove them empty. "Those were good times," says Page.

Although SOG's Chinese-flown C-123s were hit a few times by ground-fire, which downed one plane southwest of Saigon, remarkably not a single plane ever would be lost during hundreds of flights over North Vietnam.

THE BLACKBIRDS

With its expanding missions, manpower, and operational areas, SOG's transport aircraft needs quickly exceeded First Flight's capacity. Additional airlift was provided by the September 1966 assignment to SOG of the U.S. Air Force's first C-130s modified expressly for special operations. These six aircraft, designated the 15th Air Commando Squadron—changed to the 15th Special Operations Squadron (SOS) in 1968, then redesignated the 90th SOS in 1970—were co-based with the First Flight Detachment at Nha Trang. Perhaps because their classified penetration missions demanded that they fly alone, the C-130 squadron was called Project Stray Goose, which explains the strange-looking bird in their unofficial unit insignia.

These MC-130s looked strange, too, distinguished by their midnight-black and forest-green paint scheme, slide-on/slide-off insignia, and 20-foot

Fulton "Skyhook" yokes swung back against their bulbous noses. Because of their distinctive coloration, the SOG planes were nicknamed Blackbirds, which also applied to the Chinese-flown C-123s when they too adopted the dark paint scheme. Unlike the C-123s, though, these C-130s had all-U.S. Air Force crews.

The special-operations C-130s could carry more than twice the payload of C-123s at twice the speed—just under 400 mph. But payload and speed weren't key features; the C-130 Blackbirds had been tweaked and modified for special operations with cutting-edge navigation aids, Doppler radar, and the same advanced electronic countermeasures as strategic bombers. These also were the first military transports in the world outfitted with forward-looking infrared (FLIR), a revolutionary viewing system that rendered the darkest night daylight clear on a TV screen and saw through rain or fog and into foliage. Even the existence of FLIR would not be known publicly for years.

BLACKBIRD COMBAT MISSIONS

It was the amazing ability of FLIR to see through treetops and shrubs that enabled SOG to prove incontrovertibly that several agent teams were under enemy control, for the Blackbird crews could see enemy security forces and vehicles hiding in the jungle near drop zones where "doubled" agent teams awaited supplies or reinforcements.

Due to their advanced navigational gear and electronic countermeasure systems, the C-130s were assigned some of the hairiest night resupply and deception parachute drops over North Vietnam. Indeed, by mid-1967, the U.S. Air Force Blackbirds were averaging four night resupply

flights into North Vietnam per monthly moonlight period. By then U.S. Air Force fighters were over North Vietnam each day, so there was less concern about deniability; the Blackbirds weren't sterilized as stringently as the C-123s, though the Blackbirds' crews operated with a cover story. "If they went down in North Vietnam," one Blackbird veteran recalled, "the story they were to tell was that they had equipment malfunctioning, which resulted in a navigational error." To add credibility the planes carried false flight plans.

Like First Flight's C-123s, the Blackbirds slipped through the Laos backdoor into North Vietnam when the moon hung 30 degrees above the horizon and wove along carefully plotted infiltration tracks to avoid enemy radar and surface-to-air (SAM) sites. Despite their sophisticated navigation aids and electronic countermeasures, a SOG navigator said the basis for their success was careful route planning and meticulous navigation.

In addition to parachuting long-term agent teams deep into North Vietnam, the Blackbirds airdropped U.S.-led recon teams along the Ho Chi Minh Trail and dumped thousands of propaganda "gift kits" into North Vietnam, as well as millions of

pamphlets over Laos and North Vietnam offering cash rewards to anyone who could deliver a U.S. POW. These planes also have the distinction of having inserted the world's first combat high-altitude, low-opening (HALO) parachute teams.

Two C-130 Blackbirds were lost during the war. The first was destroyed while parked on the ground at Nha Trang Airbase when it caught fire during a mortar attack on 25 November 1967. The second vanished during a classified flight over North Vietnam on 29 December 1967.

Top: SOG C-130 Blackbird takes off at Nha Trang. (Photo provided by U.S. Air Force)

Above: SOG Blackbird ready for takeoff. Note the lack of insignia and the presence of a Fulton "Skyhook" yoke on the nose. (Photo provided by Bryon Loucks)

Above: SOG MC-130 coming in to land at Nha Trang. (Photo provided by Leslie Smith)

Right: A typical Blackbird crew had twice the manpower of a normal C-130. Front, left to right: Barney Dowd, Mike Connaughton, Werner Weindorf, Frank Szemere, Allen Cohen, and Hobdy Edmonson. Rear: Jimmy Riggs, Howard Rice, Billy Elliston, Donald Rhodes, and Gordon Steely. (Photo provided by Lee Hess)

Above: MC-130 Blackbird over the waters of the South China Sea. (Photo provided Leslie Smith)

Left: The burned-out hulk of the C-130 Blackbird destroyed at Nha Trang in a mortar attack, 25 November 1967. (Photo provided by Lee Hess)

Above: An unmarked SOG C-123 at low level above the South China Sea. (Photo provided by Rob Locker)

Below: Poof! A SOG C-123 becomes a Nationalist Chinese plane simply by switching insignia. (Photo provided by Rob Locker)

FIRST FLIGHT'S UNOFFICIAL EMBLEM

Below: First Flight's unofficial emblem.

Bottom: "GOM-BAY!" A SOG Chinese pilot toasts U.S. Air Force crewman Rob Locker at a Chinese banquet. (Photo provided by Rob Locker)

ALTHOUGH FIRST FLIGHT'S MISSION WAS TOP SECRET, a discerning soul with a sense of humor and familiarity with *Mad* magazine could have figured out what the unit was up to by studying its unofficial emblem: on a blue shield a bat hovered above the Big Dipper constellation, while beneath it skulked a *Mad* "Spy-Versus-Spy" white spook—in other words, First Flight flew toward the Big Dipper—*north* like a bat, and *at night* to support good-guy spooks. Apparently U.S. reporters lacked enough humor to see through First Flight's symbolic facade, because it never made the press.

THE FULTON SKYHOOK SYSTEM

SOG's C-130 BLACKBIRDS WERE OUTFITTED with the Fulton "Skyhook" system, a device for extracting intelligence agents and downed airmen from a spot where no airplane could land. The genius behind the Skyhook was Robert E. Fulton, Jr., great-great-grandson of the inventor of one of the world's first steamboats, the *Clermont* ("Fulton's Folly").

Skyhook evolved from the All-American System developed in the 1940s as a civilian mail pickup technique. Dragging a hook that resembled an aircraft carrier arresting gear, a C-47 flew a dozen feet above the ground; the hook snared a cable held between two poles and jerked an attached mailbag into the air, which was then winched into the plane, allowing mail pickup without landing. During the Korean War, the CIA-affiliated Joint Advisory Commission, Korea (JACK) modified the All-American System to snatch people up, using it to extract agents from North Korea and Mainland China. One young JACK officer, Lt. John "Skip" Sadler, a future Chief SOG, was lifted up during an All-American System demonstration in Japan in 1952. That same year, Lieutenant Sadler lobbied hard with his boss at JACK—another future Chief SOG, John "Jack" Singlaub—for permission to accompany a CIA C-47 that was going to extract a high-ranking Chinese defector in Manchuria, but

Below: Its Skyhook yoke extended, a Blackbird approaches the balloon . . .

Far right: . . . snagging the cable. The balloon breaks away, and the passenger is lifted from the ground . . .

Far right inset: . . . Then the passenger is winched into the tailgate. (Photos provided by Mike Haas)

Above: Skyhook emblem.

Right: Blackbird pilot Don James in full Skyhook suit about to be snatched away in a practice extraction. (Photo provided by Don James)

Singlaub would not allow it. The plane was shot down, and its two CIA passengers, Richard Fecteau and John Downey, were captured and imprisoned in China until President Richard Nixon's visit to Peking in 1972.

USING THE SKYHOOK

To deploy the Skyhook system, the passenger opened a casket-sized cannister dropped from a Blackbird or F-4 Phantom containing a deflated balloon, a 1,500-foot cable, and a combination suit-harness. Under ordinary conditions it took about 15 minutes to don the suit, inflate the helium balloon, and get the cable up. Meanwhile, the Skyhook airplane hydraulically swung forward its nose-mounted 20-foot yoke. Then the pilot flew the yoke into the cable beneath the balloon—which broke away—and the passenger was snatched at 125 mph and winched into the tailgate.

CIA USE OF SKYHOOK

The Skyhook system was essential to a 1961 plan to rescue a CIA contract pilot, Al Pope, from an Indonesian prison. Pope's Civil Air Transport plane had been shot down during a February 1958 CIA-sponsored coup attempt in Indonesia. But the Skyhook pilot slated to snatch Pope was killed in Laos, and then U.S. Attorney General Robert Kennedy's personal appeal—and undoubtedly a sizable gratuity—led to Pope's release.

Soon afterward, Skyhook was employed in a real-world intelligence operation. A Soviet meteorological station near the North Pole had been abandoned when the ice began breaking up, leaving behind sensors and instruments. U.S. Navy Intelligence suspected that the Soviets were testing techniques for tracking U.S. submarines under the ice, so there was great interest in recovering the Soviet gear. A U.S. team of two men was parachuted onto the abandoned site, but the ice breakup made it impossible to land an airplane to retrieve them. Finally, a Skyhook kit was dropped, and the men were snatched out with a Fulton-rigged B-17 bomber. Interestingly, this was the same plane used three years later in the James Bond film *Thunderball* to retrieve 007 and his lovely female companion.

SKYHOOK AND SOG

The first SOG member to test Skyhook was Chief SOG himself, Col. Jack Singlaub, who was snatched up at Camp Long Thanh in 1966. "The only thing I regretted was I hadn't told the pilot where to fly after he had me dangling out behind," Singlaub recalled. "I could see that we were flying over War Zone D, not more than a thousand feet up—the most heavily enemy populated part of all South Vietnam."

Skyhook was best suited for clandestine extracts, not for extractions under heavy antiaircraft fire or with hostile ground forces nearby. SOG never employed Skyhook to exfiltrate recon teams because the system could lift only two men at a time, and the antiaircraft threat usually was just too great. "To get a guy out of somewhere with a Fulton recovery system took a lot of planning," explained former Blackbird pilot, Lt. Col. Don James. "He had to be in an area where we could put this balloon up, which would alert everybody around him."

Several times SOG Blackbird crews went after downed pilots in North Vietnam, with the first on 21 May 1967. According to James "L.C." Smith, who flew aboard Maj. Sam Rose's Blackbird that day, the extraction was aborted because radio contact was lost with the downed airman before the plane arrived. In another case, a Blackbird crewman reported, the downed pilot had his balloon inflated but he'd forgotten to consider nearby obstacles, so he had to reposition himself. By the time he was ready and the Blackbird began its run in, North Vietnamese soldiers had swarmed over the downed pilot.

Another close-run Fulton Skyhook extraction personally involved another Chief SOG, Col. John Sadler, who was so concerned about the danger to a Blackbird crew that he climbed into an F-4's backseat and flew the area himself before permitting the plane to go in. Deep in North Vietnam, Sadler approved dropping a Skyhook kit from a Phantom and monitored the downed pilot's radio messages while he prepared for extraction. Then the pilot suddenly changed his call-sign to "Peter Willie"—*he was a PW*, a *prisoner of war*. It was a setup, an enemy trap to shoot down a Blackbird! There was no choice. Colonel Sadler, who as a captain had almost been drawn into an ambush in 1952 in China during an All-American extraction, aborted the pickup.

Late in the war there were several occasions when Skyhook was considered for extracting downed pilots, most notably the "Bat-21" rescue of U.S. Air Force Lt. Col. Hugh Hambleton. But in each case some critical factor or the pilot's capture precluded a Skyhook pickup.

Bottom left: Fulton Skyhook rig is airdropped by SOG Blackbird, so the passenger on the ground can don a special suit and inflate balloon for extraction. (Photo provided by Leslie Smith)

Bottom right: Its Skyhook yoke fully extended, a Blackbird makes a run in to snare a cable and snatch up a passenger. (Photo provided by Leslie Smith)

(1) C-47 dips its tail to snatch the cable and lift its passenger with its All-American System. (Photo provided by John Sadler)

(2) Then-Capt. John Sadler is snatched by the All-American System, 1952. (Photo provided by John Sadler)

(3) Future Chief SOG Sadler rides wildly beneath a C-47 while being winched aboard. (Photo provided by John Sadler)

3

THE MISSING STRAY GOOSE

On 28 December 1967, SOG Blackbird Crew S-01 penetrated North Vietnam to drop a false resupply to a Project Oodles phantom, Team Mikado. The intent was to confuse enemy counterintelligence and draw security forces away with phantom teams so that SOG's long-term agent teams would have a better chance for survival. The planned drop zone was in extreme northwest North Vietnam, a dozen miles south of Yunnan Province, China. That night, however, dense cloud cover forced the crew to abort the drop. The mission was rescheduled for the following night.

In the early morning of 29 December, the Blackbird flew southwest of Hanoi to drop propaganda leaflets, radioed an "all-OK" at 4:30 A.M., and descended to low level for the false resupply drop. That message was the last ever heard from aircrew S-01. Shot down, crashed, or hit by a SAM—the airplane simply vanished. Two weeks of overflights found nothing.

In the remarkable history of U.S. Air Force special operations, this Blackbird remains the only MC-130 ever lost operationally. As with the SOG recon MIAs in Laos, Hanoi denied any knowledge of the Blackbird crewmen's fate. In 1992, wreckage believed to be that of the Blackbird was examined, and some bone fragments were recovered, although none was identified. These were the missing U.S. Air Force crewmen:

- Lt. Col. Donald E. Fisher, Navigator
- Maj. Charles P. Claxton, Pilot
- Capt. Edwin N. Osborne, Jr., Aircraft Commander
- Capt. Gerald Van Buren, Pilot
- Capt. Frank C. Parker III, Electronic Warfare Officer
- Capt. Gordon J. Wenaas, Navigator
- T. Sgt. Jack McCrary, Flight Engineer
- S. Sgt. Gean P. Clapper, Radio Operator
- S. Sgt. Wayne A. Eckley, Flight Engineer
- S. Sgt. Edward J. Darcy, Loadmaster
- Sgt. James Williams, Loadmaster

Left: Maj. Charles Claxton, MIA aboard Blackbird, 29 December 1967. (Photo provided by family of Charles Claxton)

Below: MIA crewmen Wayne Eckley (left) and Gean Clapper at the crew door of the Blackbird that vanished over North Vietnam. (Photo provided by family of Gean Clapper)

Chapter Six

Special Helicopters and Special Crews

At the height of the Vietnam War, SOG's far-flung operations required the direct support of about 45 U.S. Army and Marine helicopters, in addition to the 15 Vietnamese H-34s and the dozen U.S. Air Force UH-1F and P-Model Hueys organic to SOG. The problem was that none of these 45 additional troop-lift helicopters and gunships was assigned to SOG.

SOG garnered these extra birds via a monthly directive from General Westmoreland or General Abrams, ordering Vietnam-based U.S. Army and Marine divisions to divert some of their own helicopters to SOG—a practice resented by major commands that had little knowledge of SOG's top-secret doings but noticed that they never seemed to get back as many birds as they sent—and the ones that did come back were frequently shot up.

Aviation commanders noted SOG's high aircraft loss rates and thought it fair to rotate their men and birds so that the danger was shared among a larger number of units. Thus, during much of the war, SOG aircrews and helicopters changed frequently—which meant constant acclimation to the Ho Chi Minh Trail's treacherous antiaircraft environment and continuing education on unique flying techniques, such as inserting personnel onto tiny LZs and extracting men on McGuire rigs.

It was not until 1970 that an alternative was practiced: that is, leaving helicopter units in direct support long enough to get past the high initial loss rates and learn lessons that could be applied to refine tactics and flying techniques. It worked. Losses declined by allowing the pilots and crews to master SOG's hazardous world.

One side effect of these frequent rotations, though, was the difficulty 30 years later in reconstructing which U.S. Army and Marine helicopter units flew for SOG and when. Many brave airmen's deeds were never attributed to SOG duty, thus creating a whole category of unsung heroes known only to the SOG recon and Hatchet Force men they rescued. For instance, a Huey doorgunner with the 155th Assault Helicopter Company, Sp4c. Ernie Plummer, shinned down a rope from his ship to rescue a Huey crew and SOG recon team that had been shot down in Cambodia. All alone, Plummer dragged the badly wounded men to an LZ for extraction. Two of the crewmen later died—Santiago Quintana and Armando Ramirez—as did two Green Berets, Phillip Strout and Howard Hill, but four men lived thanks to Ernie Plummer: Huey crewmen Richard Menzel and Jerome Green, along with Green Berets

Arthur Dolph and Mark Schneider. Eventually Plummer received a Silver Star, but he had something more valuable than a medal—the respect of men he respected.

THE KINGBEES

Undoubtedly, the war's only instance of a South Vietnamese flying unit permanently assigned to a U.S. organization was the Danang-based 219th Helicopter Squadron, whose unmarked, obsolescent H-34s would become a SOG trademark. Assigned to support cross-border reconnaissance, the 219th Squadron—nicknamed the Kingbees—parceled out helicopters to the command and control elements in Danang, Kontum, and, occasionally, Ban Me Thuot.

SOG paid the Kingbee pilots a 3,000 piastre bonus for each crossborder flight, which amounted to roughly U.S. $25 per insertion or extraction. In a month's time it approximated the flight pay, parachute pay, and combat pay Americans received—hardly a fortune.

The interiors of the bottle-nosed H-34s were grungy and oily, reminiscent of a college student's $500 "beat-

A Kingbee descends between the trees to land at Leghorn Radio Relay Site in Laos. (Photo provided by Merritte Wilson)

er" car with a case of oil in the trunk—except that the Kingbees carried cases of pink hydraulic fluid and reeked of it: the overhead lines leaked it, and the floors stayed slick with it. When enemy .50-caliber slugs hit the choppers' cavernous troop compartments it sounded like beating a washtub with a baseball bat, but these old tubs could take lots of hits. And just because they were old didn't make the H-34s bad. "The best helicopter ever made for SOG was the H-34," concluded Lt. Jim Fleming, an exceptional U.S. Air Force helicopter pilot who flew SOG Hueys. "The pilot sat right on top of that big, 32-cylinder radial engine, and when you went in, you at least had some iron between you and them. And it was really rough and tough and rugged." How tough? "You could blow cylinders out of it and still get yourself home." Because it was a taller ship, the H-34 could hover against a slope with one wheel, allowing it to lift men from steep hillsides.

A Kingbee's sole armament was a World War II belt-fed, .30-caliber machine gun hung from a bungee cord in the doorway with 1,000 rounds stacked in an old can under the gunner's seat. The doorgunner alone had an intercom connection to the pilots, and since the gunner didn't speak English it was sometimes hard to learn what was happening. Sfc. Dick Gross concluded there was a problem one day when he saw the gunner chatter excitedly into his mouthpiece, look down with widening eyes, and then make the sign of the cross. It did not instill confidence as Gross prepared to land.

At times the Kingbees' ordinary way of operating seemed fantastic. One might return from a dangerous cross-border flight with a live peacock the doorgunner had jumped out

and captured. Or as happened one afternoon at Kontum, a Kingbee returned with an elk-sized stag swinging from a rappeling rope—the main course for that night's barbecue.

They liked to fly along South Vietnamese highways with their tires skipping along the paved surface and then jerk up to keep from hitting an oncoming vehicle. Their thrill for flying bordered on the reckless, but had these pilots been cautious, they would hardly have flown through hellacious fire to rescue recon teams for years and years. "They were absolutely fearless," said former CCC commander Scotty Crerar, and this sentiment was shared by Col. Charlie Beckwith, who called the Kingbees "the cream of the Vietnamese air force and the finest pilots in the country." The respect was reciprocated. A former Kingbee pilot who made it to the United States after the war told Henry Gill that he found the SOG recon soldiers he supported "the bravest men I have ever known."

A formation of Kingbees over Laos about 15 kilometers northwest of Khe Sanh, 1967. (Photo provided by Billy Waugh)

THE GREEN HORNETS

The only other helicopter unit actually assigned to SOG was also the Vietnam War's only U.S. Air Force squadron that flew Huey helicopters, the 20th SOS, nicknamed the "Green Hornets."

Known originally as the 20th Helicopter Squadron, the Green Hornets initially flew CH-3 Jolly Greens, whose size sometimes came in handy but frequently limited their ability to land in tight LZs. Therefore, in 1967 the 20th SOS was reequipped with UH1-F model Hueys. Even though the F model's turbine was fragile and a maintenance nightmare, it also generated more power than U.S. Army Hueys, which meant that it escaped hot LZs more quickly and carried more people, features well suited to recon operations.

The 20th SOS was SOG's only U.S. helicopter unit whose crews lived with the SOG men they supported. Officially based at Nha Trang and later Cam Ranh Bay, the Green Hornet birds and crews rotated every 10 days to the CCS camp at Ban Me Thuot, and that did a lot for developing rapport. Unlike U.S. Army Hueys, which typically were piloted by 20- and 21-year-olds, these Air Force Hueys were flown by career majors and lieutenant colonels in their 30s and 40s, many of whom were on final assignment before retirement.

Half the Green Hornet Hueys were configured as UH-1P gunships with rocket pods and unique hand-controlled miniguns. Because crewmen could pivot the guns independently of the aircraft, the men would fire during the approach while passing the target and even contort the guns to shoot backward after passing. Some gunships also had hand-fired 40mm grenade launchers.

The Green Hornet gunship crews pioneered their own tactics, especially firing techniques, like "three-sixties," to exploit their hand-held miniguns.

Above: Green Hornet insignia.

Right: This 20th SOS minigunner lets his weapon roar like a fire-breathing dragon. (Photo provided by Dale Bennett)

Green Hornet minigunner Alfonso "R.T." Rivera leans from UH-1P gunship. (Photo provided by Alfonso Rivera)

Hovering above a team, the pilot spun his bird in a 360-degree pedal turn with both miniguns shooting straight down to form a circular wall of fire. "I don't give a damn who you are, you're not getting through that," recon man Ben Lyons said.

One Green Hornet gunner carried a pair of human shinbones, and after any close-run mission his bird would scream at low level over the CCS Ban Me Thuot compound, the gunner chanting and shaking those bones like a demented witch doctor. The recon men loved it.

The Green Hornets suffered their first person killed in action (KIA) on 31 March 1967 when a UH-1F was hit by 12.7mm fire, knocking it down in thick jungle and killing the aircraft commander, Maj. Robert Baldwin. On

3 January 1969 a Green Hornet Huey was shot down while trying to extract a CCS recon team, killing U.S. Air Force Sgt. R.P. Zenga. On 13 March 1969, while supporting a team extraction, a Green Hornet gunship was badly hit, killing the co-pilot, Capt. J.O. Lynch, and seriously wounding the aircraft commander, who had to make an emergency landing. Despite his own serious wounds, air crewman Sgt. Isidro Arroyo helped his comrades to the rescue bird.

There were many such stories of bravery, with about 15 Green Hornet crewmen lost in the war.

"I never met a Green Hornet I didn't like," CCS recon man Frank Burkhart said, expressing a sentiment universal among recon men. "I thought they were the absolute best."

LT. JIM FLEMING, MEDAL OF HONOR

THE AFTERNOON OF 26 NOVEMBER 1968 was 1st Lt. Jim Fleming's second day as a Green Hornet aircraft commander. Flying with his Huey co-pilot, Maj. Paul McClellan, that morning, Fleming had inserted RT Chisel near a wide Cambodian river to conduct surveillance of enemy boat traffic. By mid-afternoon his flight of two Green Hornet gunships and three trooplift birds were flying near Duc Co Special Forces border camp when they heard a desperate call from RT Chisel's radio operator, Sgt. Charles Hughes.

The six-man team, led by S. Sgt. Ancil "Sonny" Franks, was pinned in a washout on the river, surrounded by NVA troops and fighting for its life. A third Green Beret, Capt. Randy Harrison, the new CCS recon company commander, was with them.

Along with U.S. Air Force Maj. Charles Anonsen's O-2 FAC aircraft, the Green Hornets raced west into Cambodia with barely enough fuel for anything but a quick pickup. Arriving overhead they found the sky filled with intense fire. Capt. Dave Miller's gunship went down, and its crew was rescued by a Huey that, though low on fuel, headed straight for Duc Co. Then a second Huey had to head back because it was almost out of fuel. That left two helicopters: Fleming's Huey and a gunship commanded by Maj. Leonard Gonzales, both dangerously low on fuel. After Gonzales pickled rockets all around RT Chisel, Fleming noticed him trailing smoke; he'd been hit, but his bird was flyable.

Fleming ran a gauntlet of AK and machine gun fire on the river while his doorgunners, J.J. Johnson and Fred Cook, shot and scanned for RT Chisel. Just as he nosed the Huey to the riverbank, the NVA hit RT Chisel in such strength that every recon man was too busy shooting to run for the aircraft. Their radio operator screamed, "They've got us! They've got us! Get out, get out!" Fleming backed away and climbed out just as the team radioman reported, "We blew them back, but we're out of claymores and can't hold out much longer."

Orbiting at a safe altitude, Fleming took stock of the situation. Their backs against the river, the men of RT Chisel could last a few more minutes. There was not enough daylight left to refuel at Duc Co and return. The young lieutenant had been too busy flying and dodging bullets to think about the danger, but now it was clear. Fleming could have declared his fuel dangerously

Jim Fleming seconds after stepping from his Huey after the heroic rescue of RT Chisel. (Photo provided by Jim Fleming)

92

RT Chisel One-Zero Ancil "Sonny" Franks (left), whose team was rescued by Jim Fleming. (Photo provided by Cecil Carle)

low—*absolutely true*—or that the last gunship was barely flyable and almost out of ammo—*also true*. But Lt. Fleming radioed, "We'll give it one more try."

The gunship leading, the two Green Hornets swung low and fast along the river, AK bullets splashing the water all around them. Gonzales salvoed his remaining rockets and let those miniguns moan and groan. Then Fleming's right doorgunner, Fred Cook, shouted above the roar, "There he is!" and Fleming saw a Montagnard sloshing from shore with four men behind him.

Despite AK bursts and exploding rockets, Fleming held that bird rock-steady in what the U.S. Air Force later called "a feat of unbelievable flying skill." Then doorgunner J.J.

Johnson's gun jammed, AK slugs shattered the Huey's windshield, and a bursting RPG raked the helicopter's skin. With bullets slapping the water all around his helicopter, Fleming began pulling back from the bank— then the last man, Captain Harrison, jumped in the river. The Green Beret was dragged aboard amid AK fire and bursting RPGs. Then 10 seconds later they were away.

For his selfless gallantry that day, Lieutenant Fleming was awarded the Medal of Honor, SOG's lone U.S. Air Force Medal of Honor recipient. The intrepid Green Hornet gunship pilot, Major Gonzales, was awarded the Air Force Cross.

"They were great people," insists RT Chisel One-Zero Sonny Franks, and he should know.

A 20th SOS Green Hornet UH-1N high over Cambodia to avoid antiaircraft fire. (Photo provided by Rick Jalloway)

Below: SOG recon team practices ladder extraction with 20th SOS Huey at CCS. (Photo provided by Alfonso Rivera)

Top far right: Green Hornet Huey lifts away with SOG team on Cambodian frontier, 1970. (Photo provided by Rick Jalloway)

Middle far right: A 20th SOS Huey on the Cambodian border, 1969. Its only emblem is a greet hornet. (Photo provided by Rick Jalloway)

Bottom far right: CCS recon team dons gear beside Green Hornet UH-1F before a covert insertion mission in Cambodia. (Photo provided by Alfonso Rivera)

Above: The H-34 Kingbee had a single door, but its huge reciprocating engine in the nose was almost a bulletproof shield. Note the lack of insignia. (Photo provided by Bryon Loucks)

Right: A flight of Kingbees returns after inserting an RT in Laos. (Photo provided by U.S. Air Force)

155th Assault Helicopter Company Hueys carry SOG recon men near the Cambodian border. (Photo provided by Dale Boswell)

Left: Cobra pilot Mike Brovovkh, B Battery, 4th Battalion, 77th Aerial Rocket Artillery. (Photo provided by Mike Sloniker)

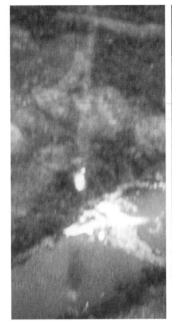

Above: FALLING FIREBALL. A Marine Corps Huey hit by enemy fire plunges into a Laotian river, killing 1st Lt. Ronald Janousek and Cpl. Bruce Kane. Surprisingly, two crewmen, Major Hill and Sergeant Dean, survived. (Photo provided by Mike Sloniker)

Top right: Huey lifts out CCC recon team from Laos despite ground fire suppressed by exploding rockets almost below the Huey and to the right at top. (Photo provided by John Plaster)

Middle: 170th Assault Helicopter Company Huey in Laotian treetops. (Photo provided by Merritte Wilson)

Bottom: 101st Airborne Division Huey weaves between trees to insert CCN team in Laos, 1970. (Photo provided by Mike Sloniker)

57th Assault Helicopter Company Huey cuts its way through brush to reach CCC recon team in Laos. (Photo provided by Mike Buckland)

Right: RT Illinois with a Kingbee at FOB-2, Kontum (Photo provided by John Plaster)

Below right: Doorgunner Terry O'Kelley (right) and RT Hatchet One-Zero Robert Bost. In an amazing display of bravery and superhuman strength, O'Kelley pulled recon man Bill Deacy from beneath a shot-down, burning Huey. Although he did not complain, O'Kelley suffered severe burns. (Photo provided by Robert Bost)

Below: CCN Khe Sanh-based insertion chopper enters a fog-shrouded Laotian valley, 1968. (Photo provided by Bob Donoghue)

Top: Recon team aboard a Kingbee. Note pilots' feet above them. (Photo provided by George Gaspard)

Middle: Surprisingly agile, the big Kingbee could spin, dip, and even go backward. (Photo provided by Jim Martin)

Bottom: Flying formation with another Kingbee over the Ho Chi Minh Trail corridor, southern Laos. (Photo provided by the family George K. Sisler)

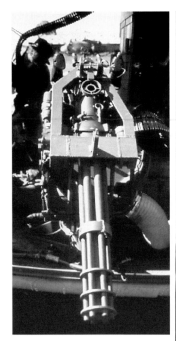

Above: Handheld firepower—a Green Hornet doorgunner's minigun on UH-1P Huey. (Photo provided by Bryan Stockdale)

Top right: The setting sun silhouetting it against the western sky, a Kingbee flies eastward back to South Vietnam after a mission in Laos. (Photo provided by Frank Jaks)

Bottom: U.S. Army Huey flies back to Kontum after a day of inserting teams from the Dak To launch site. (Photo provided by the family of George K. Sisler)

Above: The Green Hornets' unofficial unit patch. (Photo provided by Scott Kilpatrick)

The two weapon systems on a Green Hornet gunship: 2.75-inch rocket pod and hand-controlled minigun. (Photo provided by Bryan Stockdale)

PONY EXPRESS: THE 21ST SOS

Below: Carrying a SOG indigenous RT into North Vietnam, a Thailand-based, 21st SOS CH-3 Jolly Green Giant. (Photo provided by George Gaspard)

Bottom: A 21st SOS Jolly Green Giant comes in for a CCN recon team. (Photo provided by Eldon Bargewell)

Bottom right: Late in the war, the 21st SOS upgraded to the HH-53, Super Jolly Green, shown here landing in Laos. (Photo provided by Sammy Hernandez)

As Eve grew from Adam's rib, so did the Thailand-based 21st SOS evolve from a slice of SOG's Vietnam-based 20th Helicopter Squadron. In February 1966, D Flight of the 20th transferred to Thailand's Nakhon Phanom (often referred to simply as NKP) Air Base. From there, these men—nicknamed "Pony Express"—flew CH-3s similar to the Jolly Green Giant search-and-rescue helicopters already based at NKP, making for a natural cover story.

Instead of retrieving downed fliers, the Pony Express birds flew in support of the CIA secret war in Laos, flying everywhere from Site 85 on the North Vietnamese border to the Plain of Jars and Bolovens Plateau, while also inserting CIA-recruited indigenous roadwatch teams beyond SOG's area of operations. After SOG opened its own top-secret Project Heavy Hook launch site at NKP in January 1967, D Flight began inserting Green Beret-led recon teams—flown to Thailand clandestinely aboard C-130 Blackbirds—along the Ho Chi Minh Trail. When SOG inaugurated the Short-Term Roadwatch and Target Acquisition Teams (STRATA) program that same year, Pony Express CH-3s were the primary infiltration aircraft for inserting these indigenous teams into North Vietnam's southern panhandle.

By September 1967, the special operations airlift needs at NKP had grown enough that a new CH-3 unit arrived, the 21st Helicopter Squadron. Initially specializing in the emplacement of Igloo White sensors along the Ho Chi Minh Trail, its aircraft soon were combined with D Flight's to handle all the SOG and CIA helicopter missions, the combined entity redesignated in 1968 as the 21st SOS.

The 21st SOS suffered its greatest losses in May 1975, after the war, when its CH-53s landed a U.S. Marine force on Koh Tang Island, after Cambodian Communists had seized a U.S. ship, the *Mayaguez*. During the assault, three CH-53s were destroyed and two badly damaged, with two crewmen wounded, one killed, and another missing in action.

MUSTACHIO AND COWBOY

Perhaps the two greatest pilots ever to fly an H-34 Kingbee were "Cowboy" and "Mustachio," whose exploits can only be called legendary. Mustachio's real name was Nguyen Van Hoang, the nickname reflecting his finely trimmed mustache. Maj. Charlie Norton recalls that Cowboy's nickname flowed from his preference for hand-tailored, camouflaged flight suits.

According to recon man Lloyd O'Daniels, Cowboy "could make helicopters do things that they weren't designed to do, like fly backwards during takeoff. If you knew Cowboy was scheduled to come get you, you knew your stuff was right, you knew he wasn't going to back off."

Mustachio flew one of the most remarkable chopper rescues in SOG history in 1966. An RT had been hit at night and managed to slip away; but burdened with several wounded, it seemed certain the enemy would catch the team members before daylight. U.S. Hueys couldn't fly in darkness, and neither were the Vietnamese H-34s supposed to, but Mustachio said he would give it a try. Since this was all but suicidal, he went alone, taking up his Kingbee without a co-pilot or doorgunner. Despite groundfire and complete darkness Mustachio found the team and got the members out alive. "How he ever did it, I don't know," Scotty Crerar said. "It came out with 88 holes in it and the pilot's thumb shot off. The aircraft never flew again, but it got the team out."

Not all their flying stories came from combat missions. During a 1966

Mustachio (left) sits with Mecky Schuler and other Kingbee pilots in Kontum FOB-2 club. (Photo provided by Mecky Schuler)

105

Kingbee formation flight from Khe Sanh to Danang, Mustachio decided to show everyone how close he could buzz a church steeple in Hue. He accidentally knocked its crucifix off.

On 3 July 1966, Mustachio was flying RT Nevada to Kontum after a mission when his H-34 fell apart at 5,000 feet. The old bird's tail, designed to pivot for storage on aircraft carriers, had come loose, swung around, and chewed the helicopter to pieces in midair, ejecting its passengers and crew. In addition to Mustachio, everyone aboard was lost, including RT Nevada with M. Sgt. Ralph Reno, S. Sgt. Donald Fawcett, and their Nungs, plus an operations officer, Capt. Edwin MacNamara. SOG teams found all the bodies except Reno's.

On 12 July 1967, M. Sgt. Samuel Almendariz and Sfcs. Robert Sullivan and Harry Brown, plus five Nungs, were ambushed near Laotian Highway 922, about 60 miles due west of Hue. The NVA killed Sullivan and Almendariz and wounded Brown in the shoulder before he could break away and run.

At Khe Sanh the surviving half of the dynamic flying duo, Cowboy, climbed into his H-34 as quick as he got word about Brown—three SOG men, M. Sgts. Billy Waugh and Charles "Skip" Minnicks and Capt. Oliver Brin, jumped aboard after him.

Without gunship or fighter support, Cowboy slowly trolled his Kingbee above the treetops until Brown and several Nungs were spotted, and then tried to squeeze into an LZ so tiny that his rotors chewed into overhanging branches. But NVA bullets started thumping into the old Kingbee, and finally Cowboy had to return to Khe Sanh and refuel.

Ordering his co-pilot and doorgunner to stay at Khe Sanh and bringing only the insistent Skip Minnicks, Cowboy descended again into that narrow hole and hovered while Minnicks leaped off. An AK slug passed completely through Cowboy's neck, but somehow he flew the Kingbee with one hand and slowed the bleeding with his other hand while Minnicks dragged the wounded Brown aboard, and off they went. Cowboy's bravery astounded Billy Waugh, who thought, "He should get the Medal of Honor."

U.S. HELICOPTER UNITS THAT FLEW FOR SOG

SOG helicopter support came mostly from outside aviation units, which rotated frequently, resulting in incomplete records. This partial roster, assembled from many fragmentary sources, gives recognition to fine pilots and crews who saved many SOG men's lives by risking their own.

SUPPORTING COMMAND AND CONTROL NORTH:

U.S. Army
2nd Squadron, 17th Cavalry, 101st Airborne Division
17th Aviation Company, 101st Airborne Division
188th Assault Helicopter Company, 101st Airborne Division
4th Battalion, 77th Aerial Rocket Artillery, 101st Airborne Division
Co. B, 158th Assault Helicopter Battalion
Co. C, 158th Assault Helicopter Battalion
Co. D, 158th Assault Helicopter Battalion

U.S. Marine Corps
Marine aviation units began flying SOG missions from Khe Sanh in summer 1966 until the arrival of the 101st Airborne Division in I Corps following Tet 1968, with occasional support through the summer of 1970. Early missions were flown by HMM-165 with VMO-2, VMO-3, and VMO-6.

SUPPORTING COMMAND AND CONTROL CENTRAL:

U.S. Marine Corps
HMH-463 for Operation Tailwind, September 1970

U.S. Army
119th Assault Helicopter Company, 52nd Combat Aviation Battalion
57th Assault Helicopter Company, 52nd Combat Aviation Battalion
189th Assault Helicopter Company, 52nd Combat Aviation Battalion
170th Assault Helicopter Company, 52nd Combat Aviation Battalion
361st Aviation Company (Escort), The Pink Panthers

SUPPORTING COMMAND AND CONTROL SOUTH:

U.S. Air Force
20th Special Operations Squadron

U.S. Army
155th Assault Helicopter Company
195th Assault Helicopter Company

THAILAND-BASED HELICOPTER UNITS
(SUPPORTING CCN, CCC, AND THE STRATA PROGRAM):

U.S. Air Force
D Flight, 20th Special Operations Squadron
21st Special Operations Squadron

A JOLLY GREEN'S MEDAL OF HONOR

ON 8 NOVEMBER 1967 RT MASSACHUSETTS HAD BEEN ONLY A FEW HOURS in Laotian Target Oscar-Eight, when, after a quick gunfight, it was cornered by hundreds of NVA soldiers atop an elephant-grass-covered hill. The team One-Zero, Bruce Baxter, one of Special Forces' best known master sergeants, was accompanied by five Montagnards, along with One-One S. Sgt. Homer Wilson and One-Two Sp4c. Joe Kusick, new to recon.

With the NVA about to overrun the team, Kingbees and Huey gunships arrived. Aboard the first H-34, Sfc. James Scurry, a black medic built like an NFL lineman and one of the toughest men in SOG, could see that "they were in really serious trouble." Lifted aboard by Scurry's powerful hands, One-One Wilson and several 'Yards made it into the first Kingbee.

Then a second Kingbee went in, but heavy fire knocked it down. One-Zero Baxter hurriedly pulled the injured crewmen from the wreckage. A third helicopter came in, loaded a few men, and slunk away beneath tracer fire. Finally a fourth Kingbee landed, and Baxter rushed the rest of his team aboard; but he was wounded and the aircraft was shot down on the LZ.

Then the NVA made a mass assault. In the head-high elephant grass, One-Two Kusick saw Baxter get hit and die almost instantly and radioed that he was heading back for Baxter's body. A minute later and young Kusick was dead, too.

Then NVA groundfire downed a Huey gunship. By nightfall, surviving helicopter crewmen had gathered beside Baxter's and Kusick's bodies. "Instead of finishing off the survivors," a U.S. Air Force account notes, "the communists used them for bait" to bag more rescue choppers.

Two HH-3 Jolly Green Giants from the Danang-based 37th Aerospace Rescue and Recovery Squadron were dispatched to attempt a night extraction. Under the stark light of parachute flares, the first Jolly Green took severe damage from heavy fire and had to depart. The second Jolly Green was commanded by Capt. Gerald Young, 39, flying his 60th combat mission along with his co-pilot, Capt. Ralph Brower, flight engineer, S. Sgt. Eugene Clay, and pararescue man, Sgt. Larry Maysey. Asked if they'd attempt the extraction, Young answered, "Hell, we're airborne and hot to trot!"

Their Jolly Green flew a gauntlet of fire, and then Young held it steady for the survivors to scramble aboard with the Green Berets' bodies. He was just lifting out when an RPG slammed into the right engine, upending the HH-3. Seriously burned, Captain Young fell through the smashed canopy as the aircraft bounced upside down on fire. Young stumbled in the darkness, discovered an injured airman, and gave him first aid. At dawn a rescue chopper lifted away some survivors while Young and his comrade watched the enemy set up heavy machine guns within sight of them—to be bait, just like Baxter's men had been. In a display of amazing courage, Young hid his injured companion and then waved and shouted at the enemy and drew them away on a day-long chase, enabling the other survivors to escape.

That morning, a SOG Hatchet Force company landed a mile away, led by M. Sgt. Charles "Skip" Minnicks, along with Sgts. Jim Scurry, Ronald Bock, and Mike Hoglund. Seeing that NVA soldiers had dragged Baxter's and Kusick's bodies to an open spot under high ground, Minnicks knew better than to go for the bait. Later his men conducted a bloody gunfight in which Hoglund was killed and Sergeant Bock displayed such great bravery that he would be awarded the Silver Star.

Meanwhile, the injured Jolly Green pilot, Captain Young, led pursuing NVA troops deep into the jungle, and then, certain that he'd lost them and it was safe to bring in a chopper, he radioed for extraction.

Kusick's and Baxter's bodies were not recovered. Baxter's family received his posthumous Distinguished Service Cross, awarded for the selfless courage he'd shown on the LZ, repeatedly exposing himself to fire and evacuating everyone else first. For refusing extraction despite painful wounds and drawing the enemy away so the others could escape, Captain Young received the only Medal of Honor awarded to a non-SOG man for heroism while supporting a SOG operation.

Capt. Gerald O. Young. (Photo provided by U.S. Air Force)

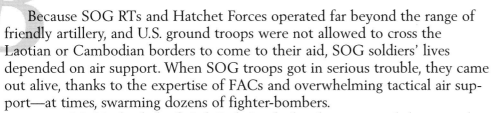

FACs and Fighters

Because SOG RTs and Hatchet Forces operated far beyond the range of friendly artillery, and U.S. ground troops were not allowed to cross the Laotian or Cambodian borders to come to their aid, SOG soldiers' lives depended on air support. When SOG troops got in serious trouble, they came out alive, thanks to the expertise of FACs and overwhelming tactical air support—at times, swarming dozens of fighter-bombers.

It was SOG's third chief, Col. Jack Singlaub, who cemented this special priority with headquarters, Seventh Air Force, in early 1967. Thanks to this arrangement, whenever SOG team members found themselves hopelessly outnumbered, in danger of being overrun, or running for their lives, the team leader had only to radio the code words "Prairie Fire! Prairie Fire!" and his tiny six-man team would have priority for all the fighter-bombers over Laos and North Vietnam.

Then the C-130 command post flying above southern Laos, known as Hillsboro in daytime and Moonbeam at night, would divert Air Force F-4s from bombing bridges in North Vietnam. Navy A-6s might even be pulled from a strike on a truck park in Laos. Within minutes anywhere from four to 24 fighters would be overhead and ready to roll in for the SOG men.

One A-1 Skyraider flashes past. (Photo provided by Newell Bernard)

COVEYS AND COVEY RIDERS

When the fighters arrived, the pilots had no idea who was on the ground, where they were, or what their predicament might be. Fortunately, there would already be an Air Force FAC plane on the scene, whose pilot could quickly brief the fighters and then direct their strike by marking the target with white-phosphorous smoke rockets. These were SOG's own assigned Air Force FACs, who overflew Laos and Cambodia during daylight hours when SOG teams were on the ground.

SOG's FACs were all volunteers, selected from among the most experienced FAC pilots in their respective squadrons, and who had already proven themselves as combat aviators. FACs from three squadrons supported SOG: the Covey FACs from Danang's 20th Tactical Air Support Squadron (TASS) with a forward element called Covey Alpha, at Pleiku; the Mike FACs of 21st TASS, flying from Ban Me Thuot; and the 23rd TASS Nail FACs based at Nakhon Phanom in Thailand.

Riding each FAC aircraft with the pilot was a SOG Special Forces liaison, popularly called a "Covey Rider." Selected from the best veteran recon men, Covey Riders brought tremendous ground experience and informed tactical judgment into the cockpit. Because they were not officially air crewmen, the Green Beret Covey Riders were not limited by crew rest regulations, allowing them to rack up prodigious numbers of combat flights.

This ideal combination—a recon vet's intimate understanding of ground operations and a FAC vet's intimate knowledge of aerial operations—gave their every decision an unequaled sophistication and effectiveness. They understood when one LZ should be passed up to extract a team from the next one, they could see when it was possible to risk a 500-pound bomb danger-close to a team, and they could tease precipitous edges of aircraft and ordnance capabilities.

SPADS AND ZORROS, HOBOS AND SANDYS

SOG's preferred close-air support fighter was not some sexy, Mach-II fighter, but rather the propeller-driven A-1 Skyraider. Perhaps because it seemed that these planes got down so low and so slow that there existed a kindred spirit between recon men and these scarf-swirling, throwback A-1 pilots whose unofficial motto, "Jets are for kids," mimicked the Kix cereal jingle.

Fuel consumption rates required jets to bomb and run within about 15 minutes, while the A-1s could loiter an hour or more, covering a team's running gunfight en route to an LZ, or a trapped team's protracted shootout. And the ordnance load! The Korean War-vintage Skyraider— a virtual flying dump truck—could lift 12,000 pounds of external stores, more than its own weight. The A-1s normally carried an ideal recon support load of cluster bombs, 20mm cannon, napalm, and 250-pound white-phosphorous bombs for masking helicopter extractions. Many a desperate recon man welcomed the distinctive roar of an approaching A-1's enormous 18-cylinder, 2,700-horsepower reciprocal engine, the most powerful ever installed in a single-seat aircraft. Helicopter pilots, too, appreciated the A-1 because it was slow and maneuverable enough to weave between helicopters. Screaming past

112

at treetop level, the A-1s laid a trail of bouncing, exploding, grenade-sized cluster bombs or fired 20mm exploding cannon slugs within 5 yards of a surrounded team. And napalm? If it didn't singe your eyebrows the napalm wasn't close enough to matter, and these A-1 pilots could drop it that close.

Four A-1 Skyraider units, having a total of about 50 aircraft, flew support for SOG. Premier among them was the Pleiku-based 6th SOS, the Spads, which flew almost solely for SOG. At Nakhon Phanom, the Hobos of the 1st SOS and Zorros of the 22nd SOS often supported SOG while also hunting trucks and interdicting roads. Split between Nakhon Phanom and Danang, the 602nd SOS specialized in escorting Jolly Green helicopter rescues of downed pilots in North Vietnam, but also flew Laotian missions for SOG operations, using the "Sandy" call sign. Late in the war, two squadrons of South Vietnamese air force A-1s based at Pleiku flew support for SOG and, like the incredible Kingbee crews, proved themselves brave and capable under the most dangerous, demanding circumstances.

Indicative of the danger inherent in supporting SOG and assisting downed pilot rescues, the Pleiku-based 6th SOS lost four Spad pilots MIA and another eight KIA, including the squadron's first commander, Lt. Col. Wallace A. Ford.

FAST MOVERS

Supplementing these A-1 "slow movers" were modern jet-powered fast movers, most often U.S. Air Force F-4 Phantoms and F-100 Supersabres and carrier-based U.S. Navy A-7 Corsair IIs and A-6 Intruders.

Most "fast movers" that supported SOG teams were diverted from other targets, steered SOG's way by the Hillsboro C-130 command bird because a team was in trouble. These redirected fast movers brought whatever ordnance they had, which most often meant "hard bombs." These could not be dropped closer than about 250 meters without seriously endangering the team. (The "book" minimum, of course, was several times that distance!)

F-100 fires a furious fusillade of 2.75-inch rockets. (Photo provided by Shelby Stanton)

The fast movers' most useful ordnance to assist running or pinned RTs was napalm canisters or 20mm cannon fire, which the planes could bring to within about 100 yards, depending on aircraft speed and terrain. After strafing and dumping napalm, the fast movers' hard bombs would be dropped ahead of the fleeing RT to sweep the terrain of enemy forces or dumped on potential enemy antiaircraft positions around the LZ. Ideally, by the time the fast movers had expended their ordnance, at least one set of A-1 Skyraiders would be on station and ready to deliver precision, danger-close strikes—with the choppers five minutes out.

During protracted situations, whole waves of fighters might be called in to save a SOG unit. In May 1968, when RT Alabama was surrounded for almost 48 hours in a bomb crater, more than 100 U.S. Air Force fighter-bombers were called in. In mid-1971, along with my Covey pilot, I directed six waves of carrier-based A-7s around a trapped ARVN team in Laos, dumping the ordnance from more than 30 fast movers in 20 minutes. Another time, while attempting to rescue a wounded U.S. trooper alone on the ground, in one hour we expended 12 sets of F-4s: 24 planes dumping almost 150 500-pound bombs!

S-P-A-F AND PROJECT FORD DRUM

In South Vietnam's Central Highlands, a handful of U.S. Army aviators wheeled about in jeeps sporting official-looking "S-P-A-F" lettering on their bumpers, which stood for "Sneaky Pete Air Force"—a fictitious unit. The jeeps had been "expropriat-ed" by SOG Green Berets and given to the Bird Dog pilots in appreciation for their vital work. The mythical S-P-A-F actually was the U.S. Army's 219th Aviation Company, whose O-1 spotter planes supported CCS, CCC, and CCN. Mainly these Bird Dogs carried recon One-Zeros on premission visual recons of cross-border targets, enabling the team leader to eyeball the terrain and check for fresh enemy activity.

Because a naked eye might whisk too quickly past something on the ground, One-Zeros carried 35mm cameras, and the resulting film occasionally disclosed surprising details. During a 1969 premission flight over Laos, M. Sgt. Norman Doney spotted a cave and several human figures, of which he snapped a few frames. Doney's enlarged pictures revealed Caucasians among NVA guards, interpreted to be U.S. POWs.

Such intelligence bonanzas eventually inspired SOG headquarters to institute Project Ford Drum, in which intelligence photographers with hand-held cameras rode Bird Dog backseats, visually recording enemy activities in Laos and Cambodia. Chugging along at treetop level, a Ford Drum flight might uncover supply stacks or the late afternoon glint off a hidden truck's windshield. Project Ford Drum proved a dramatic intelligence payoff by recording detailed information that even U-2 spy planes and satellites would have missed.

The dangerous Bird Dog flights were not without cost. Several O-1s were shot down, with crewmen killed or missing, including one Ford Drum photographer, Green Beret Sfc. Donald Armstrong, CCC, killed on 2 April 1970 by an enemy .50-caliber machine gun while he was flying at low level above Laos.

Above: Covey FAC Pleiku patch.

Left: A 20th Tactical Air Support Squadron Covey FAC over Laos. (Photo provided by Mike Cryer)

Below: A pair of OV-10 Broncos in formation. (Photo provided by Marshall Harrison)

Top: F-100 "fast mover" makes a bomb run in support of SOG team in Laos. (Photo provided by Mike Buckland)

Bottom: F-4 Phantom fast mover drops bombs on PT-76 tank on Highway 110, Laos. (Photo provided by John Plaster)

Top: A-1 "loaded for bear" over Laos—cluster bombs, napalm, and 20mm cannons. (Photo provided by John Plaster)

Bottom: A-1 Skyraider bombs NVA mortar position on ridge facing "Leghorn" radio relay site in Laos. (Photo provided by Merritte Wilson)

Skyraider lets loose its entire bomb load on a target. (Photo provided by Shelby Stanton)

Top: A-1 Skyraider at low level over Laos. Note the wingman in the rear. (Photo provided by Newell Bernard)

Bottom: A-1 Skyraider strafes in support of a recon team hidden at the edge of the jungle. (Photo provided by John Plaster)

Top: S-P-A-F Bird Dog pilots of 4th Platoon, 219th Aviation Company. Back, left to right: Captain Moccia, Captain Estell, Chief Warrant Officer 2 Lyle. Front: Chief Warrant Officer 2 Kyker, Chief Warrant Officer 2 Holmes, Platoon Sergeant (unknown), Chief Warrant Officer 2 Lugar, Chief Warrant Officer 2 Bennett. (Photo provided by Dale Bennett)

Bottom: S-P-A-F Bird Dog rolls in to fire a smoke rocket on a target in Laos. (Photo provided by Mike Buckland)

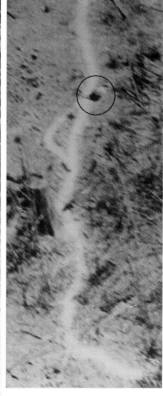

Above left: "Ford Drum" photo finds fresh NVA graves in Laos after the Battle of Dak Pek, 1970. (Photo provided by Frank Greco)

Above: NVA soldier collapses on trail after being hit in an exchange of fire with a SOG man in O-1 Bird Dog backseat. (Photo provided by Mike Buckland)

Left: O-1 Bird Dog pilot Capt. Bruce Bessor, MIA in Laos with Green Beret Sfc. Mike Scott, 13 May 1969. (Photo provided by Emery P. Johnston)

Top: NVA troops on Cambodian trail photographed by a SOG Bird Dog. (Photo provided by Brendon Lyons)

Below: THE ULTIMATE PRICE. The shot-down Bird Dog in Cambodia in which Capt. David Cinkosky died. (Photo provided by Dale Bennett)

Above: A-1 Skyraider swooping at low level in Laos. (Photo provided by Newell Bernard)

Left: AC-130 Spectre gunship, with its twin 40mm guns (right) plus 20mm Vulcans and miniguns forward. (Photo provided by John Plaster)

Inset: An OV-10 Bronco armed FAC aircraft, pilot in front seat, SOG Covey Rider in back. (Photo provided by Marshall Harrison)

Right: A pair of OV-10 Broncos in formation. (Photo provided by Marshall Harrison)

Above: Pleiku-based O-2 Covey FAC high over Laos. (Photo provided by Gerald Denison)

Top left: CCN Covey Rider Jim Martin (center), with Air Force Covey FACs, 1st Lt. Gary Pavlu (left) and 1st Lt. Bob Meadows beside O-2 Cessna Skymaster. (Photo provided by Jim Martin)

Bottom: O-2 Cessna Skymaster Covey FAC over the South China Sea after takeoff from Danang is en route to SOG's Laos area of operations. (Photo provided by Jim Martin)

Above: Locally designed patch worn by A-1H "Spad" pilots who flew Skyraiders at Pleiku. (Photo provided by Scott Kilpatrick)

Right: U.S. Army O-1 Bird Dog at treetop level, looking for enemy deep in Cambodia. (Photo provided by Marshall Harrison)

Bottom right: View through a Bird Dog's front canopy, rolling in to fire smoke rockets on a target and call in an air strike. (Photo provided by the family of George K. Sisler)

Left: Exploding bombs on an enemy position along Highway 92 in Laos. (Photo provided by the family of George K. Sisler)

Below left: A 2,000-pound bomb detonates on its target, a major enemy supply road in Laos. (Photo provided by Frank Jaks)

Below: U.S. fighter-bombers hit enemy positions astride Highway 92 in southern Laos. (Photo provided by the family of George K. Sisler)

Pleiku-based "Spad" Skyraider shrieks past SOG's "Leghorn"
Radio Relay Site in southern Laos. (Photo provided by
Newell Bernard)

Below: An A-1 Skyraider at low level over southern Laos.
(Photo provided by Newell Bernard)

Top: Pleiku-based Covey FAC banks his O-2 over southern Laos. (Photo provided by Newell Bernard)

Bottom: A-1 Skyraider over Laos in support of SOG operations. (Photo provided by Newell Bernard)

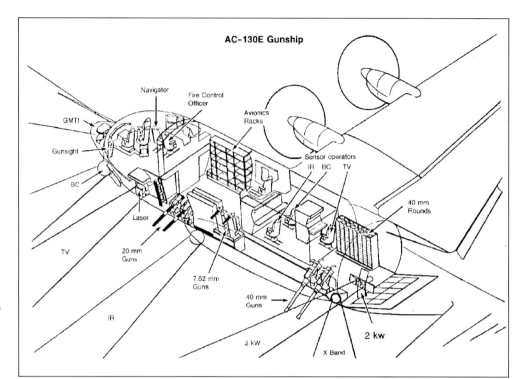

Right: AC-130E Gunship.

Below: AC-130 Spectre gunship fires 105mm howitzer and 20mm Vulcan cannon. (Photo provided by U.S. Air Force)

THE AWESOME C-130 SPECTRE

INTENDED AS A HIGH-TECH PLATFORM FOR HUNTING TRUCKS at night along the Ho Chi Minh Trail in Laos, Thailand-based Spectre C-130 gunships became SOG's finest night support aircraft.

Spectre incorporated refinements that had evolved from earlier fixed-wing gunships, all of which began as ordinary transport planes. The first of these, "Puff the Magic Dragon," a C-47 transport with only miniguns firing 7.62mm rifle-sized projectiles, evolved into "Shadow," a C-119 Flying Boxcar that added heavier Vulcan 20mm cannon to miniguns. Some Shadows hunted trucks in Laos by having a crewman lie on a mattress and handhold a night-vision scope to search for vehicles.

A still heavier transport (such as the C-130), Air Force planners realized, could be a platform for more powerful guns, along with all sorts of bulky, cutting-edge sensors and night-vision systems. The first C-130 Spectres carried the same 20mm cannon as the C-119 Shadow, but added a deadly twin-barreled Bofors 40mm cannon, specially modified from its vehicle mount for airborne firing.

Combined with night-vision aids, low-light TV, FLIR, a laser rangefinder, special heat-reading sensors, and the "Black Crow"—an electronic sensor that pinpointed enemy trucks by "reading" their ignition—Spectre became a deadly truck killer. In its final refinement (fielded in 1971), the U.S. Air Force added to Spectre's tail the heaviest gun ever mounted in an airplane, a gyro-stabilized 105mm howitzer. Its recoil was so great that it swung the enormous C-130 sideways when it fired. Day or night, orbiting at 5,000 feet, the Spectre could place its 105mm rounds with such incredible accuracy that first-round hits against stationary trucks was commonplace.

Spectre's powerful guns often fired for SOG teams along the Ho Chi Minh Trail and inside South Vietnam, with some teams carrying X-band "mini-ponder" electronic repeaters, which returned a coded signal to the aircraft for an electronic fix in total darkness. In several instances, surrounded RTs lit ration "heat tabs," on which Spectre's guns keyed as a "hot-spot" reference point for supporting fire. Despite darkness, Spectre's guns hit consistently within 50 meters of SOG RTs and Hatchet Forces, raining terrible steel and flashing explosions among NVA troops who until then had thought they owned the night.

Along with the A-1 Skyraider and OV-10 Bronco, the C-130 Spectre unquestionably helped SOG men prevail in life-or-death fights against vastly superior enemy forces.

131

SOG FAC AIRCRAFT

DURING THE SIX YEARS THAT U.S. AIR FORCE FACs supported SOG cross-border operations, they flew three generations of FAC planes—the Cessna O-1 Bird Dog, the O-2A Cessna Skymaster, and the North American OV-10 "Bronco."

The O-1 Bird Dog of 1965 had changed little since its adoption during the Korean War, where, because jet-powered strike aircraft moved too fast to see targets, targets had to be detected and marked with white smoke rockets by smaller, slower aircraft.

The O-1 chugged along at less than 100 mph, its only armament four single round tubes that carried target-marking rockets. The nimble, two-seat Bird Dog was hardly wider than the pilot and, like the O-2 that would replace it, lacked armor and self-sealing gas tanks. In SOG, the obsolescent Bird Dog initially was flown by FACs, although it was retained throughout the war by U.S. Army aviation units.

Replacing the Bird Dog FACs in late 1967 was a sophisticated civilian plane with retractable landing gear and trim control, the twin-engine Cessna 337 Skymaster. For FAC duty, the O-2 Skymaster backseat was packed with radios and electronic gear, while plastic see-through panels were installed in the doors to allow better observation, plus a seven-round rocket tube hung under each wing. The O-2's twin tandem engines allowed a maximum speed of 199 mph, but more typically the plane cruised along at about 140 mph.

Unlike the O-1 or O-2A, the North American OV-10 Bronco was laid out like a true fighter with stick controls, ejection seats, and four sponson-mounted M60 machine guns. Resembling the World War II twin-boom P-38 Lightning fighter, the highly maneuverable OV-10 raced along at 300 mph without external stores and cruised at 233 mph. When outfitted with a full combat load, its cruising speed was cut by about 75 mph. The first OV-10s reached SOG in 1969.

The U.S. armed forces' first purpose-designed FAC aircraft, the Bronco had the pilot and backseater sit forward of the engines in large bubble canopies that came down almost to their waists, affording an excellent field of view. With a typical load of four 7-round rocket pods—including 14 rounds with high-explosive warheads—the OV-10 proved to be a recon man's life-saver, bringing machine guns and explosive rockets to an RT's aid virtually within minutes of making contact. Knocking the enemy back or slowing the enemy's pursuit of an RT, the OV-10's fire filled that valuable few minutes between the FAC pilot's requesting fighters and their arrival overhead.

Late in the war, several Thailand-based "Nail" OV-10s carried "Pave Nail" first-generation laser target designators, allowing them to place an F-4 Phantom's bombs with unprecedented exactness.

Top: O-1 Bird Dog FAC over Laos. (Photo provided by Merritte Wilson)

Middle: Cessna Skymaster O-2A over Cambodia. (Photo provided by Mike Buckland)

Bottom: The OV-10 Bronco armed with four M60 machine guns and 14 high-explosive rockets. (Photo provided by Frank Greco)

LOST COVEY RIDERS

AT DESPERATE MOMENTS, a SOG recon man's final psychological lifeline was the reassuring radio voice of a former recon man, high above, flying with a U.S. Air Force FAC, doing his best to assemble the fighters and helicopters to retrieve the endangered recon team. Along with the FAC pilots, these Special Forces Covey Riders faced their own dangers—from flak traps and terrible weather to almost daily doses of heavy groundfire. Sometimes they paid the ultimate price.

From records assembled by Steve Sherman, the following roster has been constructed, although it remains incomplete. In almost each case, a U.S. Air Force FAC pilot was lost, too. Reflecting NVA antiaircraft concentrations, all were lost over Laos except Sergeant First Class Fernandez, who was shot down over South Vietnam's Ashau Valley.

Below left: Covey Rider "Sam" Zumbrun killed in action when his O-2 FAC plane was shot down. (Photo provided by Jason T. Woodworth

Below right: Roger Teeter (right) and his One-Zero, Cliff Newman. Teeter later died flying Covey. (Photo provided by Cliff Newman)

- S. Sgt. Tim Walters, CCN   9 March 1969
- Sfc. Donald Ross, CCN   23 April 1969
- Sfc. Mike Scott, CCC*   13 May 1969
- Sfc. James "Sam" Zumbrun, CCC   10 January 1970
- S. Sgt. Roger "Buff" Teeter, CCN*   28 December 1970
- Sfc. William Fernandez, CCN*   19 February 1971

* MIA

134

PART FOUR

RECON WEAPONS, MISSIONS, AND TACTICS

Recon Equipment and Weapons

Chapter Eight

A SOG recon man's basic equipment could be grouped according to where he carried it: his pockets, his web gear, or his rucksack.

No matter what happened—a helicopter crash or a surprise assault in the dead of night—a recon man would retain what he had on his person. Therefore, his pockets held a survival radio, signal mirror, flare gun, compass, folding knife, morphine injectors, salt tablets, pen light, and a bright orange signal panel. Classified materials, such as maps, codes, counterfeit money, and forged enemy documents, also would be on his person. Since he operated clandestinely, he carried no dogtags or ID, nothing that could identify him as a U.S. serviceman.

His web gear contained what he needed to fight: loaded magazines stowed in a World War II Browning Automatic Rifle belt or in stretched canteen covers, a mixture of full-size and mini-high-explosive, white-phosphorous, and tear gas grenades, along with a handgun, a knife, canteens, a gas mask, a helicopter extraction rig (the STABO or Hansen rig or a Swiss seat), bandages, rappeling "D" rings, and a strobe light.

Finally, a recon man packed his rucksack knowing that he might have to dump it if hotly pursued, so he ensured that nothing inside was essential to the mission or dependent on survival. Typically, his rucksack contained a claymore mine (in a fast-opening pouch sewn on top), a banana knife, rations, more canteens, an indigenous sleeping bag, explosives, extra smoke grenades, a

137

Top: Alex Saunders, CCS RT Hatchet, displays his homemade chopped-down M16 above a normal M16. (Photo provided by Bob Bost)

team medical kit, handcuffs or wrist restraints, and a spare radio battery.

BASIC SOG WEAPONS

When it came to weapons, SOG's armory stocked the largest collection of firearms ever assembled for a U.S. special operations unit. From German Schmeisser submachine guns to Chinese rocket launchers, from Belgian pistols to Soviet light machine guns, if it existed SOG had several or would find one—or even build one.

SOG's need for foreign weapons was driven by deniability, the need for the U.S. government to deny any knowledge of SOG activities. Therefore, SOG teams did not carry U.S. weapons in Laos until about 1967, by which time such weapons had become commonplace in Southeast Asia. However, U.S. firearms remained forbidden in Cambodia until the 1970 incursion. Always, though, weapon choice was a One-Zero's decision.

Initially, the Swedish K submachine gun was SOG's standard recon weapon. Only 21 inches long with its stock folded and weighing 6.1 pounds empty, it was superbly balanced and 100-percent reliable. With its generous 36-round magazine, a recon man carried a basic load of 12 magazines, plus one in the weapon, for 468 total rounds. Its basic shortcoming—as with all 9mm submachine guns—was the inadequate terminal ballistics of its projectile.

The Soviet-design AK, preferred over 9mm submachine guns by many SOG Green Berets, was much more ballistically effective. It also had the added benefits of visual—and audio—disguise: its distinct "ka-ka-ka-ka" report did not identify the shooter as an American. Most SOG AKs were newer AKMs, which employed stamped steel parts to reduce empty weight from 9.5 to 7 pounds. SOG recon men needed so many AK magazines that CISO deputy Ben Baker had thousands of them secretly manufactured in South Korea.

By 1967, after approval to carry U.S. weapons in Laos, the CAR-15 became SOG recon's trademark. Officially designated the XM-177 in a 10-inch barrel, or the XM-177E2 in an 11.5-inch barrel, the CAR-15 employed the same receiver as the M16 rifle, reducing its 40-inch length

A recon man's best friend: the CAR-15, shown here with an 10-inch barrel. (Photo provided by National Infantry Museum)

to 28 inches by installing a shorter barrel and tele-scoping buttstock. The resulting weapon experienced problems in muzzle rise and ear-cracking blast, corrected by installing a 4-inch compensator.

Firing 700 rpm cyclic, the only performance difference between the CAR-15 and the M16 was a slight decline in precision aiming due to the CAR-15's shortening the distance between the front and rear sights to 15 inches. A typical basic load was one 30-rounder and twenty-one 20-round magazines—"about" 450 rounds, since most recon men loaded 19 rounds per magazine to reduce tension on the follower spring, believing that this improved reliability.

As with many other weapons, SOG soldiers readily modified their CAR-15s and M16s to fit mission requirements. One notable develop-ment was a hybrid weapon: installing a CAR-15 fore-end and barrel assem-bly on a standard M16 for an excel-lent handling mini-M16.

SOG's most used handgun cer-tainly was the Browning 9mm Hi-Power. Many recon men packed the .45 U.S. Government model, although just about any handgun might be encountered, from a Walther P-38 to Colt Commando air-weight or hammerless Smith & Wesson snubnose.

The typical recon team included two indigenous M79 grenadiers, who with proper training and practice could pump out one round every

three to four seconds, twice the "book" rate of fire. Breaking open like a single-shot shotgun and weighing 6.5 pounds, the M79 presented problems in close-range shooting because its high-explosive warhead required 31 meters of flight to arm, and its canister load did not generate enough velocity for its buckshot to be very effective. Instead, some recon men loaded the canisters with dart-like metal flechettes that proved devastat-ing to exposed NVA soldiers, but achieved minimal penetration through brush.

Due to such shortcomings some team leaders didn't want to give up a CAR-15's firepower for an M79, so they sawed off the M79 barrel, whit-tled the butt into a pistol grip, and carried the resulting "pistol" as a sec-ondary weapon. This trend subsided in 1969 with the advent of the XM148 grenade launcher, which attached below the CAR-15 fore-end. When the more refined M203 grenade launcher was fielded in 1971, it too saw combat with SOG, but neither of these weapons achieved the rate of fire or consistent accuracy of the original M79.

Although seldom used, the M14 rifle and its XM21 sniping version were also part of SOG's armory. Among SOG's most distinguished M14 riflemen was Medal of Honor recipient Bob Howard, who occasion-ally carried one with green-tipped

139

RT Krait's patch. (Photo provided by Richard Claar)

IN PRAISE OF THE CAR-15

SOG RECON WAS THE ONLY UNIT IN VIETNAM armed entirely with CAR-15s, the short-barreled, folding-stock submachine gun version of the M16 rifle. So long as he had his CAR-15 and one magazine left, a SOG recon man was a force to be reckoned with—or at least he felt that way.

Many team patches incorporated CAR-15s, but RT Krait took it a step further, adding the bannered slogan, "The Lord giveth, and the CAR-15 taketh away." SOG men even sang in praise of their most popular firearm, thanks to an anonymous recon lyricist who lifted the Gospel melody from "He's Got the Whole World in His Hands":

> *I've got a CAR-15, in my hands.*
> *I've got a CAR-15, in my hands.*
> *I've got a CAR-15, in my hands.*
> *I've got the whole world in my hands.*
>
> *I've got six HEs and two Willy Petes.**
> *I've got six HEs and two Willy Petes.*
> *I've got six HEs and two Willy Petes.*
> *I've got the whole world in my hands.*
>
> *Charlie's on the radio, talking to me.*
> *Charlie's on the radio, talking to me.*
> *Charlie's on the radio, talking to me.*
> *He thinks my balls are in his hands.*
>
> *But, I've got a CAR-15. . . .*

And so on. No matter the predicament, no matter how badly outnumbered or tactically disadvantaged, in this song the recon man's CAR-15 would allow him to reign supreme.

* "HEs" are high-explosive hand grenades; "Willy Petes" are white-phosphorous grenades.

THE CAR-15 VS. THE AK

BECAUSE SOG RECON MEN FREQUENTLY CARRIED AKs IN CAMBODIA, and trained with AKs almost as much as with CAR-15s, their experience with both weapons allows a valid comparison. The criteria below are listed in the order they influenced a life-and-death SOG recon gunfight.

Ergonomics: Generally both weapons are handy and readily manipulable, but the CAR-15 points a bit more naturally. *A tie.*

Reloading: The AK bolt doesn't lock to the rear after firing the last round, adding another step and turning it into a two-hand exercise. The CAR-15 bolt locks to the rear and slams shut with a slap of the left palm against the receiver. The CAR-15 is twice as fast to reload. *The CAR-15 wins.*

Readying to Fire: The shooting hand never leaves a CAR-15's grip, but you cannot place an AK off safety without taking the shooting hand off the grip. *The CAR-15 wins.*

Firing: The lower recoil on a CAR-15 enables its 3-to-5-round bursts to stay closer to the intended impact point. The CAR-15 can switch between semiauto and full auto without taking the shooting hand off the grip. *The CAR-15 wins.*

Accuracy: Both have almost identical sight planes, but the CAR-15 has superior sights. *The CAR-15 wins.*

Ballistic Effectiveness: Both have similar maximum effective ranges and both will kill equally by proper shot placement at typical SOG engagement distances of 50 meters or less. *A toss-up.*

Magazines and Ammo Load: The 5.56mm cartridge and magazines were about half the bulk and weight of AK magazines and rounds. Although inherently a CAR-15 advantage, this was not so decisive since SOG men had to carry in all their ammo while the NVA could be resupplied in minutes from nearby units or ammo stockpiles. *Still, the CAR-15 wins.*

Reliability: This is listed last because seldom did a weapon malfunction. Like the M16, the CAR-15 had to be kept clean, but SOG men took it a step further, firing up their entire basic load before each operation so they would have tested each magazine—and replaced any mags that failed—and reloaded with completely fresh ammo. Using this procedure, my CAR-15 malfunctioned perhaps three times during practice fire but never once in a real gunfight. Yet I have never seen an AK malfunction, *ever. The edge goes to the AK.*

In summary: the CAR-15 points more naturally and is faster to get off safety, easier to fire, faster to reload, essentially as reliable, and superior overall to the AK. For those whose lives depended on it, their almost universal choice of the CAR-15 over the AK tells it all.

After extensive combat experience with both the AK and the CAR-15, recon men had no doubts about which was the superior weapon. (Photo provided by John Plaster)

141

M198 Duplex ammunition, which held two bullets in each round. The Duplex ammunition wasn't accurate at long range, but proved suitable for 50 yards or so. The XM21 was a more specialized weapon, only issued to SOG graduates of sniper courses taught by the 9th and 25th Infantry Divisions. Due to restrictive terrain and limited fields of fire, sniper rifles were seldom employed in cross-border operations.

SUPPRESSED SUBMACHINE GUNS

For prisoner snatches, sentry elimination, and chance meetings with the enemy, SOG men employed a wide variety of suppressed firearms, mostly submachine guns. Most suppressors were integral, built into weapon barrels instead of being clipped or screwed on.

The preferred submachine gun for prisoner snatches was the British Sten Mark IIS because it could be disassembled quickly and stored compactly in a rucksack. This enabled a recon man to carry a more powerful AK or CAR-15 and employ the low-powered suppressed weapon only during the prisoner snatch. A World War II development for the British Special Operations Executive (SOE)—which ran secret agents and saboteurs in Occupied Europe—the suppressed Sten was best suited for close-range shooting. In semiauto mode it was reasonably accurate and fairly quiet, although the recoiling bolt's "clack-clack-clack" seemed unnecessarily noisy.

Suppressed Swedish K submachine guns, which fired only full auto, were notably more accurate than the Sten but still presented the terminal ballistics of a 9mm. The suppressor added 6 inches in length, degrading

A suppressed Sten Mark IIS submachine gun, a SOG favorite. (Photo provided by Bill Walter)

the Swedish K's famous handiness.

The suppressed M3 grease gun proved very popular; its powerful, 230-grain, .45-caliber slug struck with lethal force, depending upon shot placement. Developed during World War II for the U.S. OSS, this suppressed gun weighed 11.5 pounds, 3 pounds more than a standard M3, which (combined with a slow cyclic rate of 450 rpm) allowed controllable single shots at full auto—and with considerable accuracy.

SOG's Uzis, manufactured under license by Belgium's Fabrique Nationale, were acquired clandestinely in Europe. They were SOG's only submachine guns issued with both a standard and suppressed barrel,

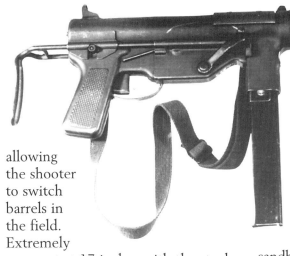

A suppressed M3 submachine gun. (Photo provided by West Point Museum)

allowing the shooter to switch barrels in the field. Extremely compact at 17 inches with the stock folded, the Uzis were especially popular with HALO parachuting teams.

SOG's most sophisticated suppressed weapon was the Sionics Silent Sniper Carbine, a much modified M1 Carbine rebarreled from .30-caliber carbine to 9mm Parabellum, and using a 13-round Browning Hi-Power magazine welded into a modified 20-round carbine magazine. The greatest mechanical difference was that this was *not* a semiautomatic, but a manually operated, straight-pull bolt-action weapon. Because the action remained closed during firing, this was SOG's quietest long gun. The Sionics Carbine came standard with a 4x riflescope. Its only major shortcoming was that it could not be carried disassembled in a rucksack—you were stuck with it for the entire mission, a 13-shot, 9mm, bolt action, hardly the choice weapon for a chance contact against AK-armed men at close range!

SUPPRESSED PISTOLS AND RIFLES

SOG stocked several suppressed pistols, but its most used was an OSS weapon of World War II, the High Standard Model HD. Firing a low-velocity, .22 Long Rifle round, the HD sounded no louder than someone snapping his fingers and inflicted such minimal injury when fired into a thigh or buttock that the disabled victim almost always survived. It had been developed by Bell Laboratories. In 1943 OSS Chief "Wild Bill" Donovan smuggled a loaded High Standard into the Oval Office, placed a small sandbag in a corner, and quietly fired 10 shots while President Franklin Roosevelt was busy on the phone. Impressed by Donovan's gift, Roosevelt put the pistol on display at his Hyde Park home. To conform with international rules of war, SOG's High Standard pistols were issued with non-expanding .22-caliber ammunition.

Another favored SOG suppressed pistol—and the quietest one I've ever fired—was a purpose-designed British SOE weapon, the .32-caliber Welrod. Developed at Welwyn Experimental Laboratory, the Welrod was simply a tubular barrel/suppressor/receiver with a bent metal rod for a trigger and a rubber-covered Colt automatic magazine as a grip. The rotary bolt turns in the palm of your hand to load or eject spent cases. In addition to its sizable suppressor, the Welrod's quietness resulted from a locked breech that allowed no gas to escape and precluded any noise from an operating mechanism. The Welrod was intended for close-range use, but it served well in Laos and Cambodia for sentry removal.

Other suppressed SOG pistols included Walther PPKs, Beretta .32 automatics, Browning Hi-Powers, and Walther P-38s.

Unlike its pistols and submachine guns, SOG's rifle suppressors

RT Pick One-Zero Bob Graham (left) with his infamous bow and arrow. Also pictured are (left to right) Sgt. Mike Cummings, 1st Lt. Mike Ash, and S. Sgt. Frank Oppel. (Photo provided by Bob Graham)

were external devices that attached to muzzles, and they represented a revolution in silencing technology. Until the late 1960s weapons experts hadn't thought that a high-powered rifle could be silenced effectively; common wisdom claimed that any suppressor capable of containing a rifle's violent muzzle blast would itself be blown apart. Georgia-based Sionics, Inc. proved the experts wrong, installing special "expansion chambers" in its suppressor, along with a spiral gas diffusor that increased the distance the gas traveled without increasing the overall suppressor size.

SOG's armory included a number of M16s and XM21s outfitted with these first-generation Sionics suppressors. Medal of Honor recipient Franklin Miller sometimes carried a

suppressed M16 as his standard long gun, with which we experimented at some length. Unfortunately, we learned that SOG lacked a subsonic 5.56mm, so an enemy would still hear the bullet's supersonic "crack"—but even this disclosed only the general direction of the shot.

Certainly SOG's most unusual silent weapon was also its least sophisticated. CCS One-Zero Robert Graham had his father ship him a hunting bow from his native Canada, along with broad-head-tipped arrows, with which he silently hunted NVA troops in Cambodia. An experienced archer, Graham actually once exchanged fire with an AK-armed NVA soldier, though he was uncertain of the result—except that the NVA foe stopped shooting, and Graham lived to tell the tale.

HEAVY WEAPONS
AND HEAVY TEAMS

Uncommitted to the firearms of any particular country, SOG's Special Forces weapons men constantly experimented and modified weapons they thought would match or outgun the NVA's, a process that led to some noteworthy developments.

Examining a captured Soviet RPD light machine gun—at 15.4 pounds, the lightest belt-fed machine gun in the world—some recon men found that its barrel could be sawed off and the gun would still function flawlessly. This SOG-customized RPD was chopped to about 31 inches, cutting its weight to 12 pounds—shorter and a bit heavier than the Thompson submachine gun, but firing the full-powered AK round. The sawed-off RPD was well balanced and handled so perfectly you could write your name with it. Then the SOG men added a jury-rigged 25-round metal belt segment to boost its capacity to 125 rounds and inserted a slice of linoleum in the drum to eliminate any rattle. At close range it was the most awesome weapon in SOG recon.

The U.S. M60 machine gun was not entirely abandoned, but it was heavy—23 pounds—and its 100-round assault bag grossly twisted it left and down, making it difficult to shoot well. The Naval Weapons Center at China Lake, California, developed a special M60 firing system nicknamed "The Death Machine," which connected an aircraft-type flexible feed belt to a 1,000-round backpack drum. The Death Machine provided incomparable firepower to a single assaulting machine gunner, but, at 75 pounds, the system required a lumberjack-sized man to wield it.

The NVA's squad-level RPG-2 rocket launcher was the rough counterpart to the U.S. M72 light antitank weapon (LAW), but the RPG produced considerably more blast and fragments than the LAW because its 4-pound 85mm rocket was approximately twice as heavy as the 66mm LAW rocket.

Looking at this math and having been at the impact side of these RPGs inspired some One-Zeros to adopt the communist weapon. Martin Bennett of RT New York modified his RPG rockets into a round he called the "Porcupine," attaching nails and tear-gas-powder packets to its warhead.

The heaviest weapon carried by recon teams was the 20-pound M19 mortar. Devoid of bipod, sight, or baseplate, this 60mm mortar was carried on a canvas sling, with rounds

DEATH MACHINE. China Lake Naval Weapons Center's 1,000-round backpack and flexible feed made for awesome M60 firepower. (Photo provided by U.S. Navy)

Frank Greco demonstrates the controllability of the sawed-off Chinese RPD machine gun. (Photo provided by Frank Greco)

either drop-fired or trigger-fired. The M19 was an excellent World War II weapon forgotten by the U.S. Army of the 1960s. Its pop-bottle-sized high-explosive (HE) round hit like a small bomb, throwing fragments in a 9 x 18-meter area. By manipulating the tube and varying the charge packets, its rounds could hit as close as 45 meters out to a maximum of 1,814 meters, or more than a mile. Since the Communist bloc had fielded no equivalent weapon and the NVA 82mm mortar was not nearly so portable or flexible for its fast-moving counterreconnaissance units, the M19 mortar represented a tremendous firepower edge.

Consider, then, what happened when all these heavy weapons went in with a 12-man "heavy" recon team, which did not sidestep or sneak away but sought out the enemy to bloody his nose in his own backyard. Thinking they were about to tangle with a lightly armed, six-man SOG team, NVA units were rocked instead by bursting 60mm mortar rounds falling at one per second, two RPD machine guns grazing the ground with 125-round belts, RPG rockets crashing, rifle grenades exploding, CAR-15s rattling—and by a force that assaulted as quickly as it gained fire superiority. Especially famous for outfighting almost every NVA unit his heavy team encountered was RT California One-Zero Joe Walker. A heavy team, however, had to fight hard and get out fast, or the NVA would mass enough troops to defeat it. Still, RTs' aggressive actions helped take some boldness out of the NVA forces so that they'd approach a typical six-man recon team more cautiously.

OTHER UNUSUAL WEAPONS AND DEVICES

Among SOG's other unusual weapons was a pump-action 40mm grenade launcher, developed by the Naval Weapons Center at China Lake. Fielded in 1967, it resembled the Winchester Model 12 shotgun, with a 3-round tubular magazine. Bulky and unbalanced, this 8.2-pound weapon was difficult to wield, and only 30 were ever made.

When it came to sawed-off shotguns, the Winchester Model 97 pump seemed a recon favorite because of its external hammer. However, few men carried a shotgun as a primary weapon because the gun is dangerously slow to reload, and, though it throws lots of projectiles, a shooter can engage only about six discrete targets in contrast to a CAR-15 shooter engaging 30. In a sustained firefight, a shotgunner spends too much time reloading and not enough time shooting; indeed, one recon man was shot dead while reloading his shotgun.

Another sawed-off backup weapon was the M1 Carbine carried as a large pistol, but compact with a 20-round magazine. Generating ballistics similar to a .357 Magnum pistol, the carbine was deadly at close quarters.

One of SOG's most novel weapons was the V-40 minigrenade, obtained from Holland by Ben Baker. Golf-ball-sized and weighing just 3.5 ounces, it was the world's smallest hand grenade, but it spawned 400 lethal fragments in a 5-meter circle. Its maximum range depended upon one's arm, with some men throwing it accurately almost 100 yards. Although not nearly as powerful as a full-sized M26 "lemon" or M33 "baseball" grenade, the minigrenade was very popular with aircrews and recon men as part of their survival gear.

Another unusual explosive device, used for trail ambushes, was a linear fragmentation charge consisting of a hose-like, half-inch-thick cord of

A SOG SEAL with radio-controlled explosive boat. (Art by Tami Odegard)

PETN high explosive encircled by steel washers. It could be strung along a trail in seconds for a quick ambush and was command-detonated with a claymore mine electrical firing device.

To interdict enemy boat traffic on the Mekong River in Cambodia, SOG acquired small radio-controlled boats, about 30 inches long, containing several pounds of high explosive packed behind a bow detonator. Controlled by SOG Green Berets or SEALs hidden on a river bank, the small boats were visually observed and steered to ram, kamikaze-fashion, into passing river barges and boats. Whether any were actually used is not noted in SOG records.

Late in the war SOG obtained Piccotex, a CIA-supplied fuel contaminant that clogs vehicle engines with a tar-like substance. The OSS had earlier developed a similar engine-sabotage chemical in 1944, Caccolube, which was slipped into a vehicle's oil intake in rubber-sheathed pouches. In 1954, while French forces were withdrawing from North Vietnam, CIA-trained teams sabotaged the Hanoi city bus system's fuel supply, apparently using Caccolube.

SOG planned to duplicate North Vietnamese fuel drums, fill them with Piccotex-contaminated fuel, and air-drop them at night into the Laotian rivers, down which the NVA floated oil drums, but first SOG needed genuine NVA barrels, and bringing them back became a major challenge. SOG recon Sgt. Jeff Mauceri photographed a 55-gallon drum during a mission in Laos, after which he was pummeled with debriefers' questions about seals, markings, and colors, but the barrel was too deteriorated to be retrieved. Eventually SOG recovered one drum, but almost a year had gone by. By then the NVA had shifted their fuel transportation to new hidden fuel pipelines, and the great sabotage opportunity had passed.

SOG's greatest sabotage effort, the insinuation of booby-trapped ammunition into enemy stockpiles, was part of a larger "black psyops" program that is covered separately.

RECON MAN'S BASIC GEAR

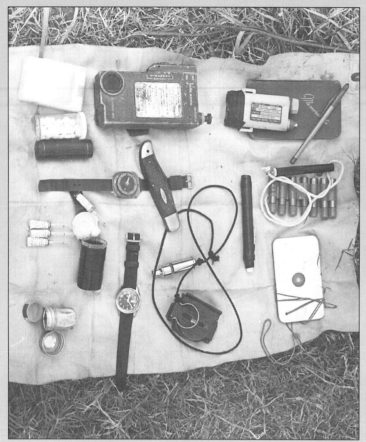

Above: Survival gear typically found in a recon man's pockets included emergency radio, penflare, mirror, morphine, whistle, and compasses, shown here laid out on a signal panel. (Photo provided by John Plaster)

Top right: On his web gear, a recon man carried 21 magazines, a pistol, canteens, a gas mask, and plenty of grenades. (Photo provided by John Plaster)

Bottom right: A recon man's rucksack contained extra grenades, more canteens, a claymore mine, a medical kit, explosives, a banana knife, handcuffs, and rations (shown here on a lightweight sleeping bag). (Photo provided by John Plaster)

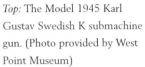

Top: The Model 1945 Karl Gustav Swedish K submachine gun. (Photo provided by West Point Museum)

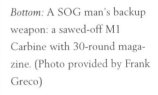

Middle: Jason "Woody" Woodworth, with a Swedish K on his shoulder, climbs into a Kingbee for an early-1965 mission into Laos. (Photo provided by Jason T. Woodworth)

Bottom: A SOG man's backup weapon: a sawed-off M1 Carbine with 30-round magazine. (Photo provided by Frank Greco)

Above: SOG's quietest suppressed weapon, the British
Welrod pistol. (Photo provided
by Will Curry)

Top right: A suppressed version
of the Swedish K submachine
gun. (Photo provided by West
Point Museum)

Middle: Disassembled, the Sten
Mk IIS fit compactly inside a
rucksack. (Photo provided by
John Plaster)

Bottom: The Sionics Silent
Sniper Carbine, a much-modi-
fied M1 carbine. (Photo provided by Donald Thomas)

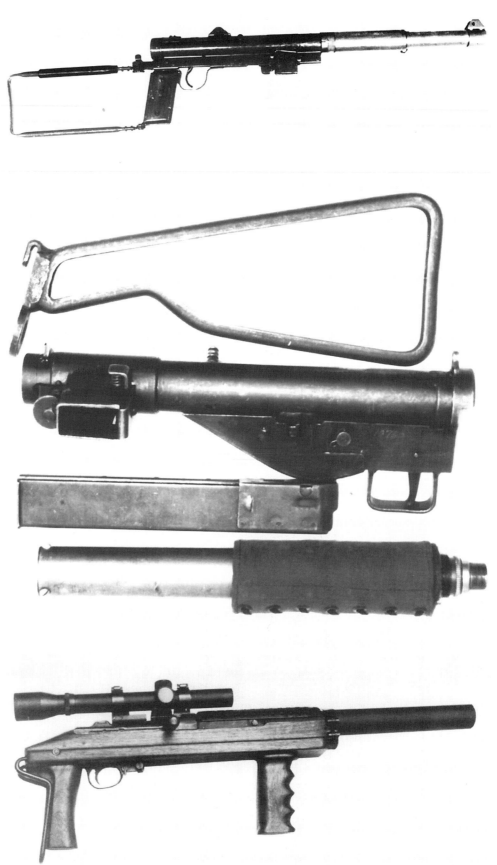

Above: Sgt. Dan Ross, RT Illinois, with suppressed M3A1 submachine gun. (Photo provided by Mike Sheppard)

Top left: A World War II OSS development, the suppressed High Standard HD .22 pistol. (Photo provided by Jim Phillips)

Middle: Suppressed pistols included the Browning, the Beretta, and (shown here) the Walther P-38. (Photo provided by National Infantry Museum)

Bottom: Hatchet Force man Craig Schmidt's M16 includes a Sionics suppressor and Swedish-made Singlepoint Night Sight. (Photo provided by Craig Schmidt)

EXPLOSIVES LADEN. RT New York One-Zero John St. Martin carried a claymore mine in his chest pouch and chain-like detonation cord covered with steel washers for quick demolition ambushes. (Photo provided by Frank Greco)

Inset: Golf-ball-sized V-40 mini-grenade. (Photo provided by Ben Baker)

One-Zero Bob Graham's auxiliary weapon was a sawed-off grenade launcher with 20 rounds in a special vest. Pith helmets were for fooling the NVA. (Photo provided by Bob Graham)

Inset: The radically chopped M79 was a bear to shoot, but desperate men ignore recoil. (Photo provided by Eldon Bargewell)

Top: Mark Kinsler, CCS, with a suppressed XM-21 sniper rifle and AN/PVS-2 night vision sight. (Photo provided by Mark Kinsler)

Middle: An experimental pump-action grenade launcher proved clumsy and temperamental. (Photo provided by Dick Johnson)

Bottom: Some teams used RPGs. A SOG team captured the first RPG-7 to appear in Southeast Asia. (Photo provided by John Plaster)

Above: "Porcupine." RPG-2 rounds modified by Martin Bennett added CS powder packets and 10-penny nails. (Photo provided by Martin Bennett)

Left: 60MM MORTARS. Full-size and sawed-off tubes with white-phosphorus (center) and high-explosive rounds. (Photo provided by Frank Greco)

Right: Hatchet Force Capt. Mecky Schuler fires 60mm minimortar. (Photo provided by Mecky Schuler)

Inset: RT New York's "Death Watch" team patch. (Photo provided by Scott Kilpatrick)

Below: HEAVY TEAM. RT New York's armament included 60mm mortar (center), RPG (left), and two sawed-off RPD machine guns. (Photo provided by Martin Bennett)

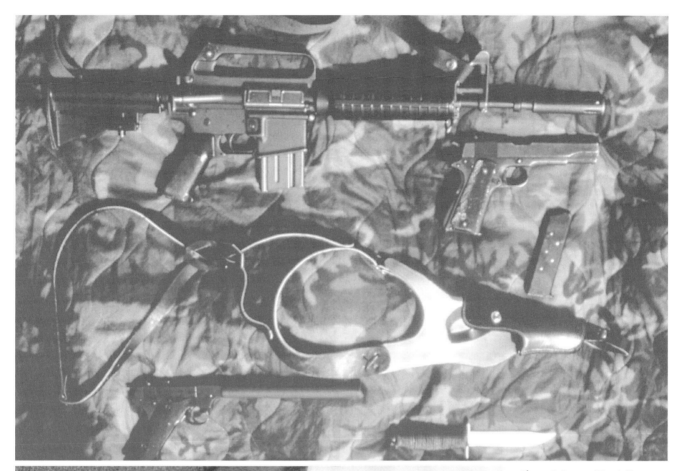

Above: A RECON MAN'S BASIC WEAPONS. CAR-15, .45 automatic pistol, suppressed .22-caliber High Standard, and a SOG recon knife. (Photo provided by Bryon Loucks)

Left: S. Sgt. Bill Deacy's CAR-15 literally saved his life by deflecting an AK slug aimed at his head, as he demonstrates here. Note the impression (circled) left by the slug on his buttstock tube. (Photo provided by Bill Deacy)

PASSIVE SIGNALING

WHEN DIRECTING AIR STRIKES or guiding incoming helicopters, SOG recon teams avoided normal ground-to-air signaling techniques, such as smoke grenades, because they'd disclose their own location to the ever-present NVA. Instead, SOG men preferred "passive" signaling techniques that could not be seen or heard by NVA troops even a few yards away.

SOG's most valuable signal device was also the oldest: the signal mirror, used in military operations since Julius Caesar's day. Unlike an ordinary mirror, a modern laminated-glass signal mirror contains a round, reflective grid in its center that glows with a bead of sunlight, thus giving the SOG man an aiming point as true as a rifle sight. All he had to do was look through the center of the mirror and manipulate that bead of light to an airplane or helicopter for his flashing mirror to be seen instantly.

On cloudy days a small luminous orange panel was employed, preferably with a recon man lying at the bottom of a bomb crater, flapping it open and closed to give it the appearance of flashing on and off. In darkness, the teams used palm-sized strobe lights—but flashed them in tin cans or M79 grenade launcher barrels to direct the light upward rather than sideways. Late in the war, infrared (IR) strobe covers arrived, which converted the flashing light to an invisible IR wavelength.

SOG's best passive signal: a signal mirror. (Photo provided by John Plaster)

A CHIEF SOG GUNFIGHTER

"A GUY WHO HAS 100-PERCENT CONFIDENCE in his ability to use his or any weapon doesn't have to worry about his personal safety—he can concentrate on his mission." These words of SOG's third chief, Col. John "Jack" Singlaub, perfectly describe the firearms training emphasis in recon—mastering your

weapons was the first step in mastering your fate. The ever-enthusiastic Singlaub imbued SOG with the spirit of his World War II days as an OSS operative fighting alongside the French Maquis, whose motto admonished Resistance fighters to conduct "*surprise, mitraillage, evanouissement*" (surprise, killing, vanishing).

Singlaub had been a "Jed"—a Jedburgh Team member, the most elite OSS element—and had parachuted into occupied France to help the Maquis demolish bridges, ambush German convoys, seize prisoners, and guide Allied units. After World War II Singlaub twice served on loan to the CIA, first to run a Manchurian intelligence network against Mao Tse-tung's communist forces, and then during the Korean War to serve with the CIA-affiliated Joint Advisory Commission, Korea, a special operations unit similar to SOG. An early advocate of freefall parachuting, Singlaub was a founding director in the 1950s of what became the nation's largest civilian skydiving organization, the U.S. Parachute Association. While serving as the 101st Airborne Division's G-3 Operations Officer in the late 1950s, Singlaub initiated the U.S. Army regulation creating sport parachute clubs on U.S. military bases.

Col. (later Maj. Gen.) Jack Singlaub, Chief SOG, 1966–1968. (Photo provided by U.S. Army)

Colonel Singlaub's two years as Chief SOG, 1966–1968, were whirlwind days of innovation and experimentation and an unrelenting search for new weapons and new techniques to fight unconventionally behind North Vietnamese lines.

159

SOG'S SILVER PISTOL

THE VIETNAM WAR'S MOST EXCLUSIVE COVERT operations memento is unknown except to the handful of Green Beret recon men who were presented with one: SOG's Boxed Presentation Browning Hi-Power Pistol.

Officially designated the "Reconnaissance Team Leader Special Recognition Award" and called the "Silver Pistol" in recon circles, each pistol was presented by then Chief SOG in a Saigon ceremony, usually to recognize an especially dramatic mission or a high award such as the Medal of Honor. These extremely rare pistols have yet to appear even in a museum.

Quite fittingly, the Browning 9mm Hi-Power was SOG's favored combat sidearm. With solid steel construction and a large magazine capacity, the Browning proved rugged, reliable, and effective. Sometime in late 1968 or early 1969, SOG headquarters arranged for a small number of these clandestinely acquired Browning pistols to be chrome plated and boxed as the "Reconnaissance Team Leader Special Recognition Award." Each pistol is boxed in a handsome, handmade black-lacquer case, lined in aquamarine velvet, and includes an engraved brass plate with the recipient's name.

Realistically, perhaps 40 or 50 SOG Silver Pistols were awarded throughout the war.

SOG's rarest memento, the boxed presentation Silver Pistol. (Photo provided by John Plaster)

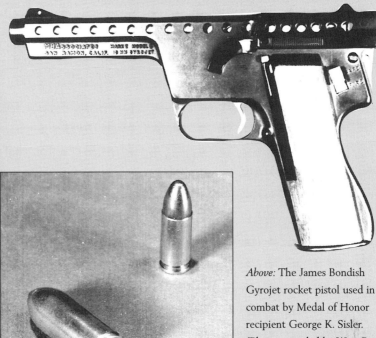

Above: The James Bondish Gyrojet rocket pistol used in combat by Medal of Honor recipient George K. Sisler. (Photo provided by West Point Museum)

Far left: Medal of Honor recipient Franklin Miller with Gyrojet pistol. (Photo provided by Richard Hoffman)

Left: The 13mm Gyrojet rocket round (front) dwarfs a 9mm cartridge. (Photo provided by Roger Kennedy)

SOG'S AMAZING ROCKET PISTOL

AMONG SOG'S MOST UNUSUAL WEAPONS was a revolutionary stamped-steel and plastic pistol that weighed only a few ounces and fired thumb-sized 13mm minirockets that impacted like .50-caliber machine gun slugs. A private development to bring small arms into the space age, the MBA Gyrojet rocket pistol was acquired by SOG as a possible suppressed or low-noise weapon. But propelled by a solid fuel that burned out in just 100 milliseconds, the minirocket emitted such a bizarre "whoosh!" that it hardly could be called silent.

Stabilized by focusing the burning fuel through two canted holes in the rocket's flat base, the round spun but never seemed very accurate. Like any recoilless weapon, the Gyrojet generated almost no recoil—but when it hit something, the effect was impressive.

In a test witnessed by J.D. Bath, a recon man fired one rocket round into an old three-quarter-ton truck door laid against a 55-gallon drum full of water. "That damned thing went through the truck door and into the drum, passed through the water, and almost poked a hole through the opposite side," recounted Bath. They also test-fired it through sandbag walls, even whole trees.

Lt. George K. Sisler, whose posthumous Medal of Honor was SOG's first, was packing a Gyrojet when he single-handedly assaulted a 40-man NVA platoon. In that wild melee, quite likely he fired his amazing rocket pistol when he retrieved two wounded comrades and fought his way out, and each powerful rocket must have astounded his foes. His great deed done, a few moments later he was killed by a sniper's bullet.

SOG'S PREFERRED COMBAT KNIVES

A SOG SOLDIER'S EDGED WEAPON WAS A MATTER of personal preference, but 95 percent or more outfitted themselves with at least one of the five knives shown here.

SOG's basic workhorse, the banana knife, was designed and manufactured clandestinely on Okinawa by CISO's brilliant deputy director, Ben Baker. It bears no markings. Combining the leverage of its curved blade with its considerable heft made it perfect for chopping bamboo on LZs, hacking through ropes, digging soil to emplace mines, or prying open cases of enemy ammunition. I kept mine tucked in the forward slit of my indigenous rucksack so that its 1/4-inch-thick blade pressed flat against my spine for protection from shrapnel—and I could pull it in a flash from behind my head.

The KA-BAR was an all-purpose combat and fighting knife, typically taped upside down on a recon man's left web gear strap. The KA-BAR dates back to 1942, when it was manufactured for U.S. Navy and Marine Corps use in the tropics. Therefore, its compressed leather disk handle was treated to resist jungle fungus, while the blade was coated with rust-inhibiting black epoxy powder. Stamped from relatively soft steel, the resilient KA-BAR could take a lot of punishment.

The most valuable collector's knife to emerge from Vietnam is another Ben Baker creation, the 7-inch-blade SOG recon knife. My SOG recon knife, shown in the photo, serial number 2263, bears a wine-red blade, although my other SOG recon knife from an earlier tour was blued and lacked a serial number.

Medal of Honor recipient Roy Benevidez—already shot repeatedly and badly bleeding—pulled his SOG recon knife in a last-ditch attempt to fight off NVA soldiers beside his rescue helicopter. "I could barely see through the matted blood in my eyes," Benevidez recounts in his book, *Medal of Honor.* "I now had only one weapon with me, my Special Forces [SOG] knife. I reached for it, and when I did [an NVA] pointed his bayonet at the front of my belly. Fortunately, he hesitated, and it gave me enough time to get to my feet. He sliced my left arm with the bayonet. . . . I stabbed him with every bit of strength I had left, and when he died, I left my S.F. knife in him." Despite seven gunshot wounds, 28 shrapnel holes, and a bayonet slash, Benevidez somehow boarded the Huey and escaped.

The Gerber Mk II, a popular Special Forces stiletto, was based on a 1966 design by retired U.S. Army Capt. C.A. "Bud" Holzmann. Its distinctive wasp-waist blade was canted 5 degrees off center to contour to its owner's body, but many SOG Green Berets believed this slight cant made it better to slip beneath an enemy's ribs. The Gerber's cast-aluminum handle was sprayed with molten stainless steel for an outstanding "cat's tongue" grip, while its semipointed pommel could be slammed effectively into an opponent's skull.

My Mk II, serial number 014333, held the best edge I've ever had on a fighting knife.

SOG Medal of Honor recipient Jon Cavaiani used an identical Gerber to kill two NVA foes when his tiny Outpost Hickory was overrun in 1971. The only surviving American among 100 or more NVA, Cavaiani used his Mk II in the first encounter to dispatch an NVA soldier who came into the bunker in which he was hiding. Later, after being shot and seriously burned—and lacking any other weapon—Cavaiani was attempting to slip away through the darkness when he came face-to-face with another NVA opponent; he slammed his Gerber so hard into the man's chest that he couldn't extract it, and only pulled burned skin from his hand. Although he escaped and evaded for several days, Cavaiani was captured and spent almost two years as a POW.

The widely admired Randall Model 14 "Attack" knife was SOG's least encountered fighting blade because it was costly—although everyone would agree that this hand-forged, hand-finished beauty was more than worth its price. Designed by W.D. "Bo" Randall, the Model 14 sported a wide, 7 1/2-inch blade and finger-grooved Micarta handle. So perfectly constructed that it was almost indestructible, the Randall held a razor-sharp edge. At Ft. Bragg's Special Operations Court of Honor, the statue of legendary recon One-Zero Dick Meadows has a Randall Model 14 on his belt.

FAVORITE SOG KNIVES. Top: banana knife; (clockwise) KA-BAR, SOG recon, Gerber Mk II, and Randall Model 14. (Photo provided by John Plaster)

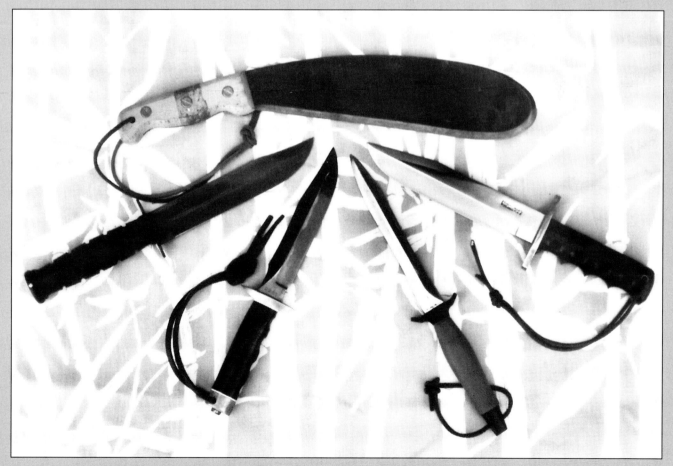

Chapter Nine

Recon Missions

SOG teams were not haphazardly dropped off into Laos or Cambodia to wander around in hopes that they might find something. Each SOG operation was formally briefed, thoroughly studied, carefully planned, briefed back to the local command and control (C&C) commander by the One-Zero, and then rehearsed and trained for as the One-Zero saw fit. His mission preparation typically required seven days to study intelligence reports and aerial photos; overfly the target area on a visual recon; rehearse special techniques his team might employ, such as rappeling or wiretapping; practice live-fire shooting drills; draw and issue food, ammo, and equipment; inspect every man's packed gear; and, finally, test-fire weapons before boarding the helicopters.

No matter the assigned mission, the team was given an area 6 kilometers square that "belonged" to that One-Zero—this 4-mile square was also a U.S. Air Force "no-bomb line" (NBL), into which no aerial ordnance would be dropped without the team leader's approval. Each such "box" had a SOG alphanumeric designator, such as Juliet-Nine, which meant a Laos target if it had a single digit, while Cambodian targets had double digits, such as Mike-Fifty-Four.

Inside his "box" a One-Zero reconned an area or point, surveilled a river or road, tapped an enemy phone line, assessed a B-52 strike, planted mines and sensors, or attempted a prisoner snatch.

AREA AND POINT RECON

SOG's most frequently assigned mission was an area recon, in which a team explored a defined zone in search of enemy activity, equipment, and installations. It could be that SOG headquarters or a requesting agency had little or no idea what was in that area or just wanted to learn if a previously detected enemy presence had ended.

A point recon, by contrast, required a team to examine a very specific grid coordinate—as small as 1-meter square—usually to verify a piece of intelligence from another source. The frustrating part of this was that the team almost never was told the source and often was not told what to expect to find there! Concerned that the recon men could be captured, the ever-security-conscious intelligence briefers withheld all but what the team absolutely needed to know. Most likely, a point recon objective was selected because a U.S. Army Security Agency radio direction-finding unit had plotted an enemy transmitter there, or perhaps a signal intercept had suggested a new supply dump was under construction. U-2 spy planes may have photographed tracked-vehicle prints, but the analysts couldn't decide whether they were tank or bulldozer tracks—sending in a SOG team to measure them was the solution.

During each hourly break in the field, recon men jotted notes of what they'd seen and heard, recording endless minutiae for their postmission debriefing. Seemingly inconsequential details might spur anything from a flash message to Saigon to a B-52 strike.

Some recon operations led to subsequent missions: finding a phone line might instigate a wiretap, while discovering an ammo stockpile could lead to a Hatchet Force raid. Sometimes, instead of merely recording an NVA location, the One-Zero radioed a FAC and had him put fighter-bombers on it. By 1968 recon teams in Laos regularly were calling air strikes on enemy facilities and troop concentrations, although tactical air strikes were not authorized in Cambodia until 1970.

ROAD AND RIVER WATCHES

As a rule, the most heavily patrolled area in enemy-occupied Laos and Cambodia was a 1-kilometer strip along each side of any convoy route. Not only did sentries and roving patrols saturate this strip, but 40-man NVA platoons and 100-man companies swept the roadsides, on line, searching for SOG surveillance teams. Penetrating that thick security screen and remaining in place took a lot of skill and more luck than many men possessed; less than half the teams targeted against highways ever made it within sight of the roads, so dense was the enemy security cordon. When a recon man somehow bypassed all that security and crawled through that last bit of jungle and found himself beside a major road, it was an eerie feeling, enough to raise the hair on the back of his neck, knowing the enemy was all around him in considerable numbers and that his only safety was silence and camouflage.

Road watch missions were fraught with danger because the team remained stationary, and, once detected, the SOG men would have to fight their way out of the cordon while the NVA quickly trucked in masses of reinforcements. Of equal danger, river watches placed surveillance teams at the tactical disadvantage of possibly being trapped against a waterway too

Inset: RT New Hampshire slips across a jungle stream during an area recon, SOG's most frequent assignment. (Photo provided by Will Curry)

Left: NVA truck rounds the corner of the Ho Chi Minh Trail. Recon teams often surveilled roads to observe and report convoy traffic. (Photo provided by DRV)

wide or too deep to use for escape if the team was detected.

Some road watch teams were assigned the additional duty of leaving behind antitruck mines when they withdrew. Typically the mines were cleverly laid by digging them into a mud puddle or concealing them underwater at a river ford; one trick to allay suspicion was to carry a piece of tire track and then press it into the freshly dug earth above a mine. Most often teams never learned whether their mines had been successful, but two One-Zeros, S. Sgts. Oliver Hartwig and David Gilmer, had the satisfaction of being nearby when NVA trucks hit their newly laid mines.

Antipersonnel mines were laid, too, but SOG men soon realized that these mines might go untripped and become a danger when SOG teams returned to the area. By 1969, it was SOG policy that each antipersonnel mine must include a self-destruct means; most often this was an acid-delay glass ampule and blasting cap from a limpet mine kit, dug in beneath the mine, which would self-detonate in a week or two.

The most clever way to kill trucks was to plant a mine underwater at a ford site. RT Ohio under Oliver Hartwig and RT Texas under David Gilmer each destroyed trucks with antitank mines.

Outriggers

WIRETAPS

The military use of wiretaps began with the telegraph's invention. During the 1862 Fredericksburg campaign, Confederate soldiers tapped into Union telegraph lines, but the Yankees detected the crude tap because it degraded their Morse code signal. Not much had changed in 100 years, because SOG wiretappers faced the same problem.

An NVA phone operator could see his multimeter needle drop when a SOG team tapped into his line. Although connected to state-of-the-art, voice-activated cassette recorders, early SOG wiretaps were primitive affairs with alligator clips that begged to be discovered.

A newer tap kit inserted a microthin wire into the line that theoretically would not drain so discernable an amount of current. But it, too, was often detected. Every time SOG team members installed a tap, they were living on borrowed time.

Eventually, the CIA supplied SOG with MS-1 wiretap devices, which employed the induction principle that had been used by the British Secret Service since late in World War II. The tap was the same size and appearance as SOG's earlier recording devices; the real difference was in the tap itself. Its two rubber-coated pads folded over the wire to glean a recordable signal purely from the electrical field. Because the MS-1 did not penetrate the phone line no voltage was drained; so the MS-1 tap was electronically undetectable.

But even without electronically compromising a tap's presence, these operations became hazardous because a phone network usually served a regiment or even a division. "The most dangerous thing we used to do was tap wires," says Sfc. Richard Gross. S. Sgt. Bryan Stockdale adds, "They checked their wire pretty close, and it just left you too exposed, too close to a trail, and too stationary."

Still the risk was deemed acceptable when weighed against the intelligence benefit, which could be considerable. Hanoi was aware of U.S. electronic intelligence gathering. In January 1967 the North Vietnamese military periodical, *Tuyen Huan*, warned about U.S. technical intelligence:

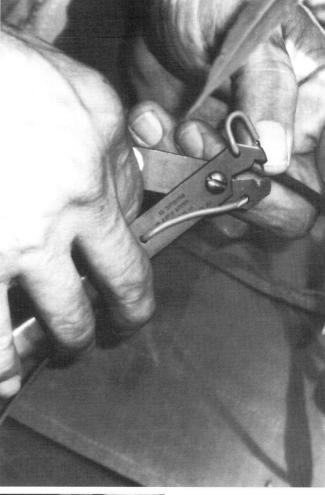

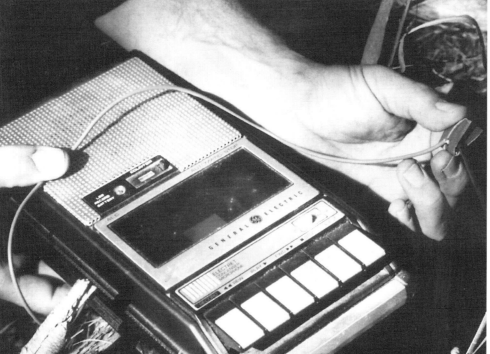

Above left: Primitive, initial taps, attached by alligator clips, were easily detected. (Photo provided by John Plaster)

Above: Second-generation taps slipped a hair-thin wire into the phone line, but they were still detected. (Photo provided by John Plaster)

Left: Eventually SOG acquried undetectable "induction" taps that merely folded over the phone line. (Photo provided by John Plaster)

They take advantage of the development of the radio and the electronic computer by collecting all the messages which we send out by radio, taking them to a research center and using computers to translate the coded messages, verify, compare, analyze, and integrate them to seek out our secrets . . . with cryptography.

North Vietnamese radio operators were scrupulous about following proper radio procedures, but the seeming privacy of a landline instigated incautious chit-chat. The Hanoi high command well understood SOG's wiretap threat and in another article urged the NVA to "guard against the enemy listening to our telephone messages," adding, "we must use the secret code and not the telephone to exchange secret talks."

SOG's first wiretap, planted near the DMZ in mid-1966 by RT Colorado, with Sgts. Ted Braden, Jim Hetrick, and J.D. Bath, yielded seven cassettes of North Vietnamese conversations, including one that analysts initially misread as an announcement that North Vietnamese Defense Minister Vo Nguyen Giap would visit 48 hours later. MACV Headquarters and 7th Air Force scrambled to hit the spot with a B-52 strike and then afterward learned the message did not refer to Giap, after all. Well, *whoever* he was, he was pounded by a flight of B-52s.

In late 1970, SOG's extremely hazardous wiretap missions were replaced by a sophisticated monitoring device, cover-named the "Department of Defense Special Repeater." A 10-foot-long, 3-inch-diameter spiked tube painted to resemble a small tree, it was air-dropped near enemy phone lines, and

could "read" conversations right out of a line's magnetic field, compress its recordings on a minitape machine, and then burst-transmit it to a passing U.S. aircraft.

BOMB DAMAGE ASSESSMENT

The first B-52 strikes of the war to hit NVA targets in Laos in late 1965 resulted from SOG Shining Brass recon operations out of Kham Duc. A year later SOG planners came up with the idea of inserting SOG teams immediately after Laotian "Arc Light" strikes to assess results.

These special recon operations, called bomb damage assessment (BDA), proved even more hazardous than wiretaps because they similarly put recon teams in heavily occupied enemy areas, but with the added factor of confronting an enemy provoked by the air strike and only too happy to vent his wrath on the SOG men. It was just such an all-out NVA reaction during a poststrike BDA mission that sparked SOG's first Medal of Honor incident. SOG recon teams also played a prominent role in the so-called secret bombing of Cambodia, having both found the targets for the unacknowledged strikes and performed BDAs after the bombings.

Inserting BDA teams directly on a target after a strike by strategic bombers was simply without precedent and had not even been attempted in World War II or the Korean War. As quickly as a B-52 strike's dust settled, U.S.-led SOG teams landed right there among hundreds, perhaps thousands, of well-armed, hostile enemy soldiers. But BDAs became the most consistently inconsistent of SOG ground missions: either teams found nothing, or all hell broke loose. About half the time SOG BDA teams encountered NVA soldiers returning from their subterranean shelters, and the recon men would have to shoot their way out. The other half of

A B-52 lets loose its load of 109 500-pound bombs from 30,000 feet. (Photo provided by U.S. Air Force)

Above inset: Fresh, still smolder-
ing craters; churned earth; and
toppled trees illustrate the devastation from a B-52 Arc Light
in Laos, moments after the last
bombs fell and a BDA team was
preparing to go in. (Photo provided by Frank Greco)

Left: B-52 Arc Light strike car-
pet-bombs an immense area,
afterward often assessed by a
SOG team. (Photo provided by
U.S. Air Force)

Right: SOG recon team peers from a fresh bomb crater in Laos. (Photo provided by Frank Greco)

Inset: Bomb damage assessment photo shot from O-2 FAC plane in northeast Cambodia. (Photo provided by John Plaster)

SOG'S FIRST MEDAL OF HONOR

ANYONE GOING INTO AN IMPACT AREA after a B-52 strike might confront masses of NVA troops eager for revenge. Just such a situation led to SOG's first Medal of Honor.

Capt. Edward Lesesne and Sfc. Leonard Tilley needed several volunteers to accompany their 40-man Montagnard platoon that was scheduled to land on a B-52 target to conduct a BDA just after the bombs stopped falling. A young recon One-Zero with a reputation for innovation and daring, 1st Lt. George K. Sisler, offered to go along.

On 7 February 1967, as soon as the B-52 strike's smoke cleared, a half-dozen Kingbee helicopters landed the BDA platoon on a heavily cratered Laotian LZ. Minutes later they were mass-assaulted by more than 100 NVA soldiers, thrown violently back, and almost overrun. Then, while the NVA force momentarily fell back to regroup, Lieutenant Sisler realized that two of his Montagnards had been wounded and left behind. Racing back alone into the jungle, Sisler picked up one man and was running with him when the NVA launched a second assault, headed directly for him. Sisler laid down the 'Yard, pulled a grenade, attacked a machine gun—destroying it—and then killed three more enemy assailants trying to slip into the platoon perimeter. He went back after the second Montagnard and just got him out when another NVA line attacked, and, all alone, George Sisler counterattacked, firing his CAR-15, throwing grenades, and quite likely blasting away with a Gyrojet rocket pistol.

With all the SOG men around him killed or wounded, Sisler almost single-handedly had repulsed the NVA attack. Meanwhile Sergeant First Class Tilley organized the rest of the platoon and brought A-1 Skyraiders within 50 feet of its position. But there was no place for extraction helicopters to land so the SOG men had to move. An RPG rocket detonated near Lesesne, and instantly he was almost bleeding to death. Tilley's expertly directed air strikes at last forced the NVA force back, and the Kingbees and several helicopter gunships arrived. George Sisler stood to direct the gunships when a lone sniper's shot cut him down. He died there.

It was only because of Tilley's leadership and skill that anyone came out. Lesesne recalls, "We were all crawling toward the LZ. How we got to the LZ, I don't know." They brought Sisler's body with them. Twice Tilley went back after wounded men and once charged directly into the enemy, which so astonished the NVA troopers that they fell back. Despite heavy groundfire, no aircraft were lost during the extraction.

A year later, the young lieutenant's widow, Jane Sisler, and her two sons, David and James, traveled to Washington to accept his posthumous Medal of Honor, the first ever awarded to a military intelligence officer. Sfc. Leonard Tilley received the second highest award, the Distinguished Service Cross.

Top: 1st Lt. George "Ken" Sisler posthumously received SOG's first Medal of Honor. (Photo provided by Jane Sisler)

Above: Sfc. Leonard Tilley was the NCOIC (noncommissioned officer in charge) of the BDA mission in which Lieutenant Sisler died. For his great courage, Tilley was awarded the Distinguished Service Cross. (Photo provided by Leonard Tilley)

Above: Secretary of the Army Stanley Resor presents George Sisler's Medal of Honor to his wife, Jane, and their sons David (left) and James. (Photo provided by Jane Sisler)

Top right: Huey gunship rockets a hillside where BDA platoon is fighting for its life and Lieutenant Sisler is displaying the incredible courage that led to his being awarded the Medal of Honor. (Photo provided by Leonard Tilley)

Bottom: Kingbee penetrates smoke and groundfire to pick up survivors of the bloody BDA mission. (Photo provided by Leonard Tilley)

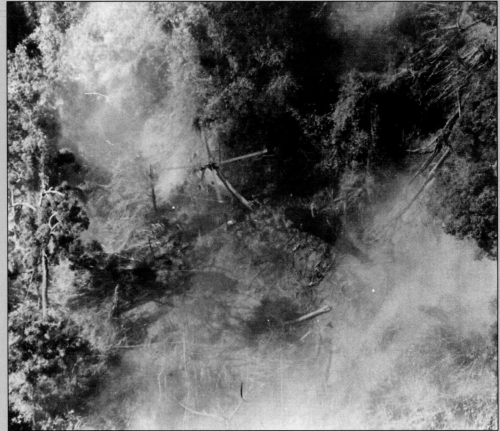

174

the time, the bombs hit only empty jungle, but even these strikes proved useful by progressively chewing away trees, bite by bite, to expose the Ho Chi Minh Trail's roads and paths.

PLANTING BEACONS AND SENSORS

SOG recon teams hand-emplaced sensors and electronic bombing beacons with a precision that could be achieved in no other way until today's generation of Global Positioning System (GPS) satellites. By exactly planting a shoe-box-sized radio transponder at a predetermined point, a SOG team allowed U.S. B-52s to aim their bomb loads electronically to achieve their greatest possible accuracy.

Precise emplacement by hand proved of great value as well for magnetic truck-counting sensors.

When a SOG team concealed a truck sensor along a highway deep behind enemy lines, at the exact spot requested by analysts, and its transmitter began sending back nightly counts, it was as if an intelligence officer could watch that road by remote control. Intelligence of immense value flowed from these devices, not because they were electronic marvels, but because the Green Beret-led teams could be relied upon to put them at an exact spot, undetected, and leave them so well concealed that they'd operate until their batteries ran out.

Of less precision but equally great value were the sabotaged ammunition SOG teams placed in enemy stockpiles and the "black" psyops materials, such as phoney letters from North Vietnam or counterfeit enemy currency that SOG teams put into circulation.

PRISONER SNATCHES

The SOG mission that demanded

THE OLD-FASHIONED WAY. Capt. Ed Lesesne and the NVA officer he had just wounded and captured beside Highway 110, Laos. (Photo provided by Ed Lesesne)

the most ingenuity and audacity was snatching enemy prisoners. Rewards and accolades were heaped upon successful snatchers because no intelligence source is as fruitful as a freshly snatched prisoner. Taking a prisoner meant a free R&R (rest and recreation) to Taiwan aboard a SOG Blackbird on maintenance rotation, a $100 bonus for each American, and a new Seiko wristwatch and cash to each Nung or Montagnard. No matter what a team's primary mission was, its secondary mission always was to seize enemy prisoners if the opportunity arose.

In 1966, SOG's first full year of Laotian operations, recon teams seized 12 prisoners. Results remained fair in 1967, with 10 NVA snatched, but expanded NVA security forces proved their worth by 1968 when Laotian seizures tumbled to one. In 1969 not a single NVA prisoner was brought out, but there was a jump to three prisoners in 1970. In Cambodia SOG teams snatched 18 prisoners between 1967 and 1970. Combined, this meant a total of 44 NVA taken from heavily defended NVA rear areas over 63 months, or one enemy POW brought out each one and a half months, which is quite high considering that a snatch meant initiating

Above: A Special Forces veterinarian fires a tranquilizer rifle. SOG tested similar rifles for prisoner snatches. (Photo provided by Robert Rounsefell)

contact in dangerous areas, against forces that often outnumbered SOG team members. And when a team grabbed an NVA soldier, the prisoner slowed the team's pace while the enemy chased all the harder knowing that a comrade had been taken.

Prisoner snatch tactics essentially came down to three: disabling the enemy with a carefully placed gunshot, knocking him senseless with explosives, or physically overpowering him.

Gunfire was tricky because the goal was to incapacitate but not kill the target. For this reason many teams preferred SOG's least powerful suppressed weapon, the .22-caliber High Standard Model HD pistol. Suppressed submachine guns were used too.

Several teams reportedly tested tranquilizer guns but only confirmed what veterinarians learned when anesthetizing dangerous animals: when a dose is sufficient to incapacitate quickly, it's enough to kill; but smaller doses act so slowly that the beast remains a

threat. SOG men were compelled to gun down NVA hit by light-dose darts or watch helplessly while a prisoner died from heavier anesthetic doses.

When tranquilizer darts failed, SOG tested chemical Mace, the non-lethal spray used by police. But in testing the Mace against each other recon men found it unreliably debilitating.

Sometimes just plain aggressiveness yielded prisoners—merely having an NVA trooper dead to rights with your weapon on him didn't ensure submission. You had to exploit that momentary edge and seize him so quickly that he had no option but surrender. Down in Cambodia's Fishhook, RT Pick One-Zero Everett Cofer and One-Two David Zack covered while One-One Bob Graham seized a lone enemy soldier. There wasn't time for anything fancy: Graham jumped out and punched the soldier right between the eyes. "It was a good catch," intelligence officers later told Graham.

Frequently teams employed explosives laid out as a demolition ambush. In theory, the blast would knock the target off his feet, wrench his AK from his hands, and render him temporarily senseless. Teams developed intricate demo ambushes using a combination of carefully placed explosive charges and claymore mines, so that overlapping fans of steel shot would kill or disable every NVA soldier in the ambush, *except one*, and he would be tossed head over heels and taken alive. With rehearsals, these demo ambushes could be laid along a trail in less than 60 seconds.

SOG's most sophisticated demo ambushes employed Astrolite, a liquid explosive discovered during rocket fuel research by the National Aeronautics and Space Administration (NASA). Astrolite came in two plastic bottles that

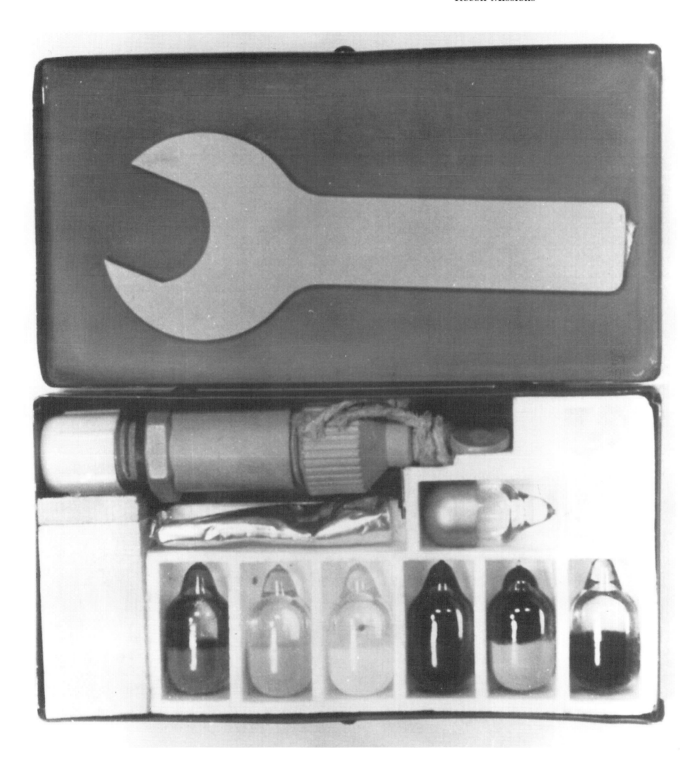

were combined on the spot and would detonate anything soaked with it—including the clay on a trail—so that literally the earth exploded beneath the prospective prisoner's feet.

Whether Astrolite or conventional explosives, a demolition ambush's unpredictable blast effects were always a grab bag—the team never knew for certain what they'd find until the smoke had cleared.

Limpet mine detonator kit contains thumb-sized blasting cap and acid-delay ampules. SOG teams used limpet kit to self-destruct mines days or weeks after they were planted. (Photo provided by Jim Phillips)

Top: TARGET OF OPPORTUNITY. A U.S. Air Force F-4 Phantom bombs an NVA unit spotted in the open by Mike Sheppard's RT Montana. (Photo provided by Mike Sheppard)

Bottom: A destroyed truck park in Laos, a major target for SOG recon. (Photo provided by U.S. Air Force)

Top: Recon man's view of Laotian Highway 110. This area was extremely dangerous because it was heavily patrolled. (Photo provided by John Plaster)

Bottom: As Close as It Gets. A recon man snapped this photo of Highway 110 after hours of careful crawling and stalking. (Photo provided by Frank Greco)

Top: To prepare demolitions for a quick prisoner snatch, Sgt. Bob Garcia and teammates tape det cord to blocks of C-4. (Photo provided by Frank Greco)

Bottom: In the field, it can be unrolled in seconds beside a trail and then command-detonated to disable a prisoner. (Photo provided by Frank Greco)

Far left inset: A HAPPY SIGHT. To a recon man even masses of NVA were not a problem if, as here, they were lax and unaware of a team's presence. (Photo provided by DRV)

Far left: MISSION ACCOMPLISHED. RT Maryland members scramble aboard a 57th Assault Helicopter Company Huey after their work is done. (Photo provided by Brendon Lyons)

These four NVA prisoners, with sandbags serving as blindfolds, were captured by One-Zero Eldon Bargewell's RT Michigan. (Photo provided by Eldon Bargewell)

Below left inset: RT Pick One-Zero Bob Graham (left) and David Paul with an NVA prisoner they just snatched in Cambodia's Fishhook. (Photo provided by Bob Graham)

Below right inset: A prolific prisoner snatcher, M. Sgt. Jerry Wareing hustles two NVA soldiers aboard a Kingbee in Laos. (Photo provided by Special Operations Association)

DICK MEADOWS—SNATCHER EXTRAORDINAIRE

ONE OF SOG'S GREATEST ONE-ZEROS—and its most accomplished prisoner snatcher—was M. Sgt. Dick Meadows. When this 34-year-old Green Beret arrived in SOG in 1966, he already had been a professional soldier for 19 years, having lied about his age in 1947 to become a 15-year-old paratrooper and then so distinguished himself in Korea that he was that war's youngest master sergeant. Quick-learning and self-taught, Meadows developed a descriptive vocabulary and sophisticated style although he had only a ninth-grade education.

"He was probably one of the best trained, best disciplined officers or NCOs I ever met in the army," says M. Sgt. Billy Greenwood. "Meadows did everything meticulously; everything was rehearsed," recalls Maj. Scotty Crerar.

According to Chief SOG Singlaub, Meadows held SOG's record of 13 prisoners. For one snatch Meadows had arrayed RT Iowa beside a trail, but five NVA soldiers strolled up rather than the desired lone man. The bold One-Zero stepped out and announced, "Good morning, gentlemen. You are now POWs." Instead of putting up their hands, three of the enemy went for their AKs, so Meadows shot them dead faster than you read this. The other two proved perfectly compliant.

Maj. Jim Rabdau recalls a time that Meadows brought out a prisoner from deep in Cambodia, and Saigon decided the man was only an ignorant rice farmer unaware of anything beyond his little valley. So SOG borrowed an untraceable civilian plane, flew the farmer into an out-of-the-way Cambodian airport, then just left him there, unsure of where he'd been and who had snatched him.

On another operation, Meadows lay beside a Laotian highway and filmed hundreds of uniformed North Vietnamese soldiers and black-clad porters as they filed past, giving the lie to Hanoi's claims that it had no troops in the war. A few months later, the resourceful recon man penetrated an enemy cache containing Soviet artillery pieces, photographed them, and presented their optical sights to Gen. William Westmoreland. The U.S. forces commander endorsed Chief SOG's recommendation that Meadows be field-commissioned as a captain.

The gallant Green Beret also led SOG's first attempt to rescue a downed pilot in the heartland of North Vietnam, which failed because his team arrived just after the pilot was captured. Instead of coming home empty-handed, Meadows set up a prisoner snatch ambush, and when four North Vietnamese soldiers walked up, he stepped out, leveled his AK, and called a friendly, "Good morning." The four NVA went for their guns, but Meadows shot first, with the usual result.

One of SOG's most extraordinary One-Zeros, in 1970 Capt. Dick Meadows would be called upon to train Green Beret volunteers for the war's greatest classified mission, the attempted POW rescue at Son Tay, North Vietnam.

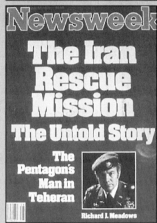

Top: Dick Meadows handcuffing an NVA prisoner for the flight to Saigon. (Photo provided by the family of George K. Sisler)

Above: Dick Meadows made the cover of *Newsweek* in 1982 after having been Delta Force's advance man in Tehran for the 1980 hostage rescue attempt.

THE ASHTRAY MISSIONS

IN EARLY 1970 GEN. CREIGHTON ABRAMS, the commander of U.S. forces, made a special request of Chief SOG Col. Steve Cavanaugh: find the destinations of an upsurge in NVA truck convoys in southeast Laos so they could be targeted for B-52 strikes.

Chief SOG Cavanaugh decided that the best bet was to kidnap an NVA convoy lead driver—no small task since enemy security had grown so vast that not a single prisoner had come out of Laos the previous year. Operation Ashtray, as the convoy ambush and prisoner snatch was named, would be led by one of SOG's most experienced officers, Maj. Frank Jaks, along with eight volunteers: Oliver Hartwig, Daniel Ster, Ray Harris, John Blaaw, Tim Lynch, Forrest Todd, Bill Spurgeon, and John Grant. After seven days of planning and rehearsals, Jaks' men ambushed a 17-vehicle convoy, but the resulting shootout was so wild that not one living NVA soldier could be seized. There were no friendly casualties.

Several One-Zeros volunteered for a second attempt, Operation Ashtray II, but security concerns overrode sending Major Jaks out a second time. I was selected to lead this two-team mission, combining my RT California with RT New Hampshire under Capt. Fred Krupa. The other six volunteers were our teammates: Rex Jaco, John Yancey, Richard Woody, Paul Kennicott, R. Michael Grace, James Galasso, and four Montagnards, for a total of 12 men.

For 10 days we planned the ambush, experimented with demolitions, and rehearsed until in our final rehearsal we could halt a truck with explosives, clear it, and seize a driver in less than 10 seconds. On the eve of Easter Sunday 1970, just before 9:30 P.M., as a Soviet-made GAZ-63 truck rolled past us on Highway 110, I blew a line of claymore mines and shouted, "Assault!" Yancey, Krupa, Woody, and I rushed the halted truck. While we covered him, Yancey jerked out the driver and pinned him, and Krupa slid a plastic restraint on his wrists. Meanwhile, our security teams 100 yards away on each flank were blocking the road.

Krupa shot a few quick photos with his Kodak Instamatic, and then it was time to get out of there—approaching NVA troops began firing, seriously wounding Richard Woody. While I shot it out with several NVA, each withdrawing American scattered a half-dozen time-delay devices, creating a minefield of fragmentation, white-phosphorous, and tear gas grenades that would cook off for 45 minutes. Meanwhile, a thermite grenade and explosive charge on the truck went off, creating a flaming beacon for arriving fighter-bombers to hit the road and our backtrail as we fled. All night we evaded and outran pursuing NVA forces; then just after dawn our extraction helicopters arrived.

That Easter Sunday night I briefed General Abrams at MACV headquarters in Saigon. When I finished he congratulated our ambushers and shook my hand. The captured driver was one of just three prisoners SOG brought out of Laos that year, and the only one in SOG history premeditatedly seized. Chief SOG Cavanaugh called Operation Ashtray II "undoubtedly our most successful operation where we had visualized doing something, planned it, then had it done."

Top: This NVA truck was ambushed on Highway 110 to snatch the driver. Note the camouflage lashed above the cab and the thermite grenade on the hood, placed there by John Plaster. (Photo provided by Fred Krupa)

Middle: Sfc. Rex Jaco (right) and S. Sgt. John Yancey lead NVA truck driver from the Huey at CCC helipad. Also pictured are (left) Lt. Col. Edgar McGowan, CCC commander, and James Galasso, Ashtray II medic. (Photo provided by Rex Jaco)

PRISONER SNATCH STATISTICS

North Vietnamese Prisoners Captured by SOG Teams

	1965	1966	1967	1968	1969	1970
Laos	0	12	10	1	0	3
Cambodia	*	*	2	3	4	9

Source: Recon Operations, 1984, U.S. Army JFK Special Warfare Center

* SOG did not begin recon operations in Cambodia until June 1967.

Above: Ralph Rodd's RT Colorado team patch. (Photo provided by Scott Kilpatrick)

Right: S. Sgt. Ralph Rodd led one of the war's most amazing ambushes. (Photo provided by Jim Jones)

RALPH RODD'S PRISONER SNATCH

THE VIETNAM WAR'S MOST SUCCESSFUL AMBUSH quite likely resulted from a 1969 attempt by RT Colorado to snatch a prisoner in Laos. One-Zero Ralph Rodd had carefully arrayed eight claymore mines so that their blasts overlapped on a heavily used trail, leaving one small, blast-free zone for their prospective prisoner.

Staff Sergeant Rodd's men had lain there motionless for a half-day when they heard approaching NVA soldiers, but soon realized that there were far too many of the enemy to attempt a snatch: Rodd counted almost 300 by the time they stopped, formed tight ranks right in front of RT Colorado's eight claymores, stacked arms, and opened their rucksacks for lunch. The RT Colorado men dared not even breathe. Then one NVA trooper stepped off the trail to urinate and saw a Montagnard. Instantly, Rodd's men detonated the mines, emptied their CAR-15s, tossed grenades, and ran with such abandon that the six of them were extracted from six different LZs. Not one SOG man was wounded.

The NVA casualties had to have been staggering—out of an NVA battalion, five full minutes passed before a single NVA round was fired in return.

Chapter Ten

NVA Counterrecon Forces and Tactics

In SOG's earliest Shining Brass days, the NVA fielded no specially tailored units to hunt RTs. NVA rear-area patrols and reaction forces were improvised by local commanders, mustering anything from clerks to hard-core infantry to track and engage the Green Beret-led teams. Certainly, with an entire field army in southern Laos, the NVA forces never had to go far to find plenty of troops.

Assisting them were Laotian native trackers, pressed into service by the North Vietnamese occupiers. Wearing only loincloths, these were game hunters, not warriors, who demonstrated such poor tactical sense that it seemed almost unsporting to ambush them.

Sometimes the NVA dispatched noisy gaggles of people to follow a discovered team at a safe distance, clacking bamboo sticks together or rapping against their metallic AK magazines to warn unknowing comrades that a team was nearby, or in hopes the team would just plain leave. Some "driving" attempts were more pointed: on two occasions, the NVA troops set afire the elephant grass in which SOG teams had fled, giving the recon men a terrible choice—burn to death or come out and fight for their lives.

For a crude but effective listening device, the NVA scooped out 4-foot-wide holes on eastern hillsides, which acted like parabolic antennas, enabling them to detect the vibration of approaching helicopters long before they otherwise could be heard.

Landing zone watchers often posted themselves on treetop platforms like this one. (Photo provided by Ben Baker)

EVOLUTION AND LAYERING

As SOG's threat became clearer—and the NVA units began suffering serious losses from SOG actions—the crude devices and improvised tactics gave way to a coherent strategy that would evolve and expand apace with the war itself.

To detect arriving recon teams, the NVA began posting one- and two-man "LZ watcher" teams near likely helicopter LZs. There weren't enough LZ watchers to cover every little open piece of ground, so wherever possible, they were placed on high ground or on platforms in tall trees. When an LZ watcher spotted a SOG helicopter landing, he reported it by phone or runner or rang a brass gong. Nearby NVA base camps or truck parks relayed the alarm, and an NVA reaction force was dispatched.

The enemy did not usually send patrols blindly into the jungle unless trackers already knew a team's whereabouts. Instead, the enemy beefed up his patrols along trails and roads throughout the area and swept the jungle beside convoy routes for SOG ambushers, usually just before dusk.

SOG teams normally stayed off enemy trails, not just because large bodies of NVA troops traveled on them but because they posted "trail watchers" to watch for RTs, somewhat as they used LZ watchers. Then, just before dusk, the enemy posted sentries along the highways, about 100 to 300 yards apart, to stand guard all night.

SPECIAL
COUNTERRECON FORCES

By 1967, the Hanoi high command had concluded that ordinary sentries and security patrols weren't enough to defend against SOG RTs and Hatchet Forces. To increase security, the enemy created another defensive layer employing "route protection battalions" and "rear security units," special organizations permanently assigned to the Ho Chi Minh Trail, whose only role was patrolling against SOG forces. Interestingly, during World War II the Soviet Union had formed identically named units under the NKVD (the precursor to the KGB) to combat German raiders and saboteurs behind Soviet lines. This indicator very strongly suggests Soviet advisors in the NVA security apparatus.

Then, in mid-July 1967, an RT near Laotian Highway 922 was ambushed by superbly trained NVA who leaped out of nowhere upon them. Two Green Berets were killed, and a third was wounded and narrowly escaped capture. About the same time, the CIA's Laotian roadwatch teams found themselves hunted by "special [NVA] units to find and destroy the 'team soldiers,' as the Lao irregular units were known to the enemy."

On 19 March 1967, North Vietnamese Premier Ho Chi Minh had attended a ceremony in Son Tay, 30 miles west of Hanoi, to congratulate the first graduates of a unique, new school, on the same day cited by postwar NVA publications as the organization of "Special Operations Forces in the Vietnamese people's war." North Vietnam's only paratroop unit, the elite 305th Airborne Brigade, had been converted into "sappers"—the night infiltrators renowned for raiding U.S. base camps wearing only shorts and carrying satchel charges—and special counterrecon units whose mission was to hunt down and kill SOG teams. During the French–Indochina War, the Communist Vietminh had similarly created the 421st Intelligence Battalion solely to oppose French

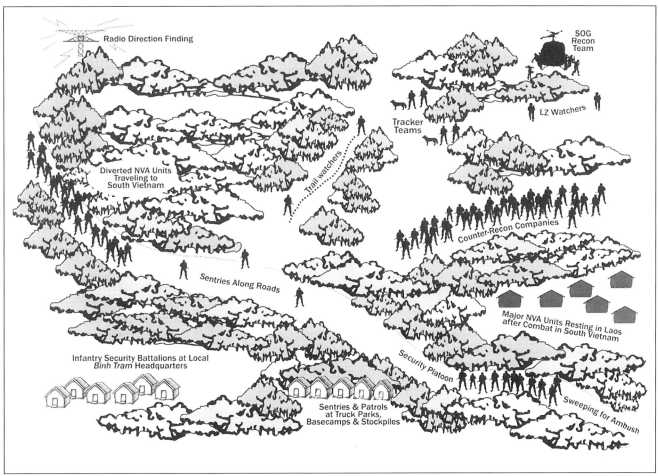

commandos with the top-secret Groupement de Commandos Mixtes Aéroportés (GCMA), a unit much like SOG that fought behind communist lines.

Unburdened by rucksacks and carrying just a few magazines and a canteen, the NVA counterrecon units usually operated as 100-man companies that split into platoons to sweep and hunt until they were closing on a SOG team. One radio message, and the other two platoons swooped in to help, while other local units operated as blocking forces.

MAN'S BEST FRIEND?

Accompanying the new counter-recon units were NVA soldiers professionally trained as trackers, who were a great deal more dangerous than the earlier Laotians in loincloths. Stationed at strategic points along the Trail, the trackers were called in when LZ watchers saw a helicopter land or when NVA patrols discovered evidence of a SOG team's presence.

The new trackers were bad enough, but some came with "man's best friend"—*dogs!* Any man who's survived it can hardly convey the unsettling emotions aroused when, already running for his life, he first hears a dog's bark—and it's not a friend. But once past that initial panic, SOG teams found the enemy's dogs just one more danger to contend with.

Actually these were not true bloodhounds, but ordinary Asian dogs taught to follow a scent, which

Top: From the moment they landed (upper right), SOG teams had to contend with layered, redundant NVA security measures.

Above: Joe Walker's RT California encountered NVA counterrecon elements with special chestboards for quick-throwing a barrage of grenades.

they did competently. One of the few recon men to observe an approaching tracker dog, One-Zero Joe Walker, was surprised to find "a little old Mickey Mouse dog, about as big as my tomcat." Still, that little dog led an enemy patrol directly to Walker's team.

HOW THE NVA TYPICALLY HUNTED A TEAM

The NVA defensive system in Laos and Cambodia matured in 1968 and 1969, with an enormous, layered program that integrated detection elements with trackers and reaction forces, along with fixed security at major installations.

Linked together by radios and landline phones—and possessing perfect knowledge of their local jungle trails—the NVA sought to determine when and where a SOG team landed, to track the team to an exact loca-

tion, and finally, to encircle and destroy or capture it.

To detect a team's arrival, the NVA dramatically expanded its LZ watcher force; by 1969, practically every usable LZ in southeastern Laos was covered by watchers. When they spotted a helicopter touchdown, the watchers called in trackers, and the local NVA commander immediately dispatched watchers and patrols to nearby trails. The NVA regional commander—perhaps heading that area's *binh tram* (communication-liasion site)—would order out a counter-recon company, which typically arrived in an hour or two, accompanied by one or more dog teams. Updated by the original tracker team, the counterrecon company would split into platoons and scour carefully selected areas for the SOG team.

This effort often was assisted by local reinforcements, either as blocking forces that laid in wait for the

Passing NVA units—sometimes numbering thousands of soldiers—could join the hunt for a SOG team. (Photo provided by DRV)

recon team, or "drivers" who noisily attempted to push the team toward an ambush. Local security, too, was beefed up, with additional sentries on the roads and patrols circling the jungle near truck parks, base camps, and stockpiles.

When the team was spotted, the NVA rushed in as many troops as it could muster, everything from rear-echelon soldiers to units on their way to South Vietnam or, the toughest of all, seasoned NVA infantry resting across the border between battles in Vietnam. Because they could quick-march along excellent high-speed trails, the NVA reinforced its units surprisingly fast to saturate the area with sweeps, ambushes, and blocking forces. In a flat-out race to an extraction LZ, the NVA often outran teams because the SOG men headed cross country, while the NVA dashed along high-speed trails.

Assuming that the SOG team could avoid, evade, or fight through all these impediments, the enemy still had a chance to get in a last blow on the team's extraction LZ by repositioning 12.7mm antiaircraft machine guns once the team's locale was first suspected. More than one SOG team thought it was home free, only to have its exfiltration helicopter shot down by freshly repositioned 12.7mm machine guns.

By 1969, this massive enemy effort tied down more than 40,000 NVA soldiers—an astounding diversion of troops from South Vietnam's battlefields. Since only about 50 SOG men were roaming Laos at any time, this means *each Green Beret was tying down 800 enemy troops*, probably the greatest economy of force in modern history.

And despite their incredible numerical superiority the NVA still could not stop SOG operations.

NVA light-armored vehicles patrolled major roads and escorted convoys. This Soviet-built BTR-60 was disabled by a U.S. air strike. (Photo provided by DRV)

Above: RT Maryland One-Zero Gunther Wald and U.S. teammates William Brown and Donald Shue were MIA after NVA counterrecon men crept into their position at night. (Photo provided by Eldon Bargewell)

Top right: A road sentry attempts to conceal himself from an airplane by pressing his body to a tree. (Photo provided by Ted Wicorek)

Bottom: The NVA's most dangerous counterrecon weapon was the Chinese B-40 RPG with reload rounds on back. This one is no longer a threat. (Photo provided by Billy Waugh)

Top: An indicator of special ops sophistication, the NVA converted this French MAT-49 submachine gun to 7.62x25mm and fitted it with a suppressor. (Photo provided by West Point Museum)

Bottom: NVA antiaircraft crews with Soviet DSh K M-1938, 12.7mm heavy machine guns, comparable to the U.S. .50-caliber Browning. (Photo provided by National Archives)

KILLERS OF AMERICANS

AMONG THE INCENTIVES FOR NVA TO HUNT DOWN and kill SOG men was a special North Vietnamese medal, the Huan-Chuong Dung-Si Diet My— Order for Heroes Who Destroy Americans—nicknamed the "American Killer Award."

Once thought by historians to be only a myth, this award is absolutely genuine and today appears in several reference volumes. Photographs of the medal are extremely rare: the photograph depicted here was provided by Edward J. Emering.

The American Killer Award was presented in three classes, apparently to distinguish among the number of Americans killed. Hanging beneath a plastic bar containing a Communist yellow star on a red-and-blue background, the starburst-shaped medal features an NVA soldier stepping on a symbolic object labeled "U.S."

In the fall of 1970, while on a mission in southern Laos, RT Washington chanced upon two NVA soldiers on a trail and quickly dispatched them with bursts of CAR-15 fire. Sgt. Jeff Mauceri hurriedly searched the enemy soldier he'd killed and scooped up a large journal from the man's rucksack. The over-sized journal was carefully examined and, lo and behold, it contained a Huan-Chuong Dung-Si Diet My certificate. Given the location, Mauceri quite likely had avenged a lost SOG recon man.

As an additional incentive, a document captured elsewhere disclosed that the North Vietnamese offered a 10,000-piastre bounty—several months' pay—to any NVA soldier who captured or killed a SOG Green Beret, with a severed head adequate proof to collect.

Right: The North Vietnamese Order for Heroes Who Destroy Americans was also called the "American Killer Award." (Photo provided by Edward J. Emering.)

Far right: ONE LESS "KILLER OF AMERICANS." This NVA sergeant major, killed by RT Washington, was a recipient of the "American Killer Award." (Photo provided by Jeff Mauceri)

THE PATHET LAO

THE LAOTIAN COUNTERPART TO THE NVA was the Pathet Lao, the military force of the pro-Hanoi Laotian Communist Party. Seldom encountered by SOG teams because the NVA usually kept them out of the Ho Chi Minh Trail corridor, members of this ragtag force existed to keep Laotian civilians in line, not to fight battles.

Blatantly dominated by Hanoi, the Pathet Lao was poorly trained, poorly led, and poorly armed, usually carrying World War II-era French or U.S. weapons. When the odd encounter between a SOG team and Pathet Lao elements did occur, it almost wasn't fair, like putting a high school football team in the Super Bowl. In one shootout with a SOG RT, the poorly maintained Pathet Lao weapons did not fire or they got off only one shot when a weapon jammed. The entire five-man Pathet Lao patrol was killed in seconds. I examined one of the Pathet Lao weapons, a French MAT-49 submachine gun, and found the magazine so badly rusted that the spring-loaded follower could not lift cartridges up to the receiver.

Hanoi's postwar suggestions that the United States must talk to the Pathet Lao to learn what happened to American MIAs is disingenuous to say the least. It was the NVA, not the Laotians, who controlled the Ho Chi Minh Trail corridor where the vast majority of Americans disappeared.

Obsolete Soviet bloc weapons captured from Pathet Lao guerrillas: PPSh-41 submachine gun (top) and Mosin-Nagant carbine (bottom). (Photo provided by Frank Greco)

LISTENERS AND MOLES

SUPPORTING THE NVA'S COUNTER-SOG STRATEGY was a parallel intelligence effort by Hanoi's Trinh Sat security agency that proved no less dangerous.

Enemy signal intelligence would not have gleaned much by studying SOG radio transmissions, since RTs encrypted almost all of their messages unless they were in a firefight. Still, a competent NVA analyst could discern a pattern in these transmissions, enough to realize when a team was being inserted or extracted and estimate the number of teams in the field, with a general idea of where they were—certainly, sufficient clues to help focus the hunt.

Without question the enemy employed radio direction finding (RDF) to plot team radios to within a few hundred yards of their location, but intervening mountains and atmospheric problems frequently would have precluded a good "fix."

Lacking advanced Western technology, the Trinh Sat admittedly relied on HUMINT (human intelligence) over SIGINT (signal intelligence). "We do not consider the scientific and technical methods of the enemy as being very important," an enemy article said in 1967, "and continue to regard the use of people as most important." This proved very true in SOG's case, where the Trinh Sat infiltrated several covert operatives—South Vietnamese staff officers—into SOG's Saigon headquarters. These "moles" did untold harm, compromising the indigenous agent teams sent into North Vietnam, and after the agent team program ended in 1968, they turned their attention to American-led recon teams on the Ho Chi Minh Trail. We will never know how many of SOG's Green Berets were killed or captured due to the traitorous work of the Saigon moles.

Enemy countermeasures included human trackers, bloodhounds, and (shown here) radio direction finders to track down recon teams. (Photo provided by DPRK)

196

CHIEF SOG CAVANAUGH AND NVA COUNTERRECON

NO ONE IN SOG WAS MORE CONCERNED about the NVA's growing counterrecon capabilities than Col. Steve Cavanaugh, SOG's fourth chief. Arriving in mid-1968, the former 10th SFG commander could see the growing casualties and SOG's difficulty at keeping teams behind enemy lines in Laos and Cambodia.

As a young paratroop officer in World War II, Cavanaugh had made two combat jumps with the 11th Airborne Division, fighting the Japanese in New Guinea and the Philippines. His second jump was on a North Luzon drop zone secured by Donald "Headhunter" Blackburn's Filipino guerrillas. And by another coincidence he was a UCLA classmate of the Chief SOG he replaced, Jack Singlaub. During Cavanaugh's first Vietnam tour in 1961, he was the senior U.S. Army training officer in the country, after which he headed the Special Warfare Development Branch at Ft. Bragg, generating Special Forces training, doctrine, and manuals. Cavanaugh was almost a fatherly figure, always supportive and a real listener, respected by the recon men whose advice he often sought.

Suspecting operational security breaches, Chief SOG Cavanaugh visited each FOB to ask One-Zeros what could be done to keep their teams on the ground. Cavanaugh concluded that radio security was a problem, so he directed teams to carry the KY-38 secure voice system, a 50-pound device as big as a shopping bag, which connected to a team's field radio. "Of course, the RTs hated this," Cavanaugh admits. Recon men believed the bulky units endangered them by slowing movement, and, besides, secure voice could not end security compromises because they knew they weren't the ones responsible. Further, they realized the KY-38 could be RDFed as easily as any radio. Many KY-38s "mysteriously" broke down just before a team insertion: One-Zero Joe Walker's KY-38 malfunctioned at the launch site five times in a row, "forcing" him to leave it behind.

Col. Steve Cavanaugh, Chief SOG, in an OV-10 FAC backseat for familiarization flight over Ho Chi Minh Trail. (Photo provided by U.S. Army)

Suspicious that enemy moles might exist among the ARVN officers in SOG headquarters, Cavanaugh started misleading his Vietnamese counterparts, letting them believe a team was to be inserted at one point when the real LZ was some distance away. "And then, when the mission went out to the field it was different," Cavanaugh said.

Another improvement, Cavanaugh thought, was inserting teams beyond SOG's 20-kilometer limit. "They had our LZs pretty well pegged. I finally went back to Washington and asked for authority to insert deeper, and I would have got it but for [Ambassador] Sullivan. We were supposed to let his embassy know every time we were putting a team in, which we did. Maybe that was where we were getting compromised, I don't know."

Chapter Eleven

Recon Tactics and Techniques

Constantly outnumbered, hunted like animals, and given no quarter by a deadly serious enemy, all of SOG's Special Forces RTs should have vanished in Laos and Cambodia. As it was, most teams accomplished their missions even though they frequently had to shoot their way out. But how could anyone have prevailed in such a dangerous environment against such terrible odds?

SOG's success began with the quality of its soldiers. Special Forces trainees had to pass a rigorous selection process, including the highest mental and physical standards of any army in the world. Then, Special Forces training culled all but the best trainees, yielding intelligent, highly motivated Green Berets who would rather die than quit. SOG's all-volunteer recon men came from among these remaining few. Dedicated to their mission and all too aware of its hazards, they trained constantly when they weren't in the field, refining and mastering tactics and techniques. There was a lesson learned, a rule, a reason, for everything they did—*everything*.

COUNTERTRACKING

Knowing that most LZs were surveilled by enemy LZ watchers, a wise One-Zero assumed from the moment he landed that the enemy was scouring for any sign of his team. To counter such LZ watchers and trackers, recon teams "sterilized" their back trail to eliminate evidence of their passage. The

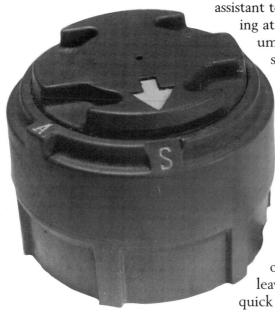

Above: The M14 "toe popper" mine, shown actual size, proved to be a handy antitracker device. (Photo provided by National Infantry Museum)

Below: DOG REPELLENT. To lose tracker dogs, recon men sprayed the backtrail with CS powder, carried in insect repellent bottles. (Photo provided by John Plaster)

assistant team leader, traveling at the rear of the column, picked up flotsam, reintertwined foliage, and obscured footprints, as well as creating false trails.

Despite their best efforts, teams sometimes still picked up trackers. In that case, one solution was to leave behind mines, a quick process using the M14 toe popper, which was slightly larger than a Copenhagen can.

Another countertracker tactic was "button hooking"—circling back to observe the team's own backtrail—and then ambushing the trackers with a suppressed weapon. This worked fine in the movies, but if the enemy got off even one shot it disclosed the action to nearby NVA elements and the race would be on.

Tracker dogs proved a bit more

difficult. During World War II, the British SOE had employed a mixture of dried-blood flakes and cocaine, which apparently worked well. The OSS used the "dog drag," a large linen wick dragged behind an operative containing equal parts of caproic acid, i-valeric acid, and castor oil. After experimenting with various concoctions to confuse tracker dogs (e.g., red pepper, exotic fragrances) SOG teams settled on CS tear gas powder, which was carried in plastic bottles and shaken on the ground like talcum powder.

DISGUISING THEIR TRACKS

Because enemy trackers would come running when U.S. jungle boot tracks were discovered, SOG devoted considerable effort to disguising boot soles. One novel solution, reputedly a CIA experiment, was outfitting jungle boots with human barefoot soles. Forwarded by CISO for testing, the smooth "footprint" boots couldn't grip and lost authenticity with wear. Besides that, they were uncomfortable.

Top inset: Human footprint boots designed to fool trackers did not work well in the field. (Photo provided by Leroy Thompson)

Bottom inset: SOG soldiers with socks pulled over their boots to obscure their trail as they examine an NVA supply road. (Photo provided by Department of Defense)

This NVA prisoner brought out of Laos is wearing U.S. jungle boots, proof that the airdrop program worked. (Photo provided by Frank Greco)

IMMEDIATE ACTION DRILLS

SOG RECON TEAMS PREVAILED IN CHANCE CONTACTS against numerically superior NVA units because of the former's immediate action (IA) drills. Executed at the instant of contact, an IA drill was rehearsed until it was mastered, so the team could pummel the enemy with a blur of fire and action, knock him off balance, and give the SOG men a decisive head start for the pursuit that was sure to follow.

Typically, an IA drill "trigger" was one shot, fired by the point man. Odd-numbered men jumped one step right, even men one step left, and faced the direction of fire. The point man emptied his weapon at the enemy in 3-to-5-round bursts, then dashed between his arrayed comrades to lead them in the opposite direction. The *split-second* the point man's weapon emptied, the next man picked up the slack; then he too ran down the middle, and so on.

One-Zeros constantly looked for new devices or techniques to enhance their IA drills. Someone devised a special rig using electrical tape and rubber bands to quick-toss grenades, so a man could grab a grenade from his harness, jerk it free, and pull the pin with one motion. Point men and tail gunners carried claymore mines in a special pouch on their rucksacks, with a 45-second time-delay fuse. The point man or tail gunner farthest from enemy contact removed his claymore and oriented it toward the enemy; then just as the last of his teammates rushed past, he'd ignite the fuse, fire his CAR-15, and withdraw.

The crowning touch was to make the NVA soliders fear that they'd stumbled onto a large unit, such as by firing lots of tracer ammunition. Since tracer rounds typically are fired by belt-fed machine guns and loaded one per five ball rounds, think of the psychological effect when four CAR-15s and two sawed-off RPD machine guns fire pure tracer. That's 370 tracers screaming past in 30 seconds, but it has the same *visual* effect as 1,850 rounds of normal machine gun fire!

Against SOG IA drills, no force, no matter its size, stood a chance—*for 30 seconds*. After that, the advantage shifted decisively to greater firepower and superior numbers.

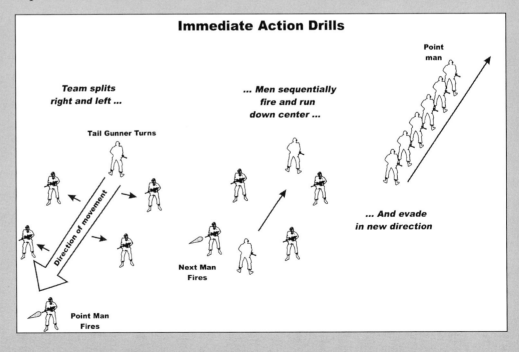

Immediate Action Drills

Point man

Team splits right and left ...

... Men sequentially fire and run down center ...

Tail Gunner Turns

Direction of movement

... And evade in new direction

Next Man Fires

Point Man Fires

Top: SOG recon team practices immediate action drill while a teammate (center) fires a 60mm mortar over them. (Photo provided by Richard Hoffman)

Bottom: RT Nevada practices immediate action drills, dryfire, on Kontum helipad. (Neil Terrell)

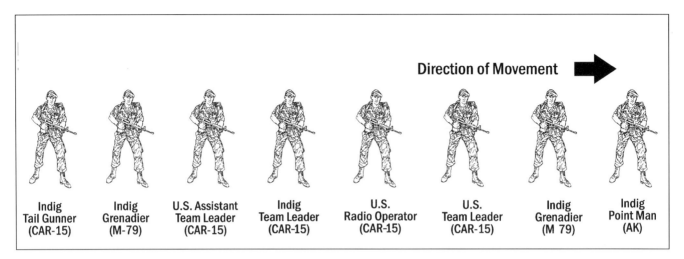

Direction of Movement

| Indig Tail Gunner (CAR-15) | Indig Grenadier (M-79) | U.S. Assistant Team Leader (CAR-15) | Indig Team Leader (CAR-15) | U.S. Radio Operator (CAR-15) | U.S. Team Leader (CAR-15) | Indig Grenadier (M 79) | Indig Point Man (AK) |

Recon team composition.

The next brainstorm was to replace the jungle boot's Vibram soles with tire treads to resemble Ho Chi Minh sandals, as worn by the Vietcong. But SOG teams weren't fighting VC—these were North Vietnamese regulars, wearing sneaker-like Bata boots with their own distinct pattern. Therefore, CISO acquired similar Bata boots in Hong Kong, which some teams wore despite the boots' weak arches and reduced ankle support.

To reduce the U.S. bootprint's distinctness, some team members pulled socks over their boots when traversing soft ground, but this had only limited application—and besides, socks wore out quickly and still left a discernable though vague track.

An especially innovative twist came under Chief SOG Col. Steve Cavanaugh. Thousands of used U.S. jungle boots left at MASH facilities by medevacked GIs were acquired and airdropped by Blackbird C-130s over Laotian and Cambodian base areas in hopes that some NVA soldiers would wear them and make the U.S. bootprint commonplace. This proved successful, with RTs observing NVA troops in jungle boots, and one RT even bringing out a prisoner in U.S. boots.

CONFUSING THE ENEMY

Realizing that contact and a subsequent gunfight would occur during more than half their missions, recon One-Zeros looked at ways to make the enemy hesitate to open fire during accidental or chance encounters, if only to gain a critical 10-second advantage.

Therefore, many SOG teams wore portions of enemy uniforms to confuse the NVA soldiers, forcing them to call out, "*Ei be do?*" (Who goes there?)—allowing the SOG men to open fire first. One-Zero Bob Graham's entire team wore NVA pith helmets, while many other One-Zeros attired their point men in complete NVA uniform with AK and chest-style web gear.

Some One-Zeros went further, outfitting their whole team in NVA clothes, weapons, and gear despite the fact that the international law of land warfare authorizes executing such men as spies. How concerned were they about losing Geneva Convention protections? RT West Virginia One-Zero Sfc. Ron Knight never gave it much thought, observing, "We never got any [SOG MIAs] back anyhow, so I reckon it didn't make any difference."

Top: Disguised in NVA uniforms and carrying Chinese weapons, RT West Virginia gained an edge in chance contacts. Shown here in NVA uniform are One-Zero Ron Knight (back row, second from right) and One-One Larry Kramer (front row, first on left). (Photo provided by Ron Knight)

Bottom: RT Pick One-Zero Bob Graham (center) confused the NVA by disguising the point man in enemy uniform (front, left) and had several other members of the team wear pith helmets. (Photo provided by Bob Graham)

STEALTH

SOG teams preferred to practice such perfect stealth that there would be no contact. In a full day, a team often advanced only 500 yards—that's just 50 yards per hour, which translates to one step per minute. During that minute each SOG man scanned to the front and sides; carefully eyeballed anyplace an enemy soldier might lurk; trained his CAR-15 at the spot contact might erupt; examined the ground where he'd next place his foot; paused, smelled, and listened; delicately pushed aside a vine with his left hand; tested the ground ahead; and with one toe slowly shifted his weight to the forward foot. He eased the vine behind him and ensured that it didn't catch on his rucksack or web gear; paused, listened, and looked around again; lifted his trailing foot; and gently brought it up to his other foot. He repeated this process hour after hour, immersed in tiny, deliberate actions, patient acts that so occupied his mind that there was nothing but the present.

Silence was the SOG men's greatest virtue. During a five-day mission teammates spoke only in whispers, but most often communicated by hand signals, facial expressions, and body language, as our speechless ancestors must have done when hunting woolly mammoths: a nod, a click of the tongue, a raised eyebrow, a shrug, a tip or shake of the head, an inquiring glance.

And then there was instinct: when a One-Zero "felt" something—danger, anticipation, hair rising on his neck—he accepted it as a subconscious warning, the gut feeling we all get that someone's watching or a foreboding about climbing a hill. Recon men learned to trust their instincts until they were almost superstitious: many a recon man *swore* the only reason a passing NVA soldier spotted him was because he'd been staring at the soldier's face.

RON PROCEDURES

Like a rabbit hiding in a briar patch, at dusk an RT squirmed into the thickest, thorniest foliage it could find, preferably on the side of a hill to make it difficult for the enemy to control night sweeps. On these so-called "rest overnights" (RONs), team members laid so close they could touch each other, eight men in a space so small the NVA wouldn't imagine that they could be there. Campfires? *Absolutely never!* Team members ate cold rations. A team member's rucksack was his pillow, and he slept in his web gear. His CAR-15 was never beyond reach.

Before dark the One-Zero squatted beside each man to designate his share of the perimeter, describing where and if to throw grenades. Claymore mines

Claymore mines—either command-detonated or left behind with a burning time fuse—disrupted enemy pursuit.

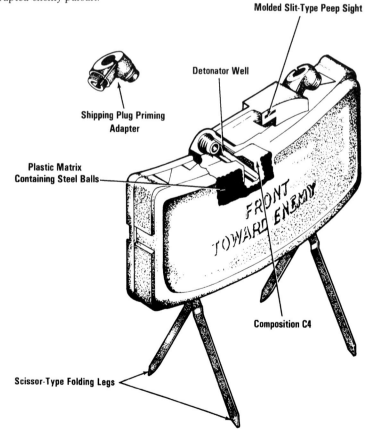

Molded Slit-Type Peep Sight

Detonator Well

Shipping Plug Priming Adapter

Plastic Matrix Containing Steel Balls

FRONT TOWARD ENEMY

Composition C4

Scissor-Type Folding Legs

were emplaced danger-close, just 5 meters away, on the reverse side of trees to absorb backblast. This way the claymore wire would not pinpoint them to NVA searchers. Relaxing at night meant death: better to stay uneasy, alert, with the tiniest sound jolting team members completely awake, hearts pounding.

By daylight they were packed and ready to go, sitting in an outward-looking circle, quietly eating rice, watching their claymores, and waiting for the FAC's morning radio check. Then they were on their way.

EVADING SWEEPS AND DRIVES

SOG men learned how a hunted animal felt because that's how the NVA scoured the countryside in search of them. Enemy signal shots, shouts, and clapping hands were intended to instill panic, like Indian coolies beating pots and pans to drive a tiger into a waiting rifleman's sights. Except the SOG men understood the game.

It demanded considerable tactical skill and good nerves to sidestep whole platoons and companies beating the bushes. Some teams boldly charged the noisemakers and shot their way through. When this worked it was brilliant; when it failed, it seemed the height of stupidity. Some tricks worked only by virtue of the team or One-Zero performing them; when another team attempted the identical technique it failed and men died.

CONTACT

A talented One-Zero anticipated enemy contact and mentally rehearsed his reactions, constantly revising contingencies to fit shifting circumstances: If we're hit right now, where's the nearest LZ? What do I do

if we take fire from uphill versus downhill? If there's a trail atop this hill, are we far enough below the crest that passing NVA troops won't hear us? Where's the nearest defensible terrain? *Upon contact, the team was executing its One-Zero's plan while the enemy was only reacting.*

When he could see that contact was inevitable, the One-Zero had his team initiate it—no matter how badly he was outnumbered—because he knew the first blow was critical. Bloody the enemy's nose and run like hell. In heavily occupied areas, 10 minutes after a chance contact a 100-man, company-sized reaction force would arrive, reinforced by another company in a half-hour, and the enemy would keep piling more on.

Typically, a recon team would dash about 200 yards through thick jungle and then slow into evasive movement to shake off pursuers. The trade-off was speed for sign: if the team moved quickly it might gain distance but would leave a more detectable trail. Evasion was preferable to an outright footrace because the numerically superior enemy carried less gear and could outrun the team or relay word ahead via radio and signal shots. Stopping was hazardous: a 30-second head start might mean a clean escape, while 10 seconds wasted could cause encirclement and annihilation.

When a team couldn't move fast or far due to wounded men, it would seize the best defensible terrain, stack magazines, and fight it out. Hopefully, this was beside an LZ so the team could be extracted as quickly as A-1 Skyraiders and Cobra gunships pushed back the enemy. But the team had to get out soon or the NVA would rush in hordes of troops and ring the area with antiaircraft guns, and the odds would shift from quality to quantity, with only one deadly result.

DIVERSIONS

THE MOST EFFECTIVE IA DRILLS INCLUDED some deception or surprise—preferably something so off the wall that the NVA wouldn't know *how* to respond.

One SOG team leader sometimes blew a shrieking whistle and shouted, "First platoon, base! Second platoon, maneuver right! Third platoon, maneuver left!" Sounding like a whole company of troops bluffed the enemy for about 30 seconds—but 30 seconds in a life-and-death shoot-out is a lifetime.

It occurred to me that a bugle sounding a cavalry charge during an IA drill might astonish NVA soldiers, but I couldn't find a bugle nor anyone who could be relied upon to pucker during a firefight. Then I recalled freon-powered airhorns, like the ones you hear at high school football games. My father shipped me one, which I spray-painted black and taped to my web gear. Soon thereafter, my RT California—with Rex Jaco, John Yancey, Galen Musselman, and four Montagnards—walked into an ambush in Cambodia, with 20 NVA soldiers firing AKs, machine guns, and RPGs. We squatted down and opened up, but heavy fire almost had us pinned in a bowl. We couldn't fall back because that meant going uphill, right into the enemy's fire. I reached for a grenade, but my hand found the airhorn instead—I depressed the plunger for 15 full seconds. *When I lifted my finger you could hear a pin drop!* Uncertain of this horrible-sounding Yankee weapon, the North Vietnamese had run for their lives!

Such tricks sometimes proved amazingly successful—but the stranger the trick, the more dangerous it was to try it twice.

SOUND DIVERSION. Even a freon-powered airhorn could be used to confuse the NVA and allow a SOG team to escape. (Photo provided by John Plaster)

DESPERATE MEN

MUCH TO THE CHAGRIN OF NVA COMMANDERS, SOG teams sometimes escaped because sheer desperation required taking risks that North Vietnamese soldiers simply would not match. For example, NVA troops had learned from battle against U.S. units in South Vietnam that they could prevent U.S. air strikes by staying so close that the bombs would endanger the Americans. But being a fatalistic lot, the SOG teams called in the air anyhow—sometimes right across themselves—preferring to chance an accidental death from U.S. bombs rather than certain death from the NVA.

One-Zero Ken "Shoe Box" Carpenter once found his team hotly pursued by NVA elements that kept driving them toward a cliff, where at last the team seemed hopelessly pinned. The doomed Carpenter peeked over that Laotian precipice while the NVA formed for the assault. Then "Shoe Box" and his teammates held hands and jumped into the treetops 30 feet below, crashing through foliage, bouncing violently between branches and spraining a few ankles, but they all hit the ground *alive*.

And not a single NVA soldier cared to follow them.

One-Zero Ken "Shoe Box" Carpenter. (Photo provided by Chuck Karwan)

Above: Sgt. James Giaco III, RT New Hampshire, touches up facial camouflage during hourly break. (Photo provided by Will Curry)

Right: Six men in black-sprayed pattern encircle a comrade in an unpainted uniform. The difference is dramatic. (Photo provided by Dale Boswell)

PERFECT JUNGLE CAMOUFLAGE

ALTHOUGH THE TIGER STRIPE PATTERN was often associated with Special Forces during the war, SOG men found that the most effective camouflage resulted from modifying plain old olive drab jungle fatigues. Just before an operation each team member donned all his field gear—rucksack, web gear, hat, scarf, weapon—over his unmarked "sterile" jungle fatigues, and then teammates would take turns spray-painting each other with black streaks to tone down the edges and blend it all together. For the shadowy world of deep jungle, creeping from shadow to shadow, this obscuring camouflage pattern fit superbly. Bits of natural foliage were not normally worn because most recon men believed that whatever concealment benefit might result was outweighed by an increase in noise and clumsiness when moving.

To break up shape and outline, faces and hands were similarly colored by using a camouflage stick; the camouflage was touched up during hourly breaks. Some blond recon men took camouflaging one step further and dyed their hair black, which also helped them appear to be Asians from a distance.

ESCAPING ENEMY PURSUERS

AFTER A FIREFIGHT, SOG TEAMS PREFERRED TO DISAPPEAR into the jungle, but NVA pursuers often were too close to shake off. In these situations One-Zeros employed special tactics to deter, divert, or delay their pursuers long enough to escape.

As shown in illustration one, teams employed the tactic of "pause and shoot," a series of quick ambushes to delay and hit the enemy with attrition until they gave up the chase. Illustration two demonstrates "button hooking," by which SOG men surprised pursuers by doubling back and ambushing them on their flank. In illustration three, a team purposely leaves strong indicators that its members headed one way, but they actually veer in a different direction. And in illustration four, a team drops one smoke, runs a short distance—perhaps 50 yards—then drops a second smoke, veers away, and radios gunships and fighters to strafe between the two smokes, with deadly effect.

All these techniques were enhanced by lacing the backtrail with specially modified time-delay fragmentary, white-phosphorous, and CS grenades, creating a temporary minefield that a pursuing enemy crossed only at great peril. Combined, these tactics were very effective—but *only* if a team kept moving.

Above: A hastily emplaced grenade and tripwire could make life difficult for pursuers. (Photo provided by Ron Mullins)

Left: Escaping NVA pursuers.

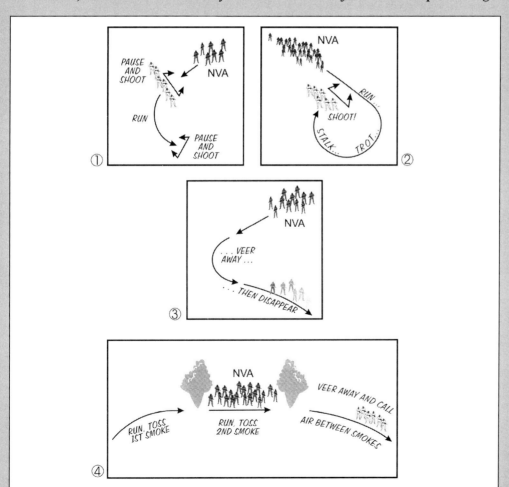

PART FIVE

RECON
OPERATIONS

Chapter Twelve

Getting Teams In and Out

Despite thousands of NVA defenders, whole belts of antiaircraft guns, layer upon layer of LZ watchers, trackers, sentries, and counterrecon units, SOG teams were inserted and extracted on a daily, almost routine basis. This could be accomplished only because SOG planners, Covey Riders, FACs, and helicopter crews developed and refined specialized tactics, techniques, and devices to bypass or penetrate or deceive the enemy.

Priorities were slightly different for an insertion versus an extraction. The key to *mission success*, it was realized, was infiltrating a team without detection, while the degree to which an extraction was speedy and unpredictable proved the key to *team survival*. SOG, of course, emphasized both mission success and team survival.

GETTING THEM IN

A successful insert began with LZ selection. SOG planners realized that NVA forces in southern Laos and eastern Cambodia were attempting to surveil every spot of open ground large enough to accommodate a helicopter—the trick, then, was to use the marginal or even "unusable" LZs that wouldn't be covered by NVA LZ watchers.

Some tiny LZs became usable due to incredible pilot skills, with a Huey

Recon man's view going into a dangerous target in Ashau Valley. Attached to the CAR-15 is a rifle grenade. (Photo provided by Ken Bowra)

teams near aircraft crash sites, rappeling was only occasionally attempted for normal recon insertions.

A bit more deceptive were "flip-flop" inserts, in which the same helicopter extracting a team at the end of its weeklong mission dropped off a fresh team at the same time. Hopefully, NVA forces would believe that the chase was over and not bother to look for the newly arrived recon men. Somewhat similar were "stay-behind" insertions, with an RT arriving aboard a helicopter resupply of a Hatchet Force platoon or company. When the Hatchet Force was extracted a day or two later, the recon men stayed behind to begin their own mission. Equally undetectable inserts were "walk-offs" from Radio Relay Sites Leghorn and Hickory whereby RTs arrived on the regular weekly resupply helicopter and then slipped away invisibly in the night.

There were outright deceptions, too, a major one being false RT inserts, which usually paralleled the insertion of a real team in the same general area. For a false insert, a Huey or Kingbee sat down briefly on an LZ and then lifted away with a few bursts by the doorgunners. Although this almost guaranteed that the NVA forces would dispatch trackers and counterrecon elements, false inserts weren't employed too often because they were just as dangerous to aircraft and crews as real inserts.

Less hazardous but very effective was airdropping a Nightingale device firefight simulator on an LZ. After a preset delay, the LZ would erupt with explosions and seeming bursts of full-auto fire that would continue a half-hour or longer, which was almost sure to draw the NVA away from a real team insertion.

Some One-Zeros requested "LZ preps"—strafing the insertion area—to

or Kingbee slowly descending, elevator-like, into a deep hole in the jungle canopy, rotors chewing through overhanging branches to reach the ground. Other times, a helicopter would hover 20 feet above an opening too small to land, while an RT scrambled down retractable aluminum ladders. Ladders worked so well that by 1970–1971, perhaps 40 percent of insertions employed them.

Riskier but even more likely to avoid LZ watchers was having a team rappel through a narrow opening in high jungle canopy—riskier because a descending recon man was at the enemy's mercy if by chance an NVA soldier was below him. Due to their rope tie-down spots and balance, Hueys were the preferred rappeling platform, with two men simultaneously kicking away from each side, all four men reaching the ground in about five seconds. Although often employed to insert Bright Light

SONG OF THE NIGHTINGALE

SOG'S MOST CLEVER DIVERSIONARY TOOL was an air-dropped firefight simulator called the Nightingale device. Named after the bird whose song captivated Chinese emperors, the Nightingale was a CIA product that attached cherry bombs and M-80 firecrackers to a waterproofed mesh screen, all linked together with slow-burning time fuse. After being lit by a fuse lighter or acid time-delay ignitor, the Nightingale powder train cooked off what sounded like grenades and bursts of automatic weapons fire, lasting about a half-hour. Even to experienced combat soldiers, a Nightingale sounded indistinguishable from the real thing, especially with its authentic pauses and peaks accented by an occasional "grenade" or two.

The Nightingale was employed very effectively for false inserts, but there were other uses. Medal of Honor recipient Bob Howard used the Nightingale one night for perhaps the most astonishing engagement of the war. Howard's assistant team leader, Robert "Buckwheat" Clough, and one Montagnard crept inside an NVA base camp among 500 sleeping enemy and left two Nightingales with a two-hour time-delay ignitor. When it erupted at 3 A.M., "It was the biggest firefight I've ever heard in my life," Howard recalled. It took NVA leaders an hour and a half to get their soldiers to stop shooting at each other in the dark. When Howard passed their abandoned encampment later that day, as he recalls, "we found dead bodies everywhere."

The Nightingale device—shown here as a replica—simulated explosions and automatic-weapon fire. (Photo provided by John Plaster)

This false insert on an Ashau Valley hilltop drew enemy attention away from a team's real LZ. (Photo provided by Mike Sloniker)

force any hidden LZ watchers to flee or go to cover so that they wouldn't see the team land. Usually this was of only questionable effectiveness. Far more effective was a powerful "prep" that not only disrupted any LZ watchers, but cut a new LZ where there had been none before—a "daisy cutter" 2,000-pound bomb whose fuse extender detonated it three feet above the ground. The resulting clearing usually was large enough to squeeze in a single helicopter.

Taking this concept to its maximum, the U.S. Air Force developed the Commando Vault, a 15,000-pound bomb—the largest nonnuclear device in the U.S. inventory—a Volkswagen-bus-sized bomb dropped from 30,000 feet by a C-130 with pinpoint accuracy. Late in the war, when SOG intelligence had indicators of a security compromise and suspected the NVA was lying in wait for an RT insertion, Commando Vault bombs were

dropped as an LZ prep, creating an incredible Hiroshima-like mushroom cloud and sweeping open a five-ship LZ—not to mention virtually vaporizing any lurking NVA ambushers.

STRIP ALERT

When a desperate RT cried "Prairie Fire!" it meant that they had to be extracted immediately, or vastly superior enemy forces would overrun them. Back at the launch site, it took only one shout from the SOG launch officer, and instantly pilots stopped pitching horseshoes or munching C-rations in the shade and dashed madly for their helicopters, where whoever was closest already had it cranking. Less than two minutes after a Covey Rider called "prairie fire" the Cobras, Hueys, and Kingbees dipped noses and screamed away, doorgunners loading machine guns as the ships climbed into the sky.

Above: STRIP ALERT. Kingbees and Green Hornets at Duc Lap Special Forces camp, only two miles from the Cambodian border. (Photo provided by Dale Bennett)

SCRAMBLE! Kingbees lift off, and Hueys crank at Dak To, going after a team in trouble in Laos. (Photo provided by Mike Sheppard)

SMART DUMMY. To fake a "string" extraction, dummies like this were suspended below Hueys. To the NVA it looked real. (Photo provided by John Plaster)

SOG teams could not have survived had it not been for such responsive aircraft, which sat dawn to dusk at a border airfield on "strip alert." Whether there were six teams on the ground or just one, all these aircraft had to be ready to launch in an instant. And that's a lot—six Hueys, two to four helicopter gunships, four to six Kingbees, and two FACs, plus a pair of A-1 Skyraiders at their own base. All these aircraft flew each insertion or extraction, a virtual air armada, yet most teams could come out aboard a single Huey. Was it lavish? Not at all.

After many lessons learned at considerable human cost, SOG planners concluded that its air assets needed *redundancy*—the leeway of losing two of anything, yet continuing—and the ability for *self-recovery*—the means to retrieve downed aircrews without halting or postponing the team extraction that brought them there in the first place. This meant that two helicopters could be shot down, yet the downed crewmen would be rescued, plus the RT would be extracted, with everyone making it home for a cold beer in the club. Lives depended upon such quick reaction. Five minutes wasted, even a minute's hesitation, and NVA soldiers would rush in enough troops to overrun an encircled team or capture a downed crew.

Lives were saved, too, by the Special Forces "chase medic" who flew aboard one Huey, ready to treat any badly wounded recon man or crewman during the flight to a MASH facility. How many men were saved by these incredibly courageous medics is beyond calculation.

Also aboard the helicopters might be the SOG Bright Light RT stationed at the same airstrip, riding along to help extract wounded men

or to rappel in and rescue injured airmen. If the rescue needed more firepower, an entire Hatchet Force platoon was on two-hour standby at Ban Me Thuot, Kontum, or Danang.

GETTING THEM OUT

Sometimes an endangered RT could be assisted in a much less dramatic fashion. If the team had only been detected or had escaped a minor contact without aggressive pursuit, it was often better to stage a false extraction. This was safest and easiest—and most credible—by simulating an extraction by McGuire rig, but instead of lifting out a real team, the Huey crew chief would toss out life-sized dummies that dangled for all the world to see as they were lifted away.

There were some "cold" extractions, with no enemy action, but "hot" extractions predominated, with even cold ones often going hot once the helicopters arrived. Most often, the hot extraction tactic was to pound the enemy with gunships and A-1s, pushing the NVA soldiers back enough to slip a Huey or Kingbee onto the LZ.

Far better, though, was the Covey Rider's directing the team to a less obvious LZ, where there was less chance that the team would be ringed by antiaircraft guns and NVA troops. As with insertions, small, seemingly unusable LZs were preferred, and here the 34-foot aluminum ladders proved themselves over and over. Having run for hours, exhausted recon men often couldn't climb all the way up to the Huey, so they rode the ladders out, escaping the NVA by a hair's breadth.

If an RT wasn't being pursued or had shaken off the NVA, it could render an "unusable" LZ usable by pulling out the excellent SOG banana

Top: Sgt. Maj. Charles McGuire is decorated for developing his namesake extraction rig, which saved may recon men's lives. (Photo provided by Steve Sherman)

Bottom: High over southern Laos, RT Maine men ride McGuire rigs beneath 57th Assault Helicopter Company Huey. (Photo provided by Clarence Long)

RT Hawaii's John Justice and Montagnard teammate chop extraction LZ, rather than use an existing open area. (Photo provided by John Plaster)

knives and hacking away at bamboo and thin trees or by lashing claymore mines to larger trees and blowing them down. Timing was crucial, though, because the noise of chopping could attract nearby NVA units, while a detonation was certain to alert any enemy troops within earshot.

String extractions—slang for any of the various rope and harness extraction systems—offered great flexibility because they required only a small treetop opening for the weighted rope bags to be dropped to the ground. But this extraction technique was inherently dangerous to both the helicopter and passengers and therefore was the least preferred extraction method.

But no matter the extraction method, close air support from A-1 Skyraiders and helicopter gunships often added the decisive touch that allowed lives to be snatched away from the jaws of death. Suppressive fire from machine guns and cannons usually forced NVA troops to find cover rather than stand up and shoot. Especially, though, cluster bombs inspired NVA antiaircraft crews to abandon their guns temporarily, while

carefully placed white-phosphorous bombs so well masked the LZ that the gunners couldn't even see the helicopters. In the most desperate situations, with special approval from MACV Headquarters in Saigon, the Skyraiders dropped special cluster bomb unit (CBU) tear gas bomblets, which disrupted the NVA soldiers' ability to see or shoot.

If ever you come upon a claim that these U.S. Air Force A-1s dropped *nerve gas*—as preposterous an allegation as ever leveled against U.S. servicemen—see this falsehood for what it truly is: a deep ignorance of tactics and ordnance, a lack of appreciation for courage, and an incredibly naive view of how special operations actually must be conducted. Hundreds of SOG men survived almost certain death due to the professionalism and great valor of those who risked their lives to extract them, employing carefully developed tactics and techniques. It was this combination of human ingenuity and personal valor—not the "magic bullet" of nerve gas—that made possible these extractions despite terrible odds.

Left: A 100-foot smoke plume from a bursting white-phosphorous bomb masks aircraft from antiaircraft gunners. (Photo provided by Shelby Stanton)

Below left: CCC RT tests a new descender for rapid rappeling. A few seconds after this photo was snapped, the device broke, killing the Montagnard on the right. (Photo provided by Gerry Denison)

Below: Recon men practice rappeling as one way to bypass enemy LZ watchers. (Photo provided by Mike Sheppard)

RT New Hampshire blasts a tree, creating a usable
LZ only minutes before extraction from Laos.
(Photo provided by Will Curry)

Above left: By using such tiny, "unusable" LZs, SOG teams avoided enemy security. (Photo provided by Jon Renegar)

Above right: Lt. George "Ken" Sisler, posthumous Medal of Honor recipient, tensely bites his lip as enemy fire drives away extraction birds. Later, air strikes pushed NVA forces back, allowing the Kingbees to land. (Photo provided by Jane Sisler)

Above: CCC Recon Company 1st Sgt. Norm Doney modified aluminum ladders to fit Hueys, making possible this infiltration/extraction technique. (Photo provided by Frank Greco)

Top right: Each SOG Huey had a special flexible aluminum ladder, allowing pickup or insertion from 28 feet above the ground. (Photo provided by Dale Boswell)

Bottom: COMING OUT HOT! CCN recon men ride the ladder coming out of Laos. The Huey is from Company C, 158th Assault Helicopter Battalion. (Photo provided by Mike Sloniker)

Inset: Holding on for his life, CCC recon man rides the ladder out of Cambodia. The helicopter is from the 57th Assault Helicopter Company. (Photo provided by Charlie Dodge)

Left: To avoid LZ watchers, CCC RT is inserted by ladder into a spot too small to land. (Photo provided by Will Curry)

Above: CCC RT members ride ladders after emergency extraction from Laos. (Photo provided by Richard Madore)

Right: CCS Lt. Mike Ash rides STABO rig 3,000 feet over Cambodia. (Photo provided by Brendon Lyons)

228

Above: An RT Idaho Montagnard's face shows understandable apprehension as he's buffeted by wind thousands of feet above the ground. (Photo provided by Ken Bowra)

Left: Wounded, exhausted, almost falling off, RT Hatchet members ride out of Cambodia after a series of running gunfights in which one 'Yard was killed and Alex Saunders and another 'Yard wounded. One-Zero Robert Bost and Ron Atwell and the rest of the team "killed a lot of bad guys on this mission." (Photo provided by Robert Bost)

Above: The 15,000-pound Commando Vault was the largest nonnuclear device in the U.S. inventory. SOG used these cataclysmic bombs to deter enemy from watching Laotian LZs. (Photo provided by U.S. Air Force)

Right: Gunship patterns.

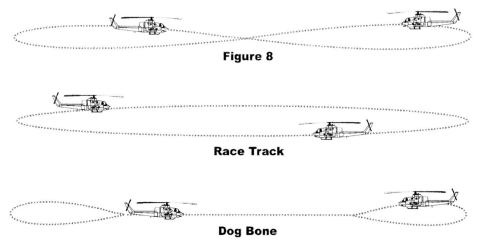

Figure 8

Race Track

Dog Bone

Top: 101st Airborne Division Huey slips through the treetops on Laotian side of the Ashau Valley to insert a CCN RT. (Photo provided by Mike Sloniker)

Bottom: A 2,000-pound "daisy cutter" bomb explodes, blowing a hole in jungle large enough for a single Huey to insert an RT. (Photo provided by Marshall Harrison)

PLAYING BALL

"PLAYING BALL" WAS SOG COVEY RIDER SLANG for the complex aerial effort involved in inserting or extracting an RT, employing up to 20 helicopters and airplanes.

It began about an hour before insertion, with a Covey FAC and Covey Rider discreetly overflying the prospective LZ to check weather, confirm the location, and look for any signs of enemy presence. Thirty minutes before insertion, the FAC called for a pair of A-1 Skyraiders loaded with cluster bombs, napalm, and smoke bombs, the planes usually being sent from Nakhon Phanom, Danang, or Pleiku. When the fighters radioed that they were about 20 minutes out, the Covey Rider called for a "launch" at a border airstrip, such as Khe Sanh or Dak To, directing these four to six gunships and 10 to 12 helicopters to a cross-border rendezvous point.

Once the helicopters and fighters had been led to the LZ, the Covey Rider's and FAC's challenge became airspace management, but the procedures were simple and well understood. One quick radio message, "White Lead, hold east, 5 miles, three grand," and the "White Flight" Hueys and Kingbees went into orbit at 3,000 feet 5 miles east of the LZ. Then the FAC held the arriving A-1s directly overhead at 5,000 feet so they could watch the insertion, ready to intervene at a second's notice. Next the Cobra gunships sped in at low level, crisscrossing the insertion area, confusing the NVA as well as watching for enemy groundfire near the LZ. Immediately, one or two helicopters carrying the RT descended from orbit and followed a Cobra gunship right on the deck to the LZ. Ideally, it was a small, one-ship LZ, and the helicopter hovered less than two seconds for the team to leap off and rush into the jungle. In all the clatter of whopping blades and whining turbines, unless an NVA soldier was right there to see the team step off, the NVA forces weren't quite sure where the team members had landed or even if a team actually had been inserted.

If the insertion aircraft took fire near the primary LZ, the helicopters immediately shifted to a designated secondary LZ in the same general area. Eventually, NVA forces became so ubiquitous that Covey Riders also designated a tertiary (third) LZ in case the helicopters took fire on both the primary and secondary zones.

After rushing off the LZ, the One-Zero hid his men for about five minutes to ensure that they had not landed in the midst of an NVA unit and then radioed a "Team OK" to the Covey Rider, releasing the aircraft and commencing his recon mission.

Although extractions were conducted similarly, more than half the time it was an emergency situation, conducted under fire amid air strikes. Yet, the great majority of times, these teams held their own, which, combined with the aviators' expertise, still allowed escape in what often seemed a hopeless situation.

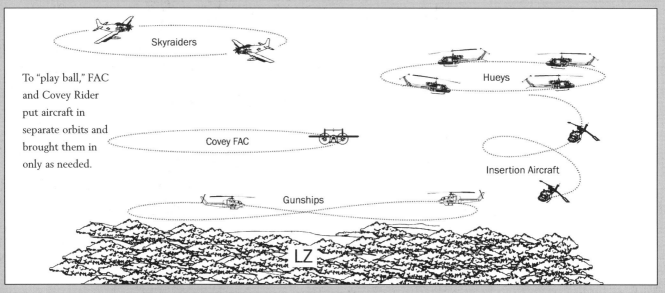

To "play ball," FAC and Covey Rider put aircraft in separate orbits and brought them in only as needed.

Skyraiders

Hueys

Covey FAC

Insertion Aircraft

Gunships

LZ

STRING EXTRACTIONS

SOG's MOST REVOLUTIONARY EMERGENCY EXTRACTION device was the McGuire rig, invented by Special Forces Sgt. Maj. Charles McGuire. A McGuire rig was simply a 100-foot rope with a 6-foot loop at the end with a padded canvas seat. A single Huey carried four rigs, or "strings," two on each side. Not only was a string extraction faster than being winched up to the helicopter, but four men could be lifted away simultaneously.

All the pilot had to do was hover at treetop level while his crew chief dropped four weighted bags containing the rigs, wait while the four recon men climbed in, and then rise vertically until his string passengers were above the jungle canopy and fly away. A team could be lifted out through any canopy hole wide enough to see the ground.

But those few seconds while lifting the men through the canopy were fraught with danger because the ropes could become snagged in the trees, or a sudden barrage of fire could threaten the aircraft. "If you got in trouble with the strings, the crew members would have to cut them," explained Sgt. Charlie Dodge, a Huey crew chief with the 57th Aviation Company. "It didn't matter if anyone was on the ends of the strings or not; if you had to cut the ropes in order to save the aircraft, you cut the ropes. That was understood by everybody."

Strings saved many recon men's lives, but several men were injured and killed when they were dragged through trees or they fell from the padded seat. Lt. Jim Bircham and Sfc. Charles White, lost in separate incidents when they fell from McGuire rigs, remain MIA today.

After several McGuire rig fatalities, 1st Sgt. Norman Doney added a wrist sliploop, which helped, but men still fell. Some recon men donned Swiss seats instead of sitting in the swing or strapped on a modified German rappeling seat called the Hanson rig. Eventually three instructors at the 5th SFG's Recondo School developed the STABO rig, an acronym for their names: Maj. Robert Stevens, Capt. John Knabb, and Sfc. Clifford Roberts. The STABO rig replaced web gear with a special webbing harness. For extraction, the recon man unfastened two straps on the back, swung them between his legs, and snapped them securely in front. When the helicopter dropped a rope with a special STABO yoke, the recon man would snap it onto two rings, one at each shoulder, and away he'd fly. It was ingenious.

Not only did the STABO rig hold its rider securely, but it left his hands free to wield weapons, a solution so well done that 30 years later the identical STABO rig is used by Green Berets, Rangers, and SEALs throughout U.S. Special Operations Command.

Top: STABO rig harness replaced recon man's normal web gear, shown here with attached pouches, canteen covers, etc. (Photo provided by Jerrald Ginder)

Above: To deploy STABO rig, the user dropped straps from the rear and clasped to the front to create a complete harness. (Photo provided by Jerrald Ginder)

Above: Recon man and Covey Rider Bill Hanson modified a German rappeling seat to create the Hanson extraction harness. (Photo provided by Bryon Loucks)

Right: SOG recon men ride strings across War Zone D, South Vietnam. (Photo provided by Dale Boswell)

Top: Special Forces noncommissioned officer rigs a SOG Huey for the STABO extraction system. (Photo provided by Dale Boswell)

Bottom: Recon men kick through low treetops as they're lifted away on STABO rigs. (Photo provided by Mike Ash)

CCC RT is lowered onto the airfield at Dak To after their last-light emergency extraction from Laos. (Photo provided by Ted Wicorek)

SOG Huey pulls away with men on STABO rigs. (Photo provided by Dale Boswell)

Sgt. Joseph Bertoni III, RT Brace, aloft over Cambodia after a "bitch of an extract," according to One-Zero Ron Mullins. (Photo provided by Ron Mullins)

RT Brace point man, Y Lup Ksor, on STABO rig coming out of Cambodia. (Photo provided by Ron Mullins)

CCS recon man rappels from a U.S. Air Force Green Hornet Huey. (Photo provided by Bryan Stockdale)

Top: Recon team loads at Dak To for a last-light insert, giving them all night to lose LZ watchers and trackers. (Photo provided by Newell Bernard)

Bottom: Sgt. Gerald Plank's RT rides ladders coming out of hot area in Laos. (Photo provided by George Gaspard)

GUNSHIP PILOTS

SOG DUTY ASSEMBLED SOME OF THE GUTSIEST men ever to wear a U.S. uniform. And no less intrepid than the recon men on the ground or the Huey crewmen who extracted them were the helicopter gunship pilots who braved incredible NVA fire right at the treetops to place rockets, grenades, and machine gun fire on the enemy.

Like any other SOG soldiers, gunship pilots volunteered for this hazardous duty, with their selection for dangerous cross-border mission attesting to their skill and esprit. Some gunship pilots took this a step further.

Like African youths who proved themselves as warriors by single-handedly spearing a lion, a number of SOG Cobra pilots teased fate by flying north of the DMZ into North Vietnam, where the NVA daringly flew an oversize communist flag just beyond a knocked-down bridge where Highway 1 crossed the Ben Hai River. As the pilots realized, the flag was a "flak trap" intended to lure U.S. aircraft into NVA gunners' sights when the pilots tried to shoot at it.

It became a Cobra pilot's ultimate coup not merely to slip through enemy antiaircraft guns and fire at the NVA flag, but to bring back a trophy photo shot through his canopy to prove it. As these amazing photos verify, SOG's gunship pilots were a bold, brassy bunch.

Top right: Cobra pilot Rick Freeman tempted fate to get this flag photo. (Photo provided by Mike Sloniker)

Bottom right: This huge NVA flag on the north side of Ben Hai River was photographed from an O-2 FAC aircraft. (Photo provided by Jim Martin)

Below: DANGER-CLOSE! This Cobra pilot almost touched the flag—and lived to talk about it. (Photo provided by Bob Coder)

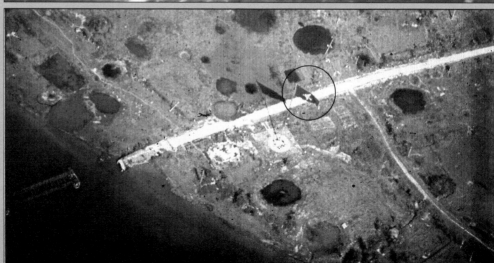

IN THE NICK OF TIME. Recon team rides strings out of Laos at sunset. (Photo provided by Richard Madore)

Chapter Thirteen

HALO: The Ultimate Infiltration Technique

One of SOG's significant contributions to military history was the world's first use of HALO parachuting in combat. HALO is the military counterpart to civilian skydiving and involves exiting an aircraft above 10,000 feet, freefalling to 1,000 or 2,000 feet, and then gliding the rest of the way using a steerable parachute. Since the first German combat jumps in 1940, paratroopers always had gone into battle using static lines to open chutes automatically as they exited the aircraft, allowing masses of troopers to land in a predictable pattern, at a predictable rate, on enormous drop zones.

By contrast, HALO offered the stealth of jumping from such high altitude that people on the ground would have no idea a jump was even under way, along with the possibility of an entire team landing in a very small clearing. Do it at night and you might really have something.

HALO had existed in Special Forces since Ft. Bragg's JFK Special Warfare Center implemented the U.S. Army's first HALO School in 1957. In its first year of operation, one gung-ho HALO graduate was none other than John "Skip" Sadler, who by 1970 was the new Chief SOG. Colonel Sadler believed that HALO offered an undetectable means to infiltrate teams into Laos.

Infiltration had become a major problem. During the second quarter of 1970 every team inserted by helicopter west of Khe Sanh was hit by

HALO TRAINING

The handful of SOG teams formed and selected for HALO jumps were each built around two or three Green Beret graduates of Ft. Bragg's HALO School, some of them having hundreds of freefall jumps under their belts. Drawn from CCN and CCC, all these volunteers were experienced recon men.

After selection, each team—both U.S. and indigenous personnel—were flown by Blackbird to Okinawa to go through basic HALO training as a team. This training was handled by the 1st SFG's finest HALO instructors, Sfcs. Joe Markham and Ben Dennis. The SOG men learned that HALO had two phases of controlled descent: first the freefall, during which a jumper had to stabilize and travel laterally to follow or group with others, and then the parachute descent, using canopy gores that open and close with toggle lines to steer the final 2,500 feet to the drop zone. Thus a 12,500-foot jump meant 60 seconds in freefall, opening the chute at 2,500 feet, and another two and a half minutes flying the canopy into the drop zone.

After a month on Okinawa, each SOG team returned to Camp Long Thanh for another 14 days of training and made more practice jumps, assisted by M. Sgt. Frank Norbury from the HALO School at Ft. Bragg, perhaps the most experienced HALO jumper in the U.S. military. Darkness produced many problems. The aircrew and jumpmaster had difficulty finding the drop zone, yet the Blackbird could make only one pass. The lead jumper, or baseman, had to see the drop zone so everyone could follow him; the parachutists had to group together in midair and then stay together during descent. They had to

Jumpmaster Ben Dennis (kneeling) signals to exit as HALO jumper Richard Gross leaps and Howard Sugar reaches the door. (Photo provided by Howard Sugar)

NVA forces; in the next quarter teams were inserted there 74 times, and two out of three made "significant contact."

As SOG intelligence reported to Sadler, the NVA did not post nighttime LZ watchers because helicopters couldn't land safely in darkness. Therefore, RTs parachuting into their targets would avoid many existing NVA countermeasures.

avoid injury while landing in the dark, and they had to link up in thick jungle. Any shortcoming at any step would quash the entire operation.

THE FIRST HALO TEAM

In July 1970, SOG's first HALO team was selected at Danang's CCN. Designated RT Virginia, it was led by S. Sgt. Cliff Newman, a seasoned civilian skydiver, with Sfc. Sammy Hernandez, a HALO graduate with 75 jumps under his belt, and Sfc. Melvin Hill, who'd been a HALO instructor at Ft. Bragg. Rounding out their six-man team were an ARVN officer and two Montagnards, none of them HALO qualified. RT Florida's target was a new NVA road just inside Laos in an area occupied by some 10,000 NVA troops.

Just after 2 A.M. on 28 November 1970, RT Virginia leaped from a SOG Blackbird cruising at 18,000 feet. Unable to spot their drop zone, their jumpmaster, Sfc. Ben Dennis, had to rely on Doppler radar because of heavy cloud cover. That darkness split them into four groups, and they landed six miles from their intended drop zone, completely off their map.

Still, they reconned the area for five days and were extracted without incident. SOG concluded that HALO had been "proven as a means of entering [Laos] undetected since an active enemy search was not made to locate the team." Of course, there was no public disclosure that the world's first combat HALO jump had been performed.

SUBSEQUENT
CCN HALO JUMPS

In early 1971 a second HALO team was selected, led by Capt. Larry Manes, a respected two-tour SOG

Sammy Hernandez, a member of SOG's first HALO team, steps from the harness after landing at Camp Long Thanh. (Photo provided by Sammy Hernandez)

recon veteran, along with Sp6c. Noel Gast, S. Sgt. Robert Castillo, and Sgt. John "Spider" Trantanella. To simplify training theirs was an all-U.S. team.

In the predawn of 7 May 1971, Manes' team jumped midway between the Ashau Valley and Khe Sanh, where NVA forces were extending Laotian Highway 921 into South Vietnam. A toe popper mine in Gast's rucksack armed itself from the sudden change in atmospheric pressure, and when he landed it exploded, seriously injuring his back. Trantanella had a bad landing too, and both had to be extracted. But Manes and Castillo slipped toward the road and reconned for five days and then came out without enemy contact. SOG concluded they were "apparently undetected."

SOG's third HALO team was led by a genuine recon legend, Sgt. Maj. Billy Waugh, who recruited S. Sgt. James "J.D." Bath and Sgts. Jesse Campbell and Madison Strohlein. After training on Okinawa, Waugh's men practiced one month at Long Thanh, including 10 jumps from Hueys and C-130s, four of them night HALO jumps.

On 22 June 1971, they leaped from a SOG Blackbird at 19,000 feet, some 60 miles southwest of Danang, into a heavily occupied enemy rear area on the Laotian frontier. Heavy rain and darkness caused them to drift away and land separately. Although Waugh and Campbell were intact, Bath hit the ground hard, injuring his back and knees, while, even worse, Strohlein broke his right arm and could not get out of the tree where he'd landed.

Bad weather delayed Strohlein's rescue, but Hueys managed to extract Waugh, Bath, and Campbell. When a Bright Light team finally reached Strohlein's tree, the 23-year-old Green Beret was gone, presumably captured. He remains MIA today.

CCC HALO JUMPS

SOG's fourth HALO jump was also its most successful, because the entire team landed without injury, assembled quickly, and conducted an entire recon mission. Led by Capt. James G. Storter, it included Sfc.

Newman Ruff, S. Sgt. Millard Moye, and Sgt. Michael Bentley. All were experienced skydivers except Storter, whose enthusiasm had caused him to exaggerate his qualifications a bit—actually, the only HALO training he ever had was the "refresher" course at Camp Long Thanh, but that proved sufficient for Storter.

SOG targeted them for the Plei Trap Valley, northwest of Pleiku, where the NVA was building new roads from Cambodia. Several thousand NVA troops were within five miles of the team's planned drop zone. On the night of 22 September 1971, Storter's team members jumped from 16,000 feet and landed within 30 yards of each other, exactly in their appointed drop zone. They reconned the Plei Trap for four days, and there was never a hint that NVA forces knew they were there. "It was picture perfect," Storter said.

CCC launched another HALO insertion three weeks later, on 11 October 1971, SOG's fifth and last. This time the drop zone was 25 miles southwest of Pleiku, in the Ia Drang Valley, site of the war's first major U.S. battle. Led by Sfc. Dick Gross, the team included Sfcs. Mark Gentry and Bob McNair, S. Sgt. Howard Sugar, M. Sgt. Charles Behler, and five Montagnards—Not, Biu, Hluih, Hmoi, and Kai. At 10 men, they were SOG's largest HALO team, designated RT Wisconsin.

Jumping from 17,000 feet, they were scattered during descent, and well before dawn NVA patrols were searching for them. Flying as Covey Rider above RT Wisconsin that night, I grew extremely concerned because bad weather precluded bringing in fighters or gunships. Just after daylight, Mark Gentry fought a one-man firefight against an enemy squad and then ran and hid in a bomb crater. A

SOG HALO skydiver steers into
the drop zone at Camp Long
Thanh. The parachute is a civilian
Paracommander, which was used
for Stateside competitions. (Photo
provided by Howard Sugar)

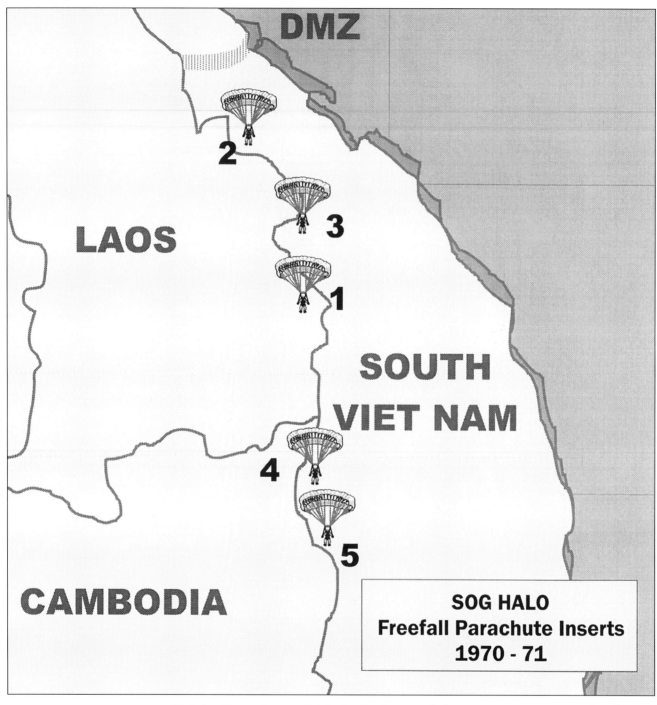

DMZ

LAOS

2

3

1

SOUTH

VIET NAM

4

5

CAMBODIA

SOG HALO
Freefall Parachute Inserts
1970 - 71

Parachutist's feet indicate the approximate site of each team's drop zone.

U.S. Air Force Covey FAC, Lt. Paul Curs, simulated an air strike, firing rockets and making low-level passes above RT Wisconsin to keep the NVA at bay. Two hours later the overcast broke, and we were able to extract them all.

SOG's top-secret HALO jumps and the courageous men who execut-ed them went unrecognized and unknown for more than 20 years. It was only in the early 1990s that these operations became entirely declassi-fied, allowing these quiet, graying veterans to attach, at last, a gold "combat" star to their HALO jump wings and receive congratulations from the entire airborne community.

Top: The world's first combat HALO team on a Blackbird tailgate, awaiting the jumpmaster's "Go!" (Photo provided by Sammy Hernandez)

Bottom: HALO student Howard Sugar practices the "frog" position before his first freefall at Camp Long Thanh. (Photo provided by Howard Sugar)

Above: High over Camp Long Thanh. SOG HALO parachutists link up beneath a Huey helicopter. (Photo provided by Jim Storter)

Right: Visiting HALO instructor Ralph Williams leaps from a SOG Blackbird to follow students during a freefall. (Photo provided by Ralph Williams)

Above: The world's first combat HALO team receives Bronze Stars—but no publicity. Left to right: Sfc. Melvin Hill, Sfc. Sammy Hernandez, and team leader S. Sgt. Cliff Newman. (Photo provided by Cliff Newman)

Left: RT Washington Montagnard Hluih is elated after one of his first HALO jumps. (Photo provided by Howard Sugar)

Above: SOG's third HALO team on the night of their jump (left to right): J.D. Bath, Billy Waugh, and Jesse Campbell. (Not shown is Madison Strohlein.) (Photo provided by Billy Waugh)

Right: Howard Sugar hours after parachuting into Ia Drang Valley in SOG's fifth HALO insertion. Note his XM-203 grenade launcher, one of the first tested by the U.S. Army. (Photo provided by Howard Sugar)

Left: Sgt. Madison Strohlein 'chuted up and ready to board a Blackbird the night of his fateful jump. (Photo provided by Cliff Newman)

Below: Sgt. Madison Strohlein was the only SOG HALO parachutist to fall into enemy hands. (Photo provided by Mike Sheppard)

THE MISSING JUMPER

THE GREATEST NIGHTMARE FOR ANY SOG HALO parachutist was that he'd land separately from his teammates, injure himself crashing violently through the trees, and then hang there helplessly, waiting for the NVA to pluck him down like a ripe apple, never to be seen again. This was indeed the tragic fate of one young HALO jumper, Sgt. Madison Strohlein.

Twenty-three-year-old Strohlein, assistant team leader for Billy Waugh's HALO jump, broke his right arm and could not descend from the tree where he hung. Despite several helicopters crisscrossing the treetops with a Bright Light team the next morning, Strohlein was unable to vector them overhead. As bad weather closed in, the desperate young Green Beret threw a smoke grenade, but the aircrews still couldn't find him.

But the NVA saw his smoke, and Strohlein reported enemy soldiers approaching. Those were the last words ever recorded from him.

Eventually the weather cleared, and a Hatchet Force platoon found Strohlein's tree. His parachute was gone, and lying on the jungle floor was AK and CAR-15 brass, along with his map and CAR-15 at the bottom of the tree. One AK slug had ricocheted off his CAR-15 stock.

Waugh and Bath are absolutely convinced that the NVA captured Strohlein, but Hanoi continues to deny knowing anything about him. The Green Beret's MIA status remains—diplomatically worded—a "discrepancy case."

Above: Six Montagnard and Vietnamese HALO graduates at Camp Long Thanh with Melvin Hill (left) and Billy Waugh. (Photo provided by Ben Dennis)

Right: COMPLETE SUCCESS. Just back from SOG's only HALO mission where the members landed together without injuries and accomplished a full-length mission. Left to right: Willard Moye, Capt. Jim Storter (team leader), Newman Ruff, and Michael Bentley. (Photo provided by Jim Storter)

Inset: After their world-first combat HALO jump, Cliff Newman (left) and Melvin Hill became SOG HALO instructors at Camp Long Thanh. (Photo provided by Cliff Newman)

Left: Sgt. Mark Gentry checks equipment for teammate M. Sgt. Charles Behler before HALO practice jump. By the early 1990s, Gentry was the sergeant major of the world's greatest counterterrorist unit, Delta Force. (Photo provided by Howard Sugar)

STATIC-LINE JUMPS

EVEN WHILE SOG'S WORLD-RECORD HALO combat jumps were under way, other Green Beret RTs were parachuting using the more conventional static-line technique, and for the same reasons: to bypass elaborate enemy defenses and to complicate NVA counterrecon measures.

Since all of SOG's Green Berets already were static-line qualified—as were many of their indigenous soldiers—their specialized training focused on night parachuting in rough terrain. Many, but not all, of these SOG jumpers wore heavy canvas smokejumper suits.

Although records are incomplete, it appears that CCS RT Augur executed SOG's first static-line jump, on 23 December 1969, into the heavily occupied Cambodian Fishhook area. One-Zero Frank Oppel, One-One Bob Graham, and four Nungs leaped from a Green Hornet Huey, landed, and linked up quickly, but one Nung had a broken ankle, requiring that the team be extracted.

Next, on 21 February 1970, CCS S. Sgt. David "Babysan" Davidson, Sgt. James "Ernie" Acre, and two Nungs parachuted from a 155th Assault Helicopter Company Huey into east-central Cambodia. CCS commander Lt. Col. Fred Lindsey called their mission "highly successful," although it was "fraught with danger and high risk."

For subsequent paradrops, SOG's night-capable C-130 Blackbirds became the jump platform. A CCC team, RT Montana—S. Sgt. Mike Sheppard, Sgt. Paul Boyd, and two Montagnards, with Sfc. Lloyd O'Daniels as jumpmaster— leaped from only 500 feet over southern Laos, landing on an enormous grassy plain nicknamed the "Golf Course." They were scattered by high winds. Just

RT Montana One-Zero Mike Sheppard (rear center) and Paul Boyd (not shown) made a night static-line jump into Laos with their Montagnards. Teammates Michael Bentley (right) and Charles Behler later made HALO jumps with other teams. (Photo provided by Billy Greenwood)

Above: SOG recon man makes a practice static-line jump. (Photo provided by Bryon Loucks)

Above left: S. Sgt. David "Babysan" Davidson (right) ready for a practice jump from a 155th Assault Helicopter Company Huey, 1970. (Photo provided by the Davidson family)

after dawn, a flight of helicopters managed to snatch up the last man just before an NVA patrol reached the tree from which he hung.

Another Kontum-based CCC team, RT Arizona, made SOG's next airborne insertion. Led by Sfc. Newman Ruff, it included his One-One, S. Sgt. Mike Wilson, two Montagnards, and 1st Lt. Jack Barton. At 3:30 A.M., 22 December 1970, a SOG Blackbird dropped RT Arizona exactly at the desired drop zone, a ridgeline a mile east of Highway 92, three miles northeast of the notorious "Bra." The three Americans broke through the trees and landed on the jungle floor, while all the 'Yards got hung up in the trees. Trying to free himself, one 'Yard fell 60 feet, breaking his neck and dying instantly. Then a dead tree fell on First Lieutenant Barton and dislocated his kneecaps. Hueys extracted the entire team seven hours later.

On 29 May 1971, RT Kansas of CCN conducted a low-level night parachute insertion northwest of the abandoned U.S. Marine Corps base at Khe Sanh near the DMZ. Led by 1st Lt. Loren Hagen with S. Sgts. Tony Anderson and George Cottrell and three 'Yards, the team was badly scattered, with most landing in trees. Anderson was hit so hard that he was knocked unconscious. "When I came to I heard dogs barking," he said, a sure sign that NVA troops were looking for them. On his own for two days, Anderson came upon fresh trails but managed to avoid contact with the enemy. Meanwhile Hagen and Cottrell had linked up and then shot their way through an enemy squad, killing three. After Covey detected three NVA formations approaching the area, RT Kansas was extracted from three separate LZs.

SOG's apparent final static-line insert came on 18 August 1971, led by CCC's Sfc. Howard Upchurch, a former U.S. Marine and Korean War veteran with a prior Vietnam combat tour in the 173rd Airborne Brigade. A tough, deep-voiced Texan, Upchurch's team jumped into a valley northwest of Pleiku, on the Cambodian frontier. His insertion and his recon mission succeeded perfectly.

Right: The drop zone in Laos used by RT Montana, known as the "Golf Course." (Photo provided by Gerald Denison)

CHIEF SOG JOHN "SKIP" SADLER

OVERSEEING THE WORLD'S FIRST HALO combat jumps was the fifth Chief SOG, Colonel John "Skip" Sadler. Sadler was one of the U.S. Army's foremost parachuting experts and had experimented with skydiving during the Korean War as a means to deliver indigenous agents behind Chinese lines.

The cigar-chewing, three-war veteran had begun his career in World War II as a combat paratrooper fighting in New Guinea and the Philippines with the same 11th Airborne Division regiment as the old friend he replaced at SOG, Col. Steve Cavanaugh. After World War II, Sadler was a paratroop instructor at Ft. Benning and served on the Airborne Department Tactics and Techniques Board. He served his first stint in the secret wars as a parachuting specialist in the CIA-affiliated JACK, where his boss was another future Chief SOG, Maj. Jack Singlaub.

After the Korean War, Sadler served with Special Forces at Ft. Bragg and then served another secret war tour with the CIA's Project White Star in Laos. He was the 8th Division chief of staff in Germany in 1970 when Colonel Cavanaugh phoned and asked if he'd care to be the new Chief SOG. Within 24 hours Colonel Sadler was on his way to Saigon.

Right: Col. John "Skip" Sadler, Chief SOG, 1970–1972. (Photo provided by U.S. Army)

HALO TEAM WEAPONS

SPACE CONSTRAINTS AND THE NEED TO REDUCE a skydiver's aerodynamic cross-section to reduce drag and improve control during freefall drove HALO teams to modify their weapons or adopt different ones. As well, though, the reality that a team might be split up and its members have to fight by themselves inspired some HALO men to become walking arsenals, with some carrying up to five firearms apiece.

Early freefall teams carried CAR-15s, while later ones came to prefer the Uzi submachine gun, primarily because it folded compactly to half a CAR-15's length. Further, unlike SOG's other submachine guns, the Uzi was issued with a quick-detach suppressor for much better tactical flexibility. Most HALO jumpers carried at least one suppressed weapon, even if it was only a pistol. The suppressed Walther PPK filled the bill perfectly for Sfc. Newman Ruff, because its .380 auto ammunition was subsonic, precluding any audible "crack."

Several HALO jumpers carried sawed-off, pump-action shotguns as back-up weapons, with a strong preference being exhibited for the Winchester Model 97 because of its external hammer. Sammy Hernandez jumped with a Model 97, although he also carried a CAR-15. Other men modified their CAR-15s to accommodate 40mm grenade launchers, such as the XM-148 on Madison Strohlein's CAR and the XM-203 on Howard Sugar's weapon, the latter launcher one of the earliest of that model ever to see combat.

Compact minigrenades were extremely popular, with up to 20 packed per man. Billy Waugh's HALO team fashioned "soap dish claymores" containing steel pellets embedded in plastic explosive, fabricated from PX-purchased plastic soapdishes. Each of Waugh's men carried four to six of these "mini-claymores."

Above: The suppressed Walther PPK .380 automatic was compact and didn't require special subsonic ammunition. (Photo provided by Ciener, Inc.)

Left: SOG's Uzis were issued with a quick-detach suppressor. (Photo provided by National Infantry Museum)

Chapter Fourteen

The Recon Ethic

SOG recon evolved into a pure meritocracy. No matter his rank or age, the most experienced man on a team served as the One-Zero team leader, period. It was not uncommon to find senior NCOs or officers led by junior sergeants, and even more common was younger men leading older ones because only experience mattered behind enemy lines. A man with 10 missions didn't know 10 times as much as a man with one mission—he knew a hundred times as much!

Paradoxically, by the time some men learned enough to operate effectively behind NVA lines, they were dead. But somewhat like the World War II British bomb disposal experts, if you could stay alive long enough to learn, you might just make it through. After that, luck weighed in, too, with each mission after about 10 teasing fate ever the more. Even a phenomenal gunfighter who can outshoot multiple opponents nine out of 10 times still dies once in every 10 gunfights.

Also militating for a recon man's demise was SOG's institutional tendency to assign the most dangerous missions to the most successful One-Zeros, upping the ante on each subsequent operation until the worsening odds might finally overwhelm even the finest leader.

A FREE ASSOCIATION

Since its members were all volunteers, each RT was a free association of

A SOG RT slips through elephant grass on the Laotian border deep behind NVA lines. (Photo provided by Ken Bowra)

men ready to face dangers together under their One-Zero. A man who could not carry his weight, who could not be relied upon to function in a firefight—or simply made too much noise in the jungle—was off the team. But it was more than just combat skills. "It's kind of hard to put into words, but it's like having somebody that you love," explained Medal of Honor recipient Bob Howard. "If you served [in SOG] and you were willing to die, you wanted to have a person there you would not mind dying for or dying with."

The One-Zero was a special case. In addition to being the team's most knowledgeable man, he had to be a true leader, ready and willing to do anything his men did. When a Montagnard point man was too fearful to go forward, the One-Zero walked point himself. By SOG ethic, the One-Zero was the first man off a helicopter during insertion and the last man coming out. The One-Zero could not long retain his One-One and One-Two if he displayed cow-

ardice or put his own welfare ahead of the mission or his teammates.

Only such mutual, absolute loyalty could hold a team together when it was completely on its own, deep behind enemy lines, with no support, no artillery, no one at the other end when it called on the radio. With the NVA all around, by the thousands, in any direction, it was only the bonds of comradeship, complete faith in each other, and trust in the One-Zero's judgment that would see the team members through. The One-Zero needed guts, fortitude, and the ability to think on his feet—plus a contradictory blend of aggressiveness and caution.

JUDGMENT AND INTEGRITY

In addition to relying upon a One-Zero's judgment, senior SOG officers had to rely upon his integrity. When he brought back important intelligence, often the only proof he possessed was his reputation—it was a PT-76 tank, *because the One-Zero said so.* There was no room for exaggeration, much less outright invention—if SOG commanders found reason to lose faith in a One-Zero, he was relieved.

When the One-Zero decided it was too dangerous to remain in his area, he requested that his team be extracted. On occasion, staff officers sitting safely behind desks in South Vietnam overruled the team leader's call—which sometimes led to disastrous results—but usually they went along with the team leader's judgment. If it was found later that he'd flinched or lost his resolve, that could be dealt with after the team was extracted.

Perhaps the greatest reward for being a One-Zero was simply being left alone to do the job. Unlike the rest of the military, once assigned a mission the One-Zero had the leeway to execute it as he saw fit—*he* decided upon the number of men he'd bring; *he* selected their weapons and equipment; *he* chose their means and time of insertion.

And when a recon man decided he'd had enough, that the fear was beginning to overwhelm him, no one said a word. He was simply reassigned to a support or staff position, and this worked well too. Since many of the NCOs in the supply room, intel shop, and operations staff were former recon men, they always did their utmost to assist those running recon and would readily run interference when some outsider's ignorance caused problems. Recon 1st Sgt. Billy Greenwood once warned a pushy operations officer, "Sir, either give these men the support they've requested or pack your rucksack, because starting tomorrow you'll have to go run these missions *yourself*." We could have kissed Billy.

This kind of camaraderie extended throughout recon and the Hatchet Forces. When word came that a team was surrounded and fighting for its life on an LZ, other recon men resting between missions grabbed their CAR-15s and headed for the helipad to go get their threatened friends. And whenever a team came out, that helipad would fill with all of Recon Company, there to greet the returning team with a handshake and a cold beer.

MEMORIALIZING LOST COMRADES

Perhaps because SOG's killed and missing warriors went unknown and their top-secret deeds could not be disclosed, their surviving comrades found personal ways to honor and remember them. Once in a while there were memorial services, sometimes even with a visiting chaplain—but that kind of formality was rare. More often all the recon men assembled at the NCO club to swap stories, share jokes, and offer toasts to the departed comrade, until someone proposed, "Let's sing 'Hey, Blue.'" Then all would stand, drinks in hand, singing that sad song in unison. To an outsider those lyrics would probably sound corny—it was a song about a dog, a boy's best friend, and calling his name after he's dead. But the club would resonate, and tears would roll down grown men's cheeks, especially when they reached that final verse when the just departed friend's name was added to that long roster of departed recon men.

Lost men were memorialized, too, by naming buildings after them. Early in the war, there were lots of unnamed buildings and only a few dead Green Berets, but by 1970 SOG's losses had so grown that just about every building had been named. There was usually an attempt to tie in the building with the lost man—for example, Peter "Fat Albert"

Below inset: One-Zero Peter "Fat Albert" Wilson (right) tends bar for recon men Dan Ster (left) and Richard Noe. (Photo provided by Frank Greco)

Right: After Wilson was MIA in October 1970, the recon bar was renamed for him, a common way to memorialize lost comrades. (Photo provided by Will Curry)

"HEY, BLUE"

I had a dog, and his name was Blue
Bet you five dollars,
He's a good dog, too.
Hey, Blue,
You're a good dog, you.

Old Blue runnin' through the
  yeller corn
Blue come a runnin'
When I blew my horn.
Hey, Blue,
You're a good dog, you.

Old Blue died, and he died so hard
Shook the ground in my backyard.
Hey, Blue,
You're a good dog, you.

Dug his grave with a silver spade
Lowered him down with a golden
  chain.
Hey, Blue,
You're a good dog, you.

Link by link, I lowered the chain,
And with each link, I called his name.
Hey, Blue,
You're a good dog, you.

Sain and Laws and Fawcett, too.
And Reno, Thorne, and
  MacNamara, too.
Hey friends,
You were good guys, you.

The words to "Hey, Blue" were sung during wakes for lost recon men.

Chaplain at CCS holding memorial ceremony for S. Sgt. Everette Cofer, recon man KIA on covert mission in Cambodia 3 April 1970. (Photo provided by Mike Ash)

Right: The bond between Green Berets and Montagnards bordered on brotherhood. RT Washington, shown here with One-Zero Robert McNeir (second from left, center row) and One-One Howard Sugar (next to McNeir) exemplified this casual attachment yet readiness to die for each other. (Photo provided by Howard Sugar)

Below: A 1st SFG "Snakebite" team, 1967. Of these 12 NCOs, five received Purple Hearts, three died, and one received a Distinguished Service Cross. Back row, left to right: Gil Hamilton, Jim Scurry, Brooke Bell, Loyd Fisher, Capt. Bill Davis, unknown, and Bruce Luttrell. Front, left to right: "Bear" Osborne, unknown, unknown, Ronald Bock, and Earl Kalani. Hamilton and Luttrell were KIA; Kalani died of his wounds. (Photo provided by Jason T. Woodworth)

Wilson often served drinks in the Recon Bar. After he became MIA the bar was renamed Fat Albert's.

SOG'S INDIGENOUS PERSONNEL

Just like the Americans, SOG's indigenous soldiers were also volunteers, and the bonds between them and the Green Berets grew strong. In the early days, most indigenous soldiers were Chinese Nungs, whose ancestors had roamed southern China. Ethnically distinct from Vietnamese, the Nungs took great pride in their combat abilities, somewhat like the Ghurkas in India, but by 1968 so many had been lost in secret operations that they were outnumbered by Montagnards and Vietnamese.

Montagnard hill tribesmen were recruited from many tribes—the Bru, Sedeng, Rhade, and Jerai—who resided in distinct geographical areas just like the North American Sioux, Cherokee, Apache, and Iroquois tribes. Due to slight differences in culture and language, the 'Yards preferred tribal integrity, with all members of their RT from the same tribe. Despite overwhelming poverty Montagnard villages were happy places, which many Green Berets visited to share *nam pei* rice wine and receive a brass bracelet, making them honorary tribal members. Mostly illiterate, the 'Yards displayed a simple approach to life in which "yes" actually meant "yes." Their loyalty was boundless, to other Montagnards and Americans alike.

Vietnamese team members tended to be the best educated and the quickest to learn, but there was always a lingering question of loyalty, especially when they were former NVA soldiers. Still, they bore the same risks as their American teammates and, if captured, would have been treated as traitors by the North Vietnamese.

South Vietnamese Special Forces-led RTs came to the fore late in the war during the "Vietnamization" of 1970–1971. Suddenly rushed through training to meet a policy date, whether ready or not they were thrown into the unforgiving caldron of cross-border operations. Many ARVN teams were made up of fine, brave men who fought as courageously as any SOG American, but others vanished on their first mission or returned with self-inflicted gunshot wounds. Like the best U.S. One-Zeros, the best ARVN team leaders found themselves assigned ever more dangerous missions until, all too often, they were lost.

Beaming with pride, RT California Montagnards pose with a heavy antiaircraft machine gun they captured under the leadership of One-Zero Joe Walker. (Photo provided by Bob Garcia)

LOST RECON TEAMS

SOG RECON'S LOSSES WERE THE GREATEST of any U.S. unit in the Vietnam War, with a very high proportion of its men missing in action. While 163 SOG Green Berets were KIA, an additional 80 were MIA, a ratio several magnitudes higher than other U.S. ground combat units. Equally telling is that *not one* of SOG's cross-border MIA Green Berets ever turned up as an enemy POW.

Of SOG's 80 missing Green Berets, 25 men belonged to 10 RTs that disappeared entirely deep in enemy territory. (The names of indigenous soldiers are not included.)

Date	Recon Team	Location	MIA Special Forces Personnel
3 Oct. 1966	Arizona	DMZ	M. Sgt. Ray Echevara, Sfc. Eddie Williams, S. Sgt. James Jones
28 Mar. 1968	Asp	Laos	M. Sgt. George Brown, S. Sgt. Alan Boyer, Sgt. Charles Huston
23 May 1968	Idaho	Laos	Sfc. Glen Lane, S. Sgt. Robert Owen
2 Mar. 1969	Saw	Cambodia	Sgt. William Evans, Sp5c. Michael May
31 July 1969	Kentucky	Laos	1st Lt. Dennis Neal, Sp5c. Michael Burns
3 Nov. 1969	Maryland	Laos	S. Sgt. Gunther Wald, Sgt. William Brown, S. Sgt. Donald Shue
13 Nov. 1969	Rattler	Laos	S. Sgt. Ronald Ray, Sp4c. Randolph Suber
24 Mar. 1970	Pennsylvania	Cambodia	1st Lt. Jerry Pool, S. Sgt. John Boronski, S. Sgt. Gary Harned
5 Oct. 1970	Missouri	Laos	S. Sgt. David Davidson, Sgt. Fred Gassman
10 May 1971	Asp	RVN	S. Sgt. Klaus Bingham, Sfc. James Luttrell, S. Sgt. Lewis Walton

Right: Team patch for RT Asp, whose men vanished twice behind enemy lines. (Photo provided by Rich Claar)

Far right: S. Sgt. Dale Dehnke, RT Alaska, KIA on 17 May 1971, along with teammates Sp4c. Gary Hollingsworth, KIA, and their One-One, 1st Lt. Danny Entrican, MIA. Intelligence suggested that Entrican was captured. (Photo provided by U.S. Army)

IN ADDITION TO THESE VANISHED TEAMS, casualty rosters and unofficial reports suggest at least an additional 14 U.S.-led RTs that were overrun and destroyed or their helicopters lost, although Bright Light teams usually managed to recover some or all of their bodies. These include the following.

Date	Special Forces Personnel on Destroyed Teams
29 July 1966	Sfc. Delmer Laws (MIA), Sp4c. Don Sain (KIA), Sgt. Maj. Harry Whalen (Survived)
22 Sept. 1966	S. Sgt. Michael Newbern, Sgt. Boyd Anderson (Both KIA)
1 Nov. 1967	Sgt. Don Hawkins, Sfc. David Woods (both KIA), Sfc. Ed Davis (Survived)
8 Nov. 1967	M. Sgt. Bruce Baxter, Sgt. Joseph Kusick (Both KIA)*
29 Jan. 1968	Sfc. Charles Tredinnick, S. Sgt. Gary Crone (Both KIA)
22 Mar. 1968	Sfc. Linwood Martin, Sfc. Esetevan Torres, Sp4c. John Wells (All KIA)
2 May 1968	Sfc. Leroy Wright, (KIA), S. Sgt. L. Mousseau (KIA), Sp4c. Brian O'Connor (WIA)
1 Jan. 1969	S. Sgt. James Hall, Sp4c. Wayne Hawes, S. Sgt. Michael McKibban (All KIA)
8 Jan. 1969	Sfc. Gerald Apperson, Sp4c. Bill Williams (Both KIA)
29 Jan. 1969	Sp5c. Larry Stephens, Sgt. Billy Simmons, S. Sgt. Charles Bullard (All KIA)**
18 Mar. 1969	Sfc. M. Fernandez (KIA), Sp5c. B. Murphy (KIA), Capt. R. Harrison (Survived)
23 May 1969	Sgt. Howard Hill, Sp4c. Phillip Strout, S. Sgt. Rudolph Machata (All KIA)
5 Jan. 1970	Sfc. Larry Bartlett, Sgt. Richard Thomas (Both KIA)
17 May 1971	1st Lt. Danny Entrican (MIA), S. Sgt. Dale Denhke, Sp4c. Gary Hollingsworth (KIA)

*Their RT Massachusetts teammate, S. Sgt. Homer Wilson, survived because his helicopter made it out of the LZ.

** This was RT New Mexico, the author's first RT. Sergeant Plaster was left behind at the Dak To launch site because the team's insertion Huey was overloaded and he was junior man. That night his teammates were overrun, and all were killed.

Capt. Dennis Neal in Kingbee doorway. He and Sp4c. Mike Burns and the rest of their team disappeared near Highway 921 in Laos. They're still MIA. (Photo provided by Eldon Bargewell)

Above: S. Sgt. John Yancey fought off the NVA single-handedly to defend wounded RT California teammate David Hayes. Tragically, although Yancey succeeded, Hayes succumbed to wounds. (Photo provided by Gerry Denison)

Left inset: Sfc. David "Baby Huey" Hayes, RT California, KIA 13 July 1970. (Photo provided by John Plaster)

273

Right: RT Washington the day before the team was almost wiped out. One-Zero Stephen Wallace (left) was badly shot. One-Two Curt Green (center rear) was killed and his body lost. Somehow One-One Jeff Mauceri (right rear) held the team together. (Photo provided by Larry Predmore)

Below: When teammate Alan Cecil was killed, Capt. Stephen Rutledge (center) suffered three serious AK wounds yet outran the NVA for an entire day before he was rescued. The initials "KKK" on his hat are the initials of a Cambodian sect, which the black officer found humorous. (Photo provided by Bobby Evans)

NO GREATER LOVE: JOHN KEDENBURG

THE RECON ETHIC OF PLACING TEAMMATES above self was never expressed more completely than by 23-year-old One-Zero John Kedenburg on 13 June 1968. Specialist Fifth Class Kedenburg's RT Nevada was evading after a firefight near Highway 110, with a 500-man NVA battalion hot on the team's heels. No stranger to tough situations, the Long Island native had carried out the body of his first team leader, Sfc. Dan Wagner, six months earlier. At one point the NVA battalion had encircled RT Nevada, but Kedenburg's men managed to shoot their way through. Any time Kedenburg's men paused, the enemy caught up and a fierce firefight ensued; finally Kedenburg sent his men ahead and conducted "a gallant rear guard fight against the pursuing enemy." Rejoining his men, Kedenburg learned one 'Yard was missing; he radioed for a string extraction and got RT Nevada beneath a hole in the canopy. A Huey dropped ropes and lifted away four men. A second Huey dropped ropes, and Kedenburg and his last three men climbed into the four McGuire rigs. Then the NVA troops broke through supporting aerial fire just as Nevada's missing 'Yard arrived, drawn by the sound of the helicopter.

Although it meant certain death, One-Zero John Kedenburg gave up his McGuire rig seat to a teammate and stayed behind alone on the ground. (Photo provided by family of John Kedenburg)

Kedenburg unsnapped himself, gave his rig to the newly arrived 'Yard, and stood guard while he climbed in. The young Green Beret turned alone to face a horde of onrushing enemy soldiers. Witnesses aboard the departing helicopter saw Kedenburg shoot six of the enemy before he collapsed, mortally wounded. The last air strike went in right on top of the fallen One-Zero.

John Kedenburg posthumously received the Medal of Honor.

Top: All of recon company is on the helipad to greet a returning team with cold beer and pats on the back. (Photo provided by Ted Wicorek)

Bottom: Stress etched on their faces, recon men wait on the CCC helipad for an in-bound Huey carrying a dead Green Beret. Left to right: Sgts. Phillip Wood and Jim Nunn, 1st Sgt. Billy Greenwood, and S. Sgt. Mike Sheppard. (Photo provided by Mike Sheppard)

Above: Prophetically, the famous "dead man's hand" was the patch of RT New Mexico, which was wiped out on 29 January 1969. (Photo provided by Rich Claar)

Top left: Gen. Creighton Abrams inspects an ARVN RT in 1971. While some ARVN teams displayed courage and talent, others failed to measure up. (Photo provided by Ted Wicorek)

Bottom: Sgt. Maj. Harry "Crash" Whalen (left) and Capt. Mecky Schuler. Whalen's RT was the first to lose men MIA, haunting the highly respected Green Beret for the rest of his life. (Photo provided by Mecky Schuler)

Top: Sgt. David "Lurch" Mixter, SOG's final MIA in Laos, lost on 29 January 1971. (Photo provided by the Mixter family)

Above: RT Alabama's team patch. (Photo provided by Scott Kilpatrick)

Right: One-Zero John Allen, the sole survivor of RT Alabama. Surrounded in a bomb crater, Allen's men fought off NVA assaults for two days until only he was left alive. Allen then ran through NVA to escape. His lost U.S. teammates were Pfc. Paul King and Sp5c. Ken Cryan. (Photo provided by Dale Boswell)

Top: CCN RT Michigan hurries through a bomb-damaged bamboo grove in Laos, 1968. (Photo provided by Ken Bowra)

Bottom: Surrounded on a Laotian LZ, RT Maine fights for its life while Cobra gunship rockets pound the earth around them. Miraculously, One-Zero John Baker's disciplined men escaped with a few minor wounds despite landing in an NVA base camp. (Photo provided by Mike Buckland)

Top: A badly wounded RT Maine Montagnard (right) awaits string extraction while his teammates prepare to receive a dropped line from a hovering Huey. (Photo provided by Mike Buckland)

Bottom: RT Montana One-Zero Mike Sheppard (left) and Green Beret medic John Padgett (right) with Soviet 85mm artillery shells they captured in an NVA cache. (Photo provided by Mike Sheppard)

Above: "THE SWASHBUCKLER LOOK." CCC recon man Richard Hoffman sports a sweatband, scarf, and earring. Note the extra pocket on his shirt sleeve, a SOG uniform modification that's become almost universal in special ops units. (Photo provided by Richard Hoffman)

Top left: RT Washington on patrol deep behind enemy lines (Photo provided by Howard Sugar)

Bottom: TAKING FIRE! Sfc. Melvin Hill (right) and Sgt. Maj. Billy Waugh just step off a helicopter 22 kilometers northwest of Khe Sanh when NVA soldiers open fire. (Photo provided by Billy Waugh)

Above: ECONOMY OF FORCE.
SOG recon was never a large
organization. In SOG's closing
days, these 38 Green Berets
made up CCN's Recon
Company, yet they tied down
many thousands of NVA defenders. (Photo provided by Ken
Bowra)

Right: NVA woodcutting party
left behind these bamboo bundles, took a lunch break, and
returned moments after this
photo only to be ambushed by
RT New Hampshire. (Photo provided by Will Curry)

Left: Recon men John Plaster (left) and Glen Uemura take cover in a Laotian bamboo grove during an air strike on an NVA antiaircraft gun that's preventing their extraction. (Photo provided by John Plaster)

BRAVEST OF THE BRAVE: BOB HOWARD

AMONG SUCH EXTRAORDINARY SOLDIERS, it is hard to single out one recon man as the very finest, yet SOG possessed a man worthy of superlatives, Sfc. Robert Howard. Unique in U.S. military annals, Robert Howard was submitted for the Medal of Honor three times in 13 months, and many thought he should have received all three.

This selfless soldier is the most highly decorated American of this or any age, his uniform displaying the Medal of Honor, Distinguished Service Cross, Silver Star, and numerous lesser awards, plus eight Purple Hearts, all earned in SOG. This is the man who one night ran alongside an enemy truck, tossed a claymore mine in back among a bunch of startled NVA troopers, and then detonated it. Another time, he saw a VC terrorist on a motorbike toss a grenade at a GI chow line; Howard snatched an M16 from an amazed security guard, dropped to one knee, carefully aimed, shot the driver, and then chased the passenger a half-mile and shot him dead.

His first Medal of Honor submission came in November 1967 for screening a Hatchet Force mission. While the Hatchet Force destroyed an enemy cache, Howard's team came upon four NVA soldiers, all of whom he shot, but then his team was pinned down by machine gun fire. Howard killed an NVA sniper and then rushed the machine gun nest and shot all its occupants at point-blank range. When a second machine gun opened fire, he crawled forward again. "Pinned down directly outside the strongpoint with a blazing machine gun barrel only six inches above his head," his award citation later read, "he threw a hand grenade into the aperture of the emplacement, killing the gunners and temporarily silencing the weapon." When more NVA took over the gun, Howard seized a rocket launcher and "stood amid a hail of bullets, fired his weapon, and completely demolished the position." Howard's one-man attack so demoralized the enemy soldiers that they abandoned the hill. Though recommended for the Medal of Honor, he was awarded the Distinguished Service Cross.

In mid-November 1968, Howard accompanied a Hatchet Force into The Bra, its mission to draw NVA forces away from a besieged CIA-supported force deeper in Laos. After four days of sporadic contact, on 19 November the Hatchet Force members were ambushed by

Sfc. Bob Howard carries a wounded NVA prisoner to the CCC dispensary. (Photo provided by Jim Shorten)

Sfc. Bob Howard with a badly shot-up Huey at Dak To in 1968. A man with a rock-hard physique and incredible courage, Howard was equally unassuming and decent. (Photo provided by Gene McCarley)

a large enemy force, the deadliest fire pouring from a PT-76 tank's turret-mounted 12.7mm machine gun. Howard crept forward to fire two LAW rockets, silencing the gun and destroying the tank. Later, when a medevac Huey was shot down, Howard ignored his own wounds to dash, all alone, 300 yards through enemy fire to scoop up a wounded doorgunner and lead the surviving pilots back to safety. During a subsequent barrage, 14 pieces of shrapnel slashed Howard, so infuriating him that he charged into the enemy soldiers; he surprised three of them, shooting two, and bringing the third back as a POW. By the night of the third day, he had been perforated 50 times and lay weak, bleeding from his arms, legs, back, and face. When a 37mm antiaircraft gun halted the force members' extraction the following morning, Howard again crept between NVA positions to pour a dozen 40mm grenade rounds on the gun, killing its crew and allowing the extraction to finish. For the second time in 12 months he was recommended for the Medal of Honor, but a combination of politics and petty jealousy got it downgraded to a Silver Star. Because he was a humble man and cared more about his comrades than any awards, Bob Howard said nothing.

Then a few weeks later, Pfc. Robert Scherdin was wounded and separated from his RT in Laos; an emergency radio beacon was detected on the hill where he had disappeared.

The next morning Howard accompanied a 40-man Bright Light platoon, led by Lt. Jim Jerson, to search the hill. After bypassing a reinforced NVA company, the platoon began climbing the hill, almost certain it'd be ambushed. It came with a terrible blast, a Chinese mine that badly wounded Jerson and Howard. When Howard awoke he ached all over, and his shredded

Above: Sfc. Bob Howard after recovering from serious wounds suffered on his Medal of Honor mission. (Photo provided by Jon Davidson)

Right: Sfc. Bob Howard receives his second Distinguished Service Cross, a temporary award later replaced by the Medal of Honor. (Photo provided by Rolland Bogguess)

fingers were almost useless, but he managed to drive away a flamethrower-wielding NVA soldier. Too injured to stand, Howard dragged himself to Jerson—he was alive. Howard clumsily carried and dragged him off the hill, pausing to fight and kill enemy soldiers on the way while himself suffering a gunshot wound to the leg. Assembling some 20-odd survivors, Howard prepared to fight to the death, that night even calling a Spectre gunship's fire through his own position. But then, miraculously, a surprise night extraction under parachute flares caught the enemy off guard, and the platoon survivors made it out. Displaying courageous leadership to the end, Howard was the last man to board a chopper.

He awoke briefly in a field hospital to find his hands bandaged and face covered with ointment and to learn that Lt. Jim Jerson had died.

This, Robert Howard's third recommendation for the Medal of Honor, was not downgraded, but when the medal was awarded American patriotism had plunged, and no special accord was given him—not one second of national TV coverage for this, the most decorated man ever to wear our country's uniform. He deserved better.

Left: CCC Bad Luck Photo. Pfc. Robert Scherdin (left) MIA on 29 December 1968; 1st Lt. Jim Jerson went in with Bob Howard and died two days later; S. Sgt. Gerald Apperson was killed one week later. (Photo provided by Craig Davis)

Below Left: The first Special Forces soldier to twice receive the Distinguished Service Cross, Bob Howard was featured on the October 1969 cover of *The Green Beret* magazine. (Photo provided by Donald J. O'Hara)

Below: Directly commissioned in 1970, Bob Howard retired as a full colonel in 1995. Few Americans realize that he's the most decorated serviceman in U.S. history. (Photo provided by U.S. Army)

THE GREEN BERET

OCTOBER 1969

LUCKY TO BE ALIVE. Sgt. Lynn Black (left) was beneath a Jolly Green awaiting extraction by winch when two NVA soldiers got the drop on him. Instead of surrendering, he pulled away one man's AK, killed the second, and escaped. Shown with him in this photo is Sgt. John Meyer. (Photo provided by Eldon Bargewell)

Top: CCN RT Georgia in the field with Sgt. William Gabbard (left) and S. Sgt. Cletis Sinyard. (Photo provided by Eldon Bargewell)

Bottom: Sgt. Randy Rhea (sitting) was killed 12 November 1969. His RT Arkansas teammates include Sfc. Fred Smith (left rear) and Sgt. Geoffrey May (kneeling). (Photo provided by Brendon Lyons)

Above: To help make up for heavy recon causalities, hand-picked 1st SFG volunteers came to Vietnam from Okinawa on 6-month temporary tours. They were code-named "Snakebite" teams. (Photo provided by Steve Cavanaugh)

Right: RT Washington trooper, Hiot, displays Montagnard cheerfulness—and a handiness with deadly weapons. (Photo provided by Bryon Loucks)

Left: Blending into shadows and foliage of the Laotian jungle, Sgt. Frank Greco on a recon mission near Highway 110. (Photo provided by Frank Greco)

SPECIAL FORCES' LONGEST RUNNING GAG

DEALING DAILY WITH DEATH, HUMOR WAS A SOG MAN'S salve of sanity. The hilariously obnoxious Walter Shumate's irrepressible sense of humor became an unending mental diversion to his sometimes grim comrades—so much so that, fittingly, Walter became the object of the longest running gag in Special Forces.

The snowball began rolling when a Green Beret gave candy to a Vietnamese girl and told her, "Here you are, my dear. My name is Walter Shumate." Word slowly spread throughout Special Forces to attribute everything and anything to Shumate—from writing a letter to a newspaper to beating the crap out of some GI. Shumate's dares, threats, boasts, and fame (infamy?) spread across the world. His name appeared on seedy hotels' registries, exceeding even those standbys "A. Lincoln" and "G. Washington," with no two signatures even faintly similar. And when word of some new misadventure would filter back, Walter would declare, for instance, "I have never been to Hong Kong in my life." But the truth was that he basked in the notoriety.

Despite Walter's passing away in 1994, the gag continues. In 1998, a Philadelphia newspaper Web site received a pointed note about its series on Delta Force in Mogadishu signed "Walter Shumate." It was datelined, of course, "Valhalla."

Above: The effervescent Walter Shumate clowns for the camera with an opium pipe. (Photo provided by Gene McCarley)

Right: What kind of man reads *Playboy*? Walt Shumate atop elephant poses as if he's to appear in the magazine's monthly promotional page. (Photo provided by Ben Baker)

Above: One of the most accomplished One-Zeros, Joe Walker narrowly survived after NVA troops overran his platoon in Laos. Badly wounded, he was brought out by Medal of Honor winner Bob Howard. (Photo provided by Billy Greenwood)

Top left: RT Maine boarding helicopters at Dak To. Pictured here are One-Zero John Baker (center) and One-One Mike Buckland (right). (Photo provided by Mike Buckland)

Bottom: RT Arizona team patch emphasized surveillance and recon via its eyeball, but its dragon was ever ready to pounce. (Photo provided by Scott Kilpatrick)

ABOVE AND BEYOND: FRED ZABITOSKY

RT MAINE ONE-ZERO FRED ZABITOSKY, 26, did not relish going into "The Bra" for his final recon mission. Named for the double river curve where Highway 110 split from the Trail's major north-south road, The Bra contained Binh Tram 37, whose hidden stockpiles and truck parks were defended by masses of antiaircraft guns, security battalions, and counterrecon units. Zabitosky recently had led two perilous Bright Lights, recovering a One-Zero's body after the NVA burned him to death and then searching for Charlie White, who'd fallen off a McGuire rig.

On 19 February 1968, Zabitosky, along with S. Sgts. Doug Glover, One-One, and Percell Bragg, One-Two, landed safely in The Bra and barely had entered a narrow canyon when an NVA platoon opened fire. Zab told Glover to lead the team back to the LZ while he bought time for fighters to get there. SOG intelligence later determined the canyon had contained a regimental command post, possibly the headquarters of Binh Tram 37, itself.

Zab repulsed the NVA platoon by blowing a claymore, tossing several grenades, and firing his CAR-15, tactics he repeated for 30 minutes until he heard A-1s overhead. In one fast dash, he ran all the way to the LZ, where he found RT Maine, but before a Huey could come in, hundreds of NVA troops attacked. No sooner had Zab's men halted one charge than another NVA company arrived and it, too, attacked through napalm and cannon fire. Then Covey had RT Maine run along a streambed and through a woodline to another LZ.

When Covey sent in a Huey, Purcell Bragg and two 'Yards made it out safely. Then 100 NVA soldiers assaulted from three sides, and Zab's men were down to two magazines apiece. Under the heavy fire of gunships and A-1s another Huey came in just as the NVA soldiers rose up again. The doorgunners and SOG men mowed down a long line of NVA, and then everyone fired as the Huey lifted off—they were 75 feet up and almost clear of the LZ when an RPG struck the helicopter, splitting it in two and dropping it. It crashed on its side, burning furiously.

Thrown free, Zabitosky forced himself awake to extinguish his burning clothes. In addition to severe burns and shrapnel wounds, he'd suffered several crushed vertebrae and broken ribs. Inside the nearby burning wreckage he could see the pilots still lashed in their seats, trapped in the flames, while in back the white-hot burning Huey already had consumed Doug Glover, four 'Yards, and the two doorgunners, Sgts. Melvin Dye and Robert Griffith.

Zabitosky stumbled to his feet and tore open the pilot's door, grabbed the semiconscious 1st Lt. Richard Griffith, and dragged him to safety. Everything was burned off Griffith except his leather gunbelt. Zab climbed back into the flames and undid WO John Cook's harness. The

Sfc. Fred Zabitosky just back at Dak To after a recon mission in Laos. (Photo provided by Gene McCarley)

Top: RT Maine One-One Doug Glover (at wheel) died in Zabitosky's burning Huey. Also shown in this photo are Lt. Jerald Henderson (center) and RT Ohio One-Zero Gerry Denison. (Photo provided by Gene McCarley)

Bottom: Sfc. Fred Zabitosky receives the Medal of Honor from President Richard Nixon, 20 February 1969. (Photo provided by Department of Defense)

Top: Huey pilot Richard Griffith, though badly burned, survived. His co-pilot, also rescued by Zabitosky, later died of his wounds. (Photo provided by Richard Griffith)

Bottom: The RT Maine patch. (Photo provided by Scott Kilpatrick)

fuel cells then exploded, blowing the two men clear.

Despite heavy groundfire, another Huey made it in, so Green Beret medic Luke Nance could help Zabitosky drag the two men into the aircraft. Evacuated to Japan, John Cook thanked Zabitosky before succumbing to the burns that covered 85 percent of his body. The other pilot, Richard Griffith, eventually recovered and spent a career with the Michigan State Police.

One year after that day in The Bra, RT Maine One-Zero Zabitosky was presented the Medal of Honor by President Richard Nixon. "I was presented and I wear the medal," he would say, "but it was earned by Doug Glover and my other Special Forces team members."

Fred Zabitosky died in early 1997 while surgeons were attempting to remove a tumor from his brain, a humble, devoted man to the very end.

THE INDEFATIGABLE BILLY WAUGH

IT IS DOUBTFUL THAT ANY MAN IN SOG FOUGHT more battles, served on more assignments, and tempted fate more often than Sgt. Maj. William "Billy" Waugh. Tough, two-fisted, whiskey drinking, and never too shy to avoid a fight, Billy Waugh was *everywhere* in SOG.

When cross-border missions turned bloody in 1966, he recovered the bodies of One-Zero Harry "Crash" Whalen's lost men. A year later he was a Covey Rider and witnessed the costly attempt to raid the enemy's Ho Chi Minh Trail headquarters in Target Oscar Eight. By 1970, he was recon sergeant major at CCN, continuing to run recon despite attaining a rank usually found behind a desk. When Chief SOG assembled a top-secret training mission to assist the surrounded Cambodian army outpost at Ba Kev, he could think of no one better to lead it than Billy Waugh, who went in with Melvin Hill, Warner "Rocky" Farr, Joe Smith, and Tomas Ruiz-Irizarry. Later in 1970 Waugh selected the world's first HALO team, and then a few months afterward, unable to watch while others were jumping, he organized and trained his own team for SOG's third HALO jump. Then he served as a HALO instructor at SOG's school at Camp Long Thanh.

During a protracted search in Laos in 1971 to find an escaped U.S. POW, Air Force Lt. Jack Butcher, Sergeant Major Waugh twice took in all-volunteer teams that nearly reached Butcher before he was recaptured. Like so many of SOG's most seasoned soldiers, Billy Waugh never received much in the way of awards—he was too busy fighting and looking out for his men—but he's deeply respected by all those who served with him.

Billy Waugh aboard a Kingbee 22 kilometers northwest of Khe Sanh about to land in Laos in 1967. (Photo provided by Billy Waugh)

Right: At Ba Kev, Cambodia, 1970, where Waugh led a SOG team that helped defend a cut-off Cambodian outpost. (Photo provided by Billy Waugh)

Below: Sgt. Maj. Billy Waugh (left) with HALO team, 1971. Also shown are (left to right): Sfc. J.D. Bath, Sfc. Charles Wesley (backup jumper), and S. Sgt. Jesse Campbell. Not shown is Sgt. Madison Strohlein. (Photo provided by Billy Waugh)

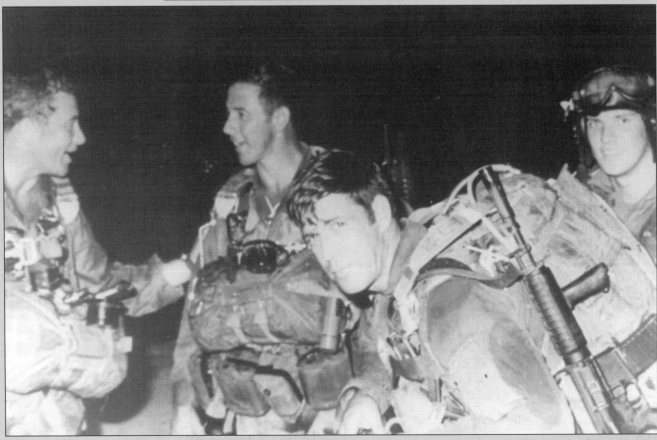

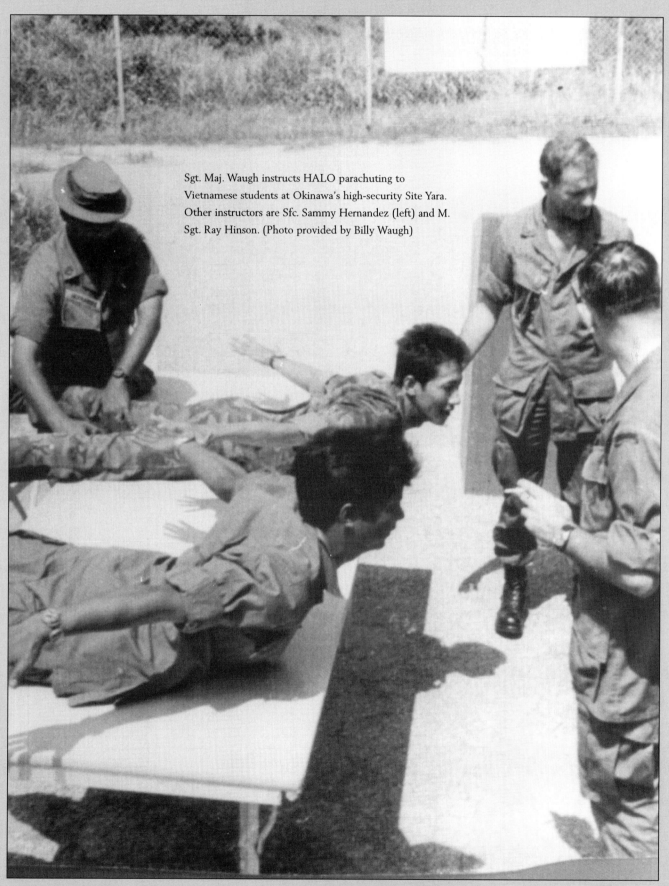

Sgt. Maj. Waugh instructs HALO parachuting to
Vietnamese students at Okinawa's high-security Site Yara.
Other instructors are Sfc. Sammy Hernandez (left) and M.
Sgt. Ray Hinson. (Photo provided by Billy Waugh)

Chapter Fifteen

Into Cambodia

From the earliest days of U.S. involvement in Vietnam, NVA forces used the neutral territory of Cambodia to launch attacks into South Vietnam. Within months of Prince Norodom Sihanouk's closing the U.S. Embassy in Phnom Penh in mid-1965, so many NVA troops were in northeast Ratanakiri Province that virtually all of the enemy troops engaged by the U.S. Army's 1st Air Cavalry Division in the war's first major battle had come from secret Cambodian sanctuaries.

For two more years the NVA presence grew and border violations became a daily affair. Not only was Hanoi secretly basing tens of thousands of troops on Cambodian soil—immune from U.S. attack—but it was purchasing rice and supplies in the open market in Phnom Penh.

Prince Sihanouk was fully aware of these neutrality violations—indeed, his fifth wife, Monique, her mother, and her half-brother were secretly peddling land rights and political protection to the NVA. Hoping to woo Sihanouk away from the Communists, the Johnson administration watched passively while thousands of GIs were killed by enemy forces operating from Cambodia. U.S. diplomats repeatedly over-ruled SOG missions into Cambodia, until by mid-1967 their threadbare objections collapsed in the face of the military need to learn what lay across that border.

RULES OF ENGAGEMENT

The rules drawn up for SOG missions into Cambodia were even more stringent than those for neighboring Laos. In addition to requiring that the Green Berets go into Cambodia without U.S. uniforms or weapons, Washington policymakers decided that no matter how dire the situation, U.S. fighters would not be allowed to come to their aid. Even if it cost the lives of an entire RT, tactical air support was absolutely forbidden—only helicopter gunships could be employed. Further, the recon men would not be allowed to ambush or engage NVA elements except in self-defense out of fear that they might mistakenly kill Cambodian soldiers.

THE DANIEL BOONE AREA

Code-named "Daniel Boone," the Cambodian area of operations was a 20-kilometer (12-mile) deep strip

Cambodia Area of Operations
Daniel Boone AO

along the border of South Vietnam. In the far south, adjacent to Vietnam's Mekong Delta, there wasn't much NVA activity beyond sampans slipping along the waterways, so there were almost no SOG missions there. Just to the north the "Parrot's Beak" jutted deep into South Vietnam, but this was heavily populated agricultural land, used only occasionally by the NVA. North of there, however, Cambodia again jutted eastward at the "Fishhook," and, SOG learned, based here were two to three enemy divisions, or more than 30,000 troops—making it the most heavily occupied area of Cambodia. Also hidden in the Fishhook, just a mile beyond the South Vietnamese border, was the COSVN, the Vietcong headquarters that ran the entire communist effort—a misrepresentation since enemy forces actually were controlled by Hanoi.

Additionally, at least two NVA regiments roamed Cambodia's northernmost tri-border area, designated Base Area (BA) 609. Operating as the NVA's B-3 Front, forces in BA 609 were the primary threat to South Vietnam's Central Highlands.

PROJECTS OMEGA AND SIGMA

Anticipating U.S. approval for cross-border missions into Cambodia, the 5th SFG organized Projects Omega and Sigma to execute them. Assuming that having these men ready to go would result in the Joint Chiefs assigning the top-secret Daniel Boone mission to them, senior 5th SFG officers were stunned when, instead, the Joint Chiefs took the fully trained Omega and Sigma men away and attached them to SOG. This bit of rivalry between senior Special Forces and SOG officers did not have much effect on the actual

Project Omega orderly room at Kontum, named for M. Sgt. Ben Snowden, the first SOG man killed on a covert Cambodian mission. (Photo provided by Cecil Carle)

operations. Soon SOG had set up launch sites at Bu Dop and Duc Co Special Forces camps and another at Quan Loi, a major 1st Air Cavalry Division base northwest of Saigon.

SOG recon missions into Cambodia commenced in June 1967, with the first Green Beret KIA, M. Sgt. Ben Snowden, suffered that same month. Snowden's Project Omega recon friends named their orderly room at Kontum after him.

Within months, SOG RTs had identified the enemy's greatest concentrations in Cambodia, along with the likely sites for major supply stockpiles and the identities of NVA units.

By 1968 SOG completely absorbed Projects Omega and Sigma and, in a major reorganization, created the structure that would exist throughout the rest of the war. The Project Sigma men were assigned to a SOG base at Ban Me Thuot for missions into Cambodia as a new unit—CCS. These CCS RTs would be named for tools, such as RT Saw and RT Hammer. Supporting CCS would be the war's only U.S. Air Force Huey squadron to fly in combat, the 20th Special Operations Squadron or Green Hornets. Meanwhile, the Project Omega men were combined with other Kontum-based SOG troops to create CCC to run missions into northern Cambodia and southern Laos. CCC teams would be named after states, such as RT California and RT Colorado. Danang-based CCN completed SOG's cross-border recon and Hatchet Force organization, with responsibility for central Laos. CCN teams usually were named after snakes, such as RT Moccasin or RT Mamba, although some were named for states.

Sgt. Paul Boyd, a recon man with CCC's RT Montana, calls for air on a rocky hillside in northeast Cambodia's Base Area 609. (Photo provided by Mike Sheppard)

THE SEAPORT OF SIHANOUKVILLE

Rather than run the Ho Chi Minh Trail gauntlet of air strikes and SOG ambushes to get supplies and munitions into central Cambodia, Hanoi found it far easier to ship its materiel clandestinely through the Cambodian seaport of Sihanoukville. Carried by East European freighters with falsified manifests, these cargoes were offloaded at Sihanoukville and convoyed to secret warehouses in the capital, Phnom Penh. There, NVA intelligence officers transferred the supplies to other trucks for delivery to a string of base camps along the border of South Vietnam, especially in the Fishhook.

It was no small-scale operation. This clandestine cargo of rockets, small-arms ammunition, and mortar rounds sustained three full enemy divisions, plus communist units across the border inside South Vietnam— some 200,000 troops.

And by virtue of doing it with the connivance of the Cambodian government, these shipments were beyond the eyes of SOG RTs or even the CIA, which had been crippled since June 1965 when Prince Sihanouk had closed down the U.S. Embassy.

THE SECRET CAMBODIAN BOMBING

Beginning in early 1969, a major SOG mission in Cambodia became BDA in support of the "secret" Cambodian B-52 strikes.

Thanks to SOG and other intelligence sources, the Nixon administration had become aware of what was happening in "neutral" Cambodia and concluded that since the NVA's greatest troop concentrations were in remote, jungled areas these could be bombed without much danger to Cambodian civilians. Due to the peculiarities of Southeast Asian politics and Cambodia's tenuous relationship with Hanoi, President Nixon decided not to acknowledge the B-52 raids unless Prince Sihanouk protested—and the prince never did. In late March 1969, Nixon turned loose the B-52s on the Fishhook. The first secret Cambodian raid set off 73 secondary explosions.

Nixon suspended further B-52 strikes in hopes that Hanoi's negotiators might begin productive discussions in Paris, but the talks droned on pointlessly. Nixon approved a second secret B-52 strike, this time against a target proposed by Gen. Creighton Abrams with Ambassador Bunker's endorsement: COSVN, the almost mythical Vietcong headquarters hidden away in the Fishhook.

MOMENTOUS DEVELOPMENTS

The story of the COSVN raid of 24 April 1969 is so intertwined with the story of legendary CCS recon man Jerry "Mad Dog" Shriver that these accounts are told together elsewhere. After the bloody COSVN raid, missions into the heavily occupied Fishhook were reduced to a case-by-case basis. And suspicions grew tenfold that SOG was being compromised by an enemy mole hidden somewhere in its Saigon headquarters.

When Prince Sihanouk was overthrown in the spring of 1970 by an anti-Hanoi coalition, the new Cambodian government immediately came under heavy NVA attack. That May, to assist the new government and clean out the border sanctuaries, U.S. forces invaded Cambodia and found every major enemy base camp exactly where SOG had said they'd

be. Communist losses were staggering: 11,349 troops, 435 vehicles, 7,000 tons of rice, 23,000 AK rifles, 2,500 machine guns and mortars, plus 143,000 rockets and mortar rounds and 15 million rounds of AK ammo. Despite these heavy losses, though, the NVA drove deeper into Cambodia, overrunning nearly half the country and seizing several major cities, including Stung Treng on the Mekong River.

With the 30 June 1970 U.S. withdrawal from Cambodia, U.S.-led SOG operations ceased there. The final CCS Hatchet Force man killed in action was 1st Lt. Vyrl Leichliter, a platoon leader lost just three weeks before the U.S. withdrawal. S. Sgt. Everette Cofer, One-Zero of RT Pick, was the final recon man killed. The last MIA was Sgt. Glenn Tubbs, a recon One-One.

By late summer of 1970, CCS' American recon men transferred to CCC and CCN, where they joined other RTs to continue fighting in SOG's top-secret wars.

Sp4c. Glenn Tubbs (shirtless), the final CCS recon man MIA in Cambodia. He was lost on 13 January 1970. (Photo provided by Mark Kinsler)

Above: A flight of Green Hornet helicopters. Assigned to CCS, they were the only U.S. Air Force Huey unit flying combat missions in the war. (Photo provided by Rick Jalloway)

Right: Cambodian Prince Sihanouk's luxurious summer palace, tucked away on a lake about 50 miles west of Pleiku, South Vietnam. Occasionally put under surveillance by SOG, the abandonded palace was hit (without authorization) by Cobra gunships in 1970 after Sihanouk announced his support for Hanoi. (Photo provided by Mike Buckland)

Left: CCS recon man Bob Bechtoldt, RT Auger, crosses a stream in heavily occupied Fishhook region of Cambodia. (Photo provided by Bob Bechtoldt)

Top inset: Project Omega One-Zero Cecil Carle, with Swedish K submachine gun in an enemy "sanctuary" in Cambodia. (Photo provided by Cecil Carle)

Bottom inset: Project Omega recon man S. Sgt. James Bolen creeps through the jungle deep behind NVA lines. (Photo provided by Cecil Carle)

Inset: BET YOU CAN'T BOMB US. Two enemy supply boats tied up on the Mekong River at Stung Treng, Cambodia, inside a U.S. Air Force "no-bomb" area. (Photo provided by Mike Cryer)

Left: But Covey FAC Mike Cryer convinced 7th Air Force that they could be hit without hitting the adjacent city. Here's the result. (Photo provided by Mike Cryer)

Top: Aerial view of thick Cambodian jungle from SOG Huey's doorway. (Photo provided by Bryan Stockdale)

Bottom: CCS RT Hammer, with One-Zero Harry Kroske (front row, third from left) and One-One Bryan Stockdale (to Kroske's right). First Lieutenant Kroske was killed on Stockdale's first mission. Alone, Stockdale had to crawl around and through dozens of NVA, who even set fire to elephant grass where he was hiding. The resilient young Green Beret went on to become a respected One-Zero. (Photo provided by Bryan Stockdale)

COSVN, the Control Office for South Vietnam, was hidden in the Fishhook, Base Area 353.

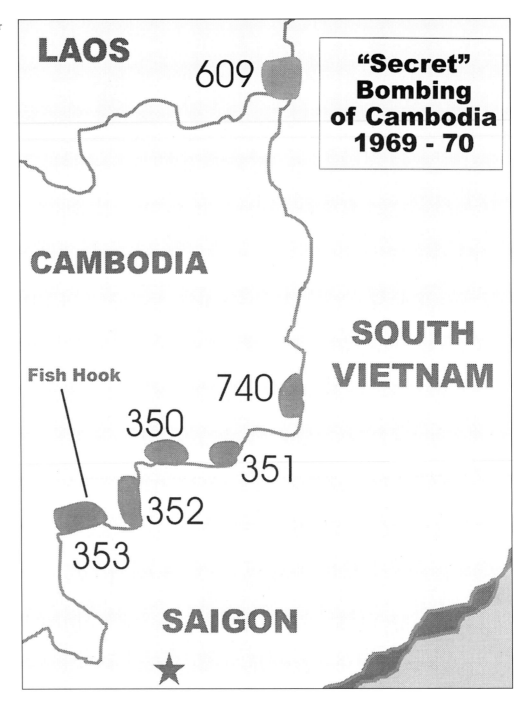

MAD DOG SHRIVER—
THE MAN AND THE MYTH

THERE WAS NO ONE AT CCS QUITE LIKE THE LEGENDARY Jerry "Mad Dog" Shriver. The 28-year-old Green Beret rarely spoke and walked around camp for days wearing the same clothes. In the club he'd buy a case of beer, open every can, then go alone to a corner and drink them all. In his sleep, he cradled a loaded rifle. Medal of Honor recipient Jim Fleming, who flew Green Hornet Hueys at CCS, found Shriver "the quintessential warrior-loner, antisocial, possessed by what he was doing, the best team, always training, constantly training."

No recon man was better in the woods than Mad Dog. "He was like having a dog you could talk to," Bill O'Rourke thought. "He could hear and sense things; he was more alive in the woods than any other human being I've ever met." Mad Dog seemed a walking arsenal with an imposing array of sawed-off shotgun or suppressed submachine gun, pistols, knives, and grenades. "He looked like Rambo," Project Omega 1st Sgt. Billy Greenwood thought. Rather than stand down after an operation, Shriver would go out with another team. "He lived for the game; that's all he lived for," Dale Libby, a fellow CCS man, said.

By 1969 Shriver was into his third continuous year in SOG, and though he'd been awarded a Silver Star, five Bronze Stars, and the Soldier's Medal, he didn't care about decorations—only the Montagnards mattered, and he spent all his money on them. He was the sole American at CCS who lived in the Montagnard barracks.

Sfc. Jerry "Mad Dog" Shriver with a suppressed M3 submachine gun and a Gerber MK II stiletto, boarding a Green Hornet Huey. (Photo provided by Jim Fleming)

Mad Dog projected an image of perfect prowess—but the truth was he feared death and, having escaped so many close calls, didn't think he'd live much longer. "He wanted to quit," Medal of Honor winner Fred Zabitosky could see. "I said, 'Why don't you just tell them, "I want off, I don't want to run any more?"' He said he would, but he never did, just kept running."

On the morning of 24 April 1969, following a top-secret B-52 strike into Cambodia's Fishhook, Jerry Shriver accompanied a 60-man SOG raiding force that landed directly upon COSVN—the enemy headquarters responsible for the entire war. But no sooner had the SOG BDA force landed than fire began exploding from all directions, horrible fire that skimmed the ground and mowed down anyone who didn't dive into a bomb crater or roll behind a fallen tree trunk.

Below: Shriver in the early days of Project Omega suited up and ready to go. Note the suppressed High Standard HD pistol. (Photo provided by Gene McCarley)

Below right: Shriver sharing a crock of *nam pei* rice wine with Montagnards. More so than most Green Berets, Shriver "went native" and even lived with his Montagnards. (Photo provided by Gene McCarley)

A machine gun pinned down Mad Dog's men. Skittish 'Yards looked to Shriver, and his half-grin inspired confidence. Then they were on their feet, charging, Shriver and his 'Yards dashing through the flying bullets, into the tree-line, into the very guts of COSVN. *And Mad Dog Shriver was never seen again.*

Pinned down at the other end of that hellhole LZ, Sgt. Ernest Jamison was killed, and the acting Hatchet Force commander, Capt. Paul Cahill, was badly wounded. First Lieutenant Greg Harrigan directed helicopter gunships for 45 minutes, and then he, too, was killed. Finally, after hours of fighting, three Hueys raced in and picked up 15 wounded men. CCS 1st Lt. Dan Hall carried out a wounded radio operator and then managed to drag Lieutenant Harrigan's body to an aircraft.

Thus ended the bloody COSVN raid and the story of Mad Dog Shriver. Killed or captured, Jerry Shriver's fate remains a mystery known only to Hanoi.

Above: Unit patch for CCS Hatchet Force Company that assaulted COSVN when Shriver was lost. (Photo provided by Harry Pugh)

Top left: A SIDE SELDOM SEEN. Shriver grieves with Montagnard teammates over the wrapped body of a killed tribesman. (Photo provided by Cecil Carle)

Bottom: Shriver's dog, Klaus, was unable to understand when his master did not return. (Photo provided by Dale Bennett)

M. Sgt. Roy Benavidez suffered seven gunshot wounds, 28 shrapnel holes, and a bayonet wound. (Photo provided by U.S. Army)

ROY BENAVIDEZ, ONE-MAN BRIGHT LIGHT TEAM

ON 2 MAY 1968, SOG MEN GATHERED in the Quan Loi launch site tent to listen to radio reports of a team in trouble. The situation sounded grim.

A few hours earlier, Sfc. Leroy Wright's RT had been inserted into the Fishhook in Cambodia, 75 miles northwest of Saigon. Going in with Wright were S. Sgt. Lloyd "Frenchie" Mousseau, One-One, and Sp4c. Brian O'Connor, One-Two, along with nine Nungs. Now they were all pinned down on an LZ by several NVA companies blasting away with mortars, RPGs, and machine guns. One-Zero Wright was dead, One-One Mousseau was badly wounded, and One-Two Brian O'Connor had been shot several times. All their Nungs were dead or wounded, and everybody was about to be overrun.

Back at the CCS launch site, an old friend of Wright's, Sfc. Roy Benavidez, knew something had to be done—but there were no Bright Light teams or reaction forces.

Weakened by loss of blood, One-Two O'Connor heard a Huey coming in and saw a hefty figure in the doorway make repeated signs of the cross and roll to the ground. It was Roy Benavidez, a one-man Bright Light team who'd come so spontaneously that he'd brought just the SOG knife on his belt.

Benavidez dashed 75 yards through withering enemy fire and, despite an AK round through the leg, dove into the brush where Wright's men lay. Benavidez could see that Wright was dead, while Frenchie Mousseau had a serious head wound. O'Connor was coherent but barely able to crawl. Benavidez bound their wounds, injected morphine, and, ignoring NVA bullets and grenades, passed around ammunition he'd taken off several bodies. At last he armed himself with an AK. Benavidez was calling in a Huey when an enemy AK slug hit his right thigh, his second wound.

When the Huey landed, Benavidez gave his AK to O'Connor and struggled to bring along Wright's body. Something threw him to the ground—he'd been shot through one lung, his third wound. Benavidez almost passed out. Then a Huey was shot down.

Coughing blood, Benavidez stumbled onto the LZ to help survivors get free before the Huey's gas tanks exploded. While mortar shells burst everywhere he called air danger-close. Benavidez was shot yet again. He tried to ignore it. Five minutes later he took still another slug. And another gunship was downed.

Then amid heavy aerial supporting fire, a lone Huey landed. Assisted by Green Beret medic Ronald Sammons, Benavidez was dragging his injured comrades to the helicopter when a berserk NVA soldier clubbed him and tried to bayonet him. Benavidez pulled his SOG knife, just as the bayonet poked through his left forearm. The Green Beret threw his body against the North Vietnamese soldier, driving his knife into his assailant's side with such force that it couldn't be pulled out. When two more NVA soldiers materialized just then, Benavidez shot them both. Powerful hands dragged Benavidez aboard, and the Huey lifted off. Mousseau died en route to the medevac hospital.

Wright and Mousseau received Distinguished Service Crosses posthumously, and Benavidez spent almost a year recovering from seven gunshot wounds, 28 shrapnel holes, and a bayonet wound. His incredible bravery was written up—but the paperwork was lost. The U.S. Congress passed special legislation 13 years later, and retired M. Sgt. Roy Benavidez was flown to Washington, where President Reagan draped the Medal of Honor around his very deserving neck.

Far left: One-Zero Leroy Wright, an old friend, died before Benavidez could get to him. (Photo provided by Roy Benavidez)

Left: One-One Lloyd "Frenchie" Mousseau died en route to the medevac hospital. (Photo provided by Roy Benavidez)

Below: On 24 February 1981 President Reagan said, "Sergeant Benavidez, a nation grateful to you and to all your comrades, living and dead, awards this highest symbol of gratitude, for service above and beyond the call of duty, the Congressional Medal of Honor." (Photo provided by Ronald Reagan Presidential Library)

FRANKLIN "DOUG" MILLER—ONE-MAN ASSAULT FORCE

S. Sgt. Franklin Miller with the Medal of Honor, awarded for single-handedly delaying a large NVA force so that his wounded teammates could escape. (Photo provided by JFK Special Warfare Museum)

THE TRI-BORDER AREA OF NORTHEASTERN Cambodia's Ratanakiri Province—dubbed Base Area 609 by U.S. intelligence—typically contained at least two NVA infantry regiments of about 1,000 men each. Almost any SOG team venturing into that heavy jungle was likely to find trouble.

That was the case when CCC's Kontum-based RT Vermont landed there on 5 January 1970 to search for enemy base camps. RT Vermont's One-Zero, S. Sgt. Franklin "Doug" Miller, had been in SOG for a little over six months, but he was hardly new to recon. Although Miller was trained as a Special Forces demolitions man, when he originally arrived in Vietnam in 1966 he'd been assigned to the 1st Air Cavalry Division where he spent two and a half continuous years in a long-range reconnaissance patrol company. With that much time in combat, especially in recon, he was instantly accepted when he volunteered for top-secret SOG duty in 1969.

Miller soon adjusted to SOG's most demanding environment and became One-Zero of RT Vermont. His One-One, Sgt. Robert Brown, was a Special Forces medic with one previous mission, while his One-Two radio operator, Sgt. Edward Blythe, was on his first mission.

Not long after RT Vermont left its LZ, an indigenous soldier noticed a thin cord tied across a trail and, not believing the enemy would booby-trap his own rear area, he yanked on it. Instantly there was a tremendous roar, and four team members collapsed, seriously wounded. Worse yet, the hastily emplaced booby trap had been put there by a reinforced NVA squad, which now rushed forward to assault the disorganized SOG men.

Unwounded, One-Zero Miller and Montagnard point man Hyuk let loose a heavy volume of fire at almost point-blank range, buying time for Brown and Blythe to lead the injured men to safety.

With half his men incapacitated and more NVA troops now rushing into the area, Miller hastily helped bandage the wounded. Then, leaving most of their rucksacks behind, they made their way across a stream and 150 meters up a small hillside to a bomb crater. Taking cover there to watch their back-trail, Miller and his point man could see to where they'd left their rucksacks—a North Vietnamese leader looked through the backpacks and then waved over more of his men and signaled for a wide sweep toward where Miller and his teammates were hiding.

Knowing he could not move his men because of their wounds, Miller opened fire with his CAR-15, knocking down several enemy soldiers. Then Hyuk added more fire, forcing NVA troops to fall back, but soon still more of the enemy arrived. Fanning out right and left, an estimated NVA platoon-strength body rushed up the hill, aggressively advancing despite Miller's and Hyuk's well-aimed CAR-15 bursts.

Meanwhile, Sergeant Brown, a medic, was bandaging the wounded and radioing for air support. Then the NVA assaulted again, their massed fire killing the point man and seriously wounding One-Zero Miller. By now an evacuation Huey was inbound, but heavy enemy fire drove it off.

Again Miller exposed himself on that dangerous downhill flank and, despite taking an AK round through his left arm, placed effective CAR-15 fire on the NVA forces, repelling their assault. By now every member of RT Vermont had been wounded.

Despite his condition, One-Zero Miller led the team to a more protected position, where a Huey was at last able to land a Bright Light team that helped to evacuate the wounded men.

Staff Sergeant Miller was awarded the Medal of Honor, SOG's second such award for a covert ground action in Cambodia.

Above inset: Patch of RT Vermont, the team of Medal of Honor recipient Franklin Miller. (Photo provided by Harry Pugh)

Left: S. Sgt. Franklin "Doug" Miller during a recon mission in Laos. (Photo provided by John Plaster)

THE GREEN BERET MURDER CASE

ON 10 MAY 1969, A FAMILIAR FACE WAS NOTICED among photos captured by Special Forces' 3rd Mobile Strike Force. One group photo of enemy political officers included a perfect likeness of Thai Khac Nguyen. It explained a lot.

Thai was an agent of 5th SFG's Project Gamma, which ran operatives into Cambodia as early warning for border camps. Not long after hiring Thai, Gamma agents had begun disappearing. Gamma officers confronted Thai with the photograph, interrogated him by using sodium pentathol, and then subjected him to a polygraph test. He failed.

They'd found their mole but wondered what to do with him. If they gave him to the ARVN, it would disclose Gamma operations, which they'd kept compartmented. They could not play Thai as a double because he wouldn't cooperate. The CIA offered no help. The last option was to execute him as a spy—permissible under the Geneva Convention but contrary to U.S. Army regulations. Certainly, that's what the NVA would have done with any mole it discovered, and after terrible torture.

The matter landed on the desk of Col. Robert Rheault, the dynamic new 5th SFG commander, one of the finest officers ever to wear a green beret. Rheault told the Gamma men, "I've got to trust you guys to run your own show." If it was necessary to dispose of this mole, he told them, make it so—after all, that's what the OSS had done in World War II. Thai Khac Nguyen was anesthetized and shot, and his body was dumped in Nha Trang Bay.

There the affair might have ended except that General Abrams had been growing irritated by his inability to control Special Forces, which often seemed to serve other masters at the CIA, Joint Chiefs, SOG, SACSA, and Commander in Chief, Pacific Command (CINCPAC.) A straitlaced armor officer, after General Abrams learned about the Thai's execution, he had U.S. Army criminal investigators jail Colonel Rheault like some common thug.

For those fighting the secret wars, Colonel Rheault's arrest was an ill-advised legitimizing of their worst enemy—an enemy mole who killed by treachery—and an egregious misunderstanding of the secret wars by the very leadership that sent them on their missions. Not a single Johnson administration figure had said a thing about enemy use of Cambodia nor Sihanouk's duplicity. No one had said anything about SOG men being captured, tortured, and probably murdered; yet here a communist agent was seen as a "victim" of those he'd victimized.

Rumors abounded of Green Berets plotting Rheault's rescue from Long Binh Jail, and indeed some men were working for his release, among them the courageous S. Sgt. Ken Worthley. One-Zero Worthley's RT Florida—including

Sgts. Robert Garcia and Dale Hanson—had been inserted in northeast Cambodia on 25 August and the next day ambushed two NVA soldiers on a trail. SOG later determined they'd bagged the highest-ranking intelligence officer ever killed by recon men, an NVA full colonel—*and carrying an impressive leather satchel*. Grabbing the bag, team members ran for their lives, with dozens of NVA troopers in pursuit. Coming out on strings, young Ken Worthley was killed, and Garcia and Hanson were wounded by enemy fire.

The satchel contained a roster of spies operating inside South Vietnam and a warning that they must lie low, because, a document warned, *the Americans had unmasked Thai Khac Nguyen*!

Had this critical evidence been needed to assist Colonel Rheault's defense, Ken Worthley would have been proud, even at the cost of his life, to have supplied it. As it was, after a series of stinging speeches on the floor of Congress, Secretary of the Army Stanley Resor announced that all charges had been dropped; however, General Abrams refused to return Colonel Rheault to command of the 5th SFG. Denied official vindication, the Green Beret officer retired.

Above left: Col. Robert Rheault, commander of 5th SFG. (Photo provided by U.S. Army)

Above: One-Zero Ken Worthley, RT Florida, seized documents proving the "mole's" guilt. The Minnesota native was shot and killed during his team's extraction. (Photo provided by Robert Garcia)

319

THE PRESS EXPOSES SOG

During 1969's Green Beret murder case, the media mistakenly assumed that Project Gamma was a SOG element and that the dead agent was a SOG operative. For the first time in the war, a spate of publicity came SOG's way, along with a couple of other articles later. SOG men especially got a chuckle out of the Associated Press claim that they wore eye putty to look like Orientals.

"The organization known as S.O.G. is said to work only on delicate assignments ordered directly by high officials. . . . [SOG] conducts clandestine operations, ranging from intelligence gathering to kidnaping, on special assignments from the United States military command in Vietnam and the Central Intelligence Agency."
—*New York Times* (15 August 1969)

"SOG—the Studies and Observations Group—is about as spooky an outfit as there is. . . . There is, to my knowledge, neither a SPECTRE nor a SMERSH in Vietnam, but there really is a SOG."
—*Baltimore Sun* (24 August 1969)

". . . [W]hile almost all Green Berets are potentially intelligence agents, only a relative few are involved in purely covert activities. Those who are so employed belong to SOG. . . ."
—*Newsweek* (25 August 1969)

"All wear North Vietnamese uniforms and carry North Vietnamese weapons. The Americans sometimes dye their skin and wear eye putty to look like Orientals."
—Associated Press (June 1971)

". . . [SOG] is all very hush-hush. Many . . . carry British-made weapons with silencing devices. In some cases, the soles of their boots carry a special tread that leaves an imprint like that of the sandals worn by the Vietnamese."
—*Newsweek* (23 March 1970)

BABYSAN DAVIDSON

SECOND ONLY TO JERRY SHRIVER IN RESPECT and achievements while running recon at CCS was S. Sgt. David "Babysan" Davidson. Even though he was 23, Davidson looked barely 16, with his red hair and freckles, and his 5-foot, 6-inch frame that weighed only 130 pounds. "If you didn't know who he was, you'd think he was just a baby-face kid that got stuck up in the draft like all the other baby-face kids," Ben Lyons said. "When they tagged him 'Babysan,' they tagged him right."

Davidson was among the first U.S. combat troops to serve in the war, arriving as an 18-year-old paratrooper in 1965. After a stint with the 101st Airborne Division, he volunteered for Special Forces and served another year, as a parachute rigger with the 5th SFG. In June 1967 he was among the very first Project Omega recon men to penetrate Cambodia and continued running recon until May 1968. Babysan went back to Ft. Bragg's 7th SFG but apparently didn't care for stateside duty. He returned to SOG in August 1969. "He was good in the woods," fellow One-Zero Sonny Franks said, "but he didn't mind a scrappin', and when he got in a firefight he always got 'em out."

Understandably nicknamed "Babysan," David Davidson displayed boundless courage and became one of SOG's finest One-Zeros. (Photo provided by Cecil Carle)

On 21 February 1970, Davidson's team made one of SOG's rare static-line parachute inserts, jumping deep into Cambodia in the middle of the night. By October 1970, though only 23 years old, he had spent one out of every five days of his life in Vietnam and was into his third year of running SOG recon. When Cambodian cross-border missions ended that summer, Babysan transferred to Danang-based CCN and continued running recon, this time leading RT Fer de Lance.

On the afternoon of 5 October 1970 RT Fer De Lance was on a Laotian ridge just south of Route 922, 10 miles west of where the road entered the northern Ashau Valley at Hamburger Hill. A FAC arrived as Babysan reported NVA forces sweeping for the RT, but solid clouds covered the area. The FAC had to refuel, and by the time he returned the team had been in one firefight—Babysan had been shot and fallen down a slope—and his One-One, Sgt. Fred Gassman, reported that many NVA troops were advancing on him from three sides. Then Gassman called, "I've been hit and in the worst possible way." The radio went dead.

The next morning six FACs scoured the ridge at tree-top level but found nothing. To this day, the North Vietnamese have refused to acknowledge any information about Babysan Davidson and his teammate Fred Gassman.

Top: S. Sgt. David Davidson is presented the Silver Star for gallantry. (Photo provided by the Davidson family)

Bottom right: CCS intelligence officer leads away a blindfolded NVA prisoner (left) who had just been snatched in Cambodia by "Babysan" Davidson. (Photo provided by Mark Kinsler)

Bottom left: MIA along with Babysan was his One-One Sgt. Fred Gassman, shown here riding strings at CCS. (Photo provided by Bill Deacy)

Hanoi denies any knowledge of "Babysan," but his family found two images of a U.S. POW that bears a striking resemblance to the missing One-Zero. (Photo provided by the Davidson family)

PART SIX
SOG's HATCHET FORCES

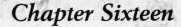
Chapter Sixteen

Hatchet Force Operations

The Hatchet Forces were SOG's strike arm—quick-reaction platoons and companies that attacked NVA installations or seized cache sites when recon teams discovered them. Later in the war they also performed deliberate, planned operations of longer duration.

A Hatchet Force platoon contained 42 indigenous soldiers and four Green Beret NCOs plus one lieutenant, while a Hatchet Force company combined three such platoons under a U.S.-led headquarters section with a Special Forces captain in command. Each of SOG's three major FOBs—CCN, CCC, and CCS—included at least one Hatchet Force company. Hatchet Force indigenous troops initially were Chinese Nungs, but by the time strength peaked at about nine companies in 1970, they all were Montagnard hill tribesmen.

Although Hatchet Forces frequently raided behind enemy lines in Laos, U.S. policy did not normally allow them in Cambodia's "Daniel Boone" area until 1970, so CCS companies operated on the South Vietnamese side of the border. Still, CCS companies saw heavy combat, such as in March 1969, while screening the Laotian border southwest of Khe Sanh for the U.S. Marine Corps Operation Dewey Canyon. This SOG CCS task force, led by Dick Meadows, fought with distinction and suffered five American wounded—Lts. Bill O'Rourke and Bob Killebrew, along with M. Sgt. Tom Twomey and Sfcs. Jerry Shriver and Nathaniel Johnson.

Throughout the war Hatchet Force operations were limited by a shortage of helicopters. A dozen troop-carrying Hueys or Kingbees were required to insert a single company—any less and the SOG men would be stuck beside their insertion LZ for hours while the rest of their comrades arrived piecemeal. The entire time they were on the ground, helicopters had to remain on strip alert, committed solely to the Hatchet Force. Further, because even a few days' unflyable weather might allow the NVA to surround and destroy a Hatchet Force, their largest operations were normally in fair-weather months. Under such operational and weather constraints, each FOB could mount about two major company-sized operations per year.

HATCHET FORCE RAIDS

Early Hatchet Force operations were mostly quick-reaction raids, one of the primary missions conceived by the Chief SOG who organized them, Col. Donald Blackburn. These short-duration attacks usually followed the discovery of a lucrative enemy target, as was the case in early 1967 when a platoon led by M. Sgt. Bill "Country" Grimes landed on a Laotian hilltop near Highway 110. After a short fight, Grimes' platoon captured a staggering 250 tons—*100 truckloads*—of rice. After that great success, the NVA dispersed stockpiles and increased security around all their caches.

Another success was a company-sized raid on a North Vietnamese way station, some 25 miles northwest of Khe Sanh. In addition to overrunning the enemy base, the SOG force captured a stockpile of antiaircraft machine gun mounts, which the force destroyed with explosives.

Hatchet Forces also performed Bright Light missions—such as the attempted POW rescue in Operation Crimson Tide, described elsewhere—and poststrike BDAs on B-52 bomber targets. In mid-1967 SOG experimented with a combined Hatchet Force BDA and raid, landing a 100-man company on the NVA headquarters overseeing the entire Laotian Ho Chi Minh Trail immediately after a B-52 strike. The 3 June 1967 mission took place in Target Oscar-Eight, some 23 miles southwest of Khe Sanh, but when the CCN Hatchet Force landed it was pinned on its LZ with hundreds of NVA streaming out of underground bunkers to attack. Between incessant enemy assaults and thick antiaircraft fire, only about a platoon made it back. In all, 23 Americans were lost in Oscar-Eight—SOG raiders, U.S. Air Force pilots, and U.S. Marine helicopter crewmen—plus twice that many Nungs. Although six Americans became MIA—including Hatchet Force men Billy Laney and Ron Dexter—Hanoi admitted capturing just one doorgunner, Marine L. Cpl. Frank E. Cius, Jr. He was released in 1973.

The tactic of following a B-52 strike with a Hatchet Force raid was attempted again 24 April 1969 on the enemy's most important headquarters in Cambodia, COSVN—with equally devastating effect to the assault force, including the loss of SOG legend Jerry "Mad Dog" Shriver. Many SOG men suspected that these two crucial raids had been compromised by an enemy spy in SOG's Saigon headquarters.

RECONNAISSANCE IN FORCE

Instead of waiting for a recon team to find a target, Hatchet Forces sometimes conducted their own

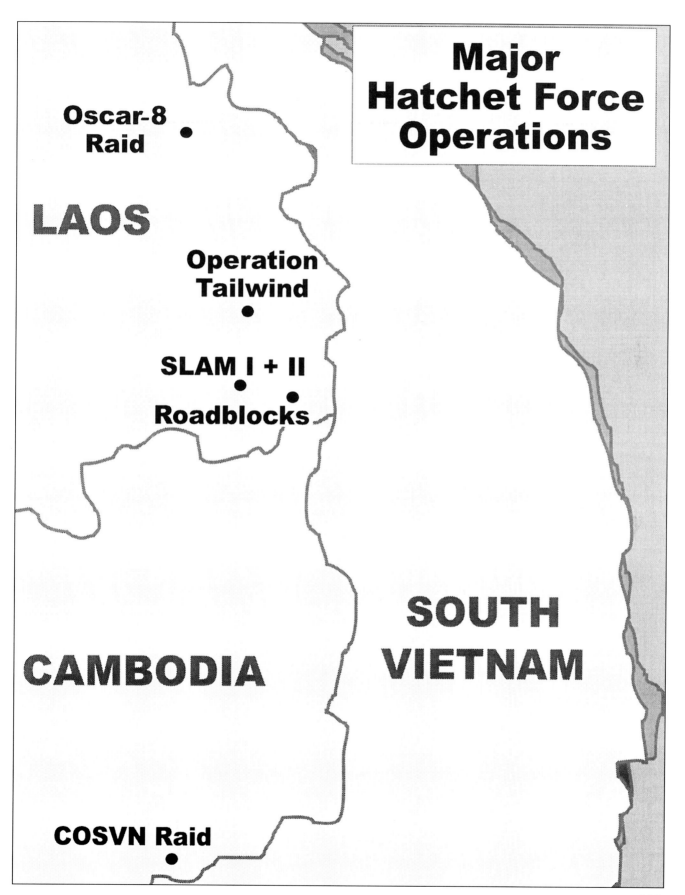

Major
Hatchet Force
Operations

Oscar-8
Raid

LAOS

Operation
Tailwind

SLAM I + II
Roadblocks

CAMBODIA

SOUTH
VIETNAM

COSVN Raid

THE ORDEAL OF CHARLES WILKLOW

THE 3 JUNE 1967 RAID IN TARGET OSCAR-EIGHT proved a terrible disaster, with the Hatchet Force raiders pinned on the LZ and several of their extraction helicopters shot out of the sky. Aboard one downed helicopter was Sfc. Charles Wilklow, who'd suffered a serious gunshot wound in his right leg. Emerging from the wreckage of a Marine CH-46, Wilklow forced himself to crawl a few yards and then collapsed with dozens of enemy soldiers all around him. Unarmed and too weak to move, he expected to be seized, but the NVA merely walked over, noticed his condition, and left him there. Wilklow passed out.

By the time he awoke, he'd been dragged into a clearing with an orange panel lying beside him. NVA machine guns covered the spot, their gunners hoping that U.S. helicopters would come to his rescue. All day, Wilklow lay motionless in the tropical sun, resolved to appear dead so that no one would fall into the trap.

Sfc. Charles Wilkow, the only SOG man to escape captivity in Laos. (Photo provided by the Wilkow family)

The second day he thirsted mightily, but no NVA soldier offered him any water. He probably would have died but lapped water from a muddy puddle. Enemy soldiers strolled over, urinated in the puddle, chuckled, and walked away. By the third day Wilklow was dying; it rained for hours, and he shivered uncontrollably.

On the fourth day, shriveled up and shaking, Wilklow was barely clinging to life. His usefulness was about over; perhaps he'd look convincing enough to be bait for one more day. That night Wilklow's strength ebbed, and he knew that death was imminent. For the first time in his adult life Wilklow prayed, begging God to help him live and see his wife and three children again. He felt a twinge of energy and forced himself to start crawling. Weak and feverish, he passed out several times, but he always woke up and started crawling again. By sunrise he must have crawled nearly two miles, but by then he was completely spent and slipped into unconsciousness.

When next he awoke, SOG S. Sgt. Lester Pace was dragging him to an awaiting helicopter. During the flight to Danang, Wilklow shook and sobbed and tried to talk, but he could not, thinking only of his family—which, indeed, he did see again.

His escape can only be called miraculous: Charles Wilklow was the only one of SOG's 57 Green Berets MIA in Laos and Cambodia ever to return.

Hatchet Force heavy-weapon squad members, with 60mm mortar and M60 machine gun, cross a river in Laos, deep behind enemy lines. (Photo provided by Bob Donoghue)

reconnaissance-in-force operations, roaming behind enemy lines with enough firepower to attack almost anything they discovered. Typically, this meant landing a heavily armed platoon near a major enemy highway and then walking the road until the platoon encountered the NVA. In the enemy's absence the SOG men would sow dozens of antitruck and antitank mines. If the enemy showed up in strength, it would be pummeled with tactical air strikes, and the SOG men would be extracted before they could be surrounded—at least that was the concept.

Each FOB launched about 15 platoon-sized cross-border operations annually, with most being recons in force. Typifying these was an early-1969 CCN Hatchet Force platoon

mission to prowl the jungle west of Khe Sanh for a week. Accompanied by Capt. Jim Storter, their company commander, Lts. Peter McMurray and Vincent Sabatinelli performed impressively, discovering an enemy truck park and destroying it with air strikes. But their enjoyment of the achievement was short-lived: both Hatchet Force lieutenants were killed within six months of the mission.

In 1968, SOG modified the company-sized recon-in-force concept with search, locate, annihilate, and monitor (SLAM) missions. The SLAM operations were similar to search-and-destroy missions performed by U.S. forces in South Vietnam except that they were supported by continuous heavy air strikes. The first company-size

331

SLAM, begun on 1 May, was commanded by Capt. Eugene McCarley, accompanied by two recon teams, one led by One-Zero Robert Van Hall with One-One David Cheney. For several days the Hatchet Force walked Highway 110, skirmishing with NVA. At one point, an RPG rocket killed Lt. Joseph Shreve. When the situation became untenable, Captain McCarley piled explosives on the highway, blew a 20-foot-deep crater, and had his force extracted. Of 12 Americans on SLAM-I, eight earned Purple Hearts. The wounded included Eugene McCarley, David Davidson, John Probart, Horace Ford, Terry Hamric, David Hause, and David Cheney.

Six months later, in mid-November 1968, SLAM-II was conducted, again along Highway 110. For eight long days, a Hatchet Force company fought its way westward until overwhelming NVA numbers bogged it down and surrounded it. During the ensuing fight more than half the Americans were wounded. Bob Howard was recommended for the Medal of Honor for his actions in the fight, though it was downgraded to a Silver Star. Wounded men included Bob Howard, Lee Swain, Robert Price, William Groves, Tony Dorff, and Joe Parnar. Bill Kendall was wounded while resupplying them. Silver Stars were awarded to Lloyd O'Daniels, Lee Swain, and Robert Price.

BLOCKING THE TRAIL

For sheer audacity, no other operations could match the Hatchet Force's roadblocks conducted along Highway 110 at the peak of the dry season in 1969 and 1970. During each of these three company-sized operations, SOG helicopters landed more than 100 men atop a hill into which they dug furiously and toppled trees with chainsaws. By nightfall, the SOG men were dug in with perfectly positioned firing lanes covering the road with machine guns, mortars, and recoilless rifles.

The first roadblock, held by Company A from CCC, commanded by Capt. Barre R. McClelland, cut Highway 110 for a full week, 18–24 March 1969. Once Company A was in place, not one truck, bicycle, or even a porter got past, despite the enemy's pounding them day and night with mortars and light artillery. When NVA fire wounded Company A's only 90mm recoilless rifle gunner, RT South Carolina One-Zero Tom Waskovich volunteered to take his place. He subsequently hit several NVA trucks. Whenever enemy trucks tried to sneak past, the SOG men called in AC-119 and AC-130 gunships.

Only one week after Company A came out, it went back in to the same hill, this time led by Capt. Bobby Evans, and kept the road closed for another week. Due to the roadblocks, dozens of NVA trucks were backed up far along Highways 110 and 92; the regional NVA forces were so desperately short of storage space that they had to pile tons of supplies in the open, creating a perfect bombing target.

Company A's wounded included Captain Evans, Henry Kemp, Tom Flynn, Ed Garbett, and Franklin Roe, along with about 25 Montagnards. The only deaths were among the Montagnards. The overworked medic, Sgt. Verlon Cantrell, was awarded the Silver Star, as were Captain Evans, Roy Lamphier, and Henry Kemp.

One year later, on 23 February 1970, SOG attempted to repeat the previous success with Operation Spindown, again blocking Highway 110 by placing CCC's Hatchet Force Company B on top of the same hill that its sister company had occupied.

In addition to daytime support by fighters and nighttime support from AC-130s and AC-119s, U.S. Army 175mm guns at Ben Het fired hundreds of rounds to support Company B. However, quicker to react than the previous year, the NVA soon were pounding Company B's strongpoint with mortars and recoilless rifles and ringing the area with antiaircraft guns. Then a signal intercept disclosed that the entire 1,500-man NVA 27th Infantry Regiment was en route: clearly, after five days of intense fighting, it was time to extract the Hatchet Force.

Covey Rider Lloyd O'Daniels used 32 F-4 Phantoms with 200 tons of ordnance to assist Company B's 1-kilometer march to an extraction LZ. Under such constant heavy bombardment, the NVA were unable to maneuver or disrupt the extraction.

About half of Company B's Americans were wounded, with Lt. Billy Potter seriously hit by an AK. The single U.S. fatality was Special Forces medic Bill Boyle, whose Kingbee was shot down when he attempted to extract wounded SOG men; his body was not recovered. Also lost were two Kingbee crews and about 10 Montagnards. U.S. Air Force photo interpreters credited Company B with killing or wounding 800 NVA soldiers and disrupting road traffic. For his gallantry under fire, Bill Blankenburg was awarded a Silver Star.

Just six months later, this same Company B would conduct what many thought the greatest Hatchet Force success in SOG history— Operation Tailwind—the subject of the next chapter.

Besieged Ben Het Special Forces camp, only 15 miles from Hatchet Force roadblock, was totally cut off and dependent on aerial resupply. (Photo provided by U.S. Air Force)

333

Top: These knocked-out NVA tanks hit Ben Het only hours before Hatchet Force cut Highway 110. (Photo provided by Shelby Stanton)

Bottom: Hatchet Force roadblock (right) faced Highway 110, about 300 meters away. (Photo provided by Frank Greco)

Above: The patch of Company A, CCC, unit that blocked Laotian Highway 110 in 1969. (Photo provided by Scott Kilpatrick)

Top left: Hurriedly digging trenches and bunkers, Hatchet Force cut the road and fought off all attempts to seize the hilltop, which was occupied in 1969 and 1970. (Photo provided by Frank Greco)

Bottom: View of Highway 110 from Hatchet Force hilltop position. (Photo provided by Gene McCarley)

335

Top: Denuded trees and shell-pocked ground attest to the heavy incoming fire on road-block position. (Photo provided by Gene McCarley)

Bottom: The Hatchet Force constantly called air strikes on the enemy. Observed and adjusted here by Rich Ryan (right) during the 1970 roadblock. (Photo provided by Rich Ryan)

Cobra gunship turns tight on
perimeter, firing into NVA
trenches just outside the roadblock position. (Photo provided
by Gene McCarley)

Hit by enemy fire, H-34 Kingbee autorotates into the Hatchet Forces perimeter. (Photo provided by Gene McCarley)

Sergeant First Class Brinkmiere mans the heaviest weapon on the roadblock, a 60mm mortar. (Photo provided by Gene McCarley)

Top: Lt. Frank Longaker (right) laughs during a lull in the fighting while readying belts of machine gun ammo. (Photo provided by Frank Longaker)

Bottom: An F-100 rolls into bomb trucks on Highway 110, backed up by Hatchet Force roadblock. (Photo provided by Frank Greco)

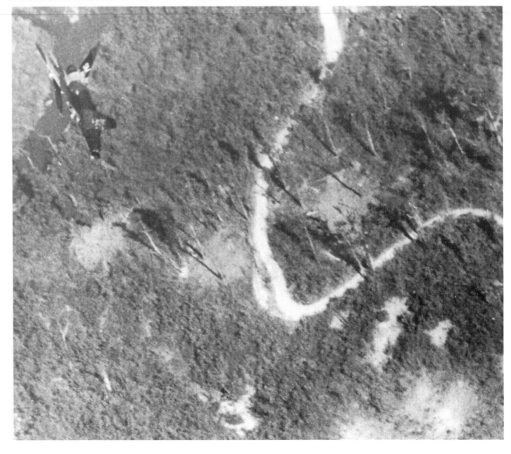

Bombs pound NVA trucks and supplies that have been trapped by a SOG roadblock. (Photo provided by Frank Greco)

Inset: Destroyed NVA trucks and scattered supplies about 1 1/2 miles west of the roadblock. (Photo provided by Frank Greco)

Top: Special Forces medic Bill Boyle (right), who was killed in the helicopter shootdown, standing here with actress Martha Raye, Capt. Bud Williams (left), and Medal of Honor winner Fred Zabitosky. (Photo provided by Gene McCarley)

Bottom: The H-34 Kingbee Bill Boyle was aboard, shown here seconds after impact. The H-34 crashed hard after its tail was shot off. (Photo provided by Mike Buckland)

Top: U.S. fighters bombed (left) the area, hoping that Hatchet Force men could rush from the roadblock perimeter (right) to retrieve Boyle and the air crewmen. (Photo provided by Mike Buckland)

Bottom: But H-34 exploded and burned furiously, reducing all aboard to ashes within minutes. Boyle's body was not recovered. (Photo provided by Mike Buckland)

Capt. Mecky Schuler's Hatchet
Force company overran this
NVA way station 25 miles
northwest of Khe Sanh. Sign
says, "Defeat the American
aggressors and the Vietnamese
traitors." (Photo provided by
Mecky Schuler)

Top: Cache of antiaircraft machine gun mounts demolished by Schuler's Hatchet Force. (Photo provided by Mecky Schuler)

Bottom: Hatchet Force Co. B, CCC, marches cross country in Laos, 1969. S. Sgt. Mike Sheppard is in the center. (Photo provided by Mike Sheppard)

Ready for his Hatchet Force combat assault, Bru tribesman Cum Ba sits in Huey door. (Photo provided by Bob Donoghue)

Top: Sgts. Bob Donoghue (center left) and Bob Shippen with Hatchet Force Montagnards on Laotian highway with NVA they have just killed in an ambush. Note the security man in the rear. (Photo provided by Bob Donoghue)

Bottom: Green Berets of CCC Hatchet Force savor a cold beer on the helipad after a dangerous operation in Laos, 1970. In the rear row, second from left is 1st Sgt. Richard Carnagey and to his right is Sfc. Ken "Shoe Box" Carpenter. (Photo provided by Chuck Karwan)

CCS Hatchet Force's 1st Exploitation Company displays seven battle streamers on its unofficial unit colors. (Photo provided by Dick Johnson)

Top: A shell-shocked Hatchet Force Montagnard decompresses after days of hard fighting. Note the shrapnel damage to his helmet and the bullet hole in the forearm of his CAR-15. (Photo provided by Frank Greco)

Bottom: VICTORY PARTY. Sgt. Jan Brady (left) and S. Sgt. Earl Savage hold a captured AK and a Soviet 12.7mm heavy machine gun after an operation in Laos, September 1969. (Photo provided by Frank Longaker)

Inset: CCN Hatchet Force preparing for an operation in Laos. (Photo provided by George Gaspard)

Left: Hatchet Force troops advance along a Ho Chi Minh Trail side road, 1967. (Photo provided by Mecky Schuler)

LOST HATCHET FORCE COMMANDERS

FIGHTING SIDE BY SIDE WITH THEIR NUNGS, Montagnards, and fellow Green Berets, three Hatchet Force company commanders paid the ultimate price.

Captain Dick Legate's company was exploring a recently abandoned enemy base camp in Laos on 25 March 1967 when they discovered freshly washed NVA uniforms hanging from a clothesline. Mindful of their intelligence value, Captain Legate was photographing the uniforms when a hidden NVA shot and killed him.

Capt. Ronald Goulet had been CCC's Recon Company commander, but that meant too much desk time so he volunteered to lead Hatchet Force Company B. Enthusiastic and fearless, he saved Mike Sheppard's life by pulling him from a crashed and burning Kingbee on 24 September 1969. Two days later, after his men had seized a large enemy cache in Laos, Goulet was killed when an RPG round detonated beside him.

When a recon team sighted a convoy of three-wheeled bicycles carrying supplies from Cambodia into South Vietnam's Plei Trap Valley, Capt. Fred Krupa's Hatchet Force was ordered to raid the spot as a likely enemy logistics stockpile. On 27 April 1971 Captain Krupa was riding the lead Huey, ready to be the first man to step out onto the LZ when a burst of enemy fire hit his helicopter. He was wounded and fell onto the LZ, even as heavy enemy fire drove his damaged Huey away. Although an attempt was made to mount a rescue mission, Fred Krupa—living or dead—was never recovered. He is the only Hatchet Force company commander among SOG's MIAs.

Chapter Seventeen

Operation Tailwind

In the late summer of 1970, the North Vietnamese seized the most critical terrain in southern Laos, the Bolovens Plateau, and overran several CIA airfields and forward bases. Two CIA-supported Hmong battalions attempted to recapture the most important strongpoint, but the more numerous NVA forces repelled attack after attack.

In this critical situation, the CIA asked Chief SOG John Sadler for a Hatchet Force company to land 40 miles northeast of the Bolovens and kick up such a ruckus in the enemy rear that Hanoi would pull some troops off the plateau. No SOG Hatchet Force had ever been so deep into Laos, so the possibilities seemed lucrative. With the approval of the U.S. ambassador in Vientiane and the concurrence of Gen. Creighton Abrams in Saigon, Operation Tailwind was a "go."

Company B, CCC, led by Capt. Eugene McCarley, was assigned the diversionary mission. On 11 September 1970, McCarley's 126 SOG raiders launched from Dak To aboard four huge CH-53 Sikorskys of the U.S. Marine Corps' HMH-463 squadron, escorted by 12 Marine Cobra gunships. Almost immediately upon crossing into Laos, NVA gunners began spraying the air with heavy machine guns. Inside the semitrailer-sized cargo compartments, bullets cracked through the floors amid the din of whining turbines, but the huge choppers just kept lumbering between the jungled hills and limestone

Sfc. Denver Minton leads a B-Company platoon to the helipad for departure for Operation Tailwind. (Photo provided by Gene McCarley)

bluffs. Then the CH-53s circled down and landed, disgorging the SOG company. For the next three days, all day, Cobras or A-1 Skyraiders or AC-130 Spectres would be overhead.

Captain McCarley immediately began advancing northwest because he knew any hesitation would allow the NVA to fix and overrun his unit. As quickly as they left the LZ, they ran into an NVA squad that fired a few rounds and fled. Then the SOG point squad reported bunkers.

McCarley had several squads sweep through to see what they'd found—a 500-yard-long line of bunkers crammed with 122mm and 140mm rockets, *thousands of rockets*. Hurriedly, Sp5c. Craig Schmidt and

Sfc. Jim Brevelle laid a demolition charge in each of the 20 bunkers, dual-priming each charge with a time-delay detonator.

Company B had marched 1,000 yards when an explosion that shook the ground was followed by 30 secondary explosions; rockets would continue cooking off for 12 hours with the resounding echoes announcing a challenge: *Come on down and try to stop us.*

One NVA platoon took the challenge. McCarley and his men shot it out and then backed off, called in fighters on the NVA unit, and continued west. Hatchet Force attempted to medevac several seriously wounded Montagnards, but before a chop-

per could land, 150 NVA soldiers attacked. The Hatchet Force fought them off, called in air strikes, and, carrying its wounded along, kept going west.

By now it was almost dark, time to set up a perimeter for night—that's what the NVA would expect. But, determined not to stop long enough for the enemy to mass superior forces, McCarley kept Company B moving. All night the men of Company B bumped into NVA squads, and each time either a salvo from AC-130 gunships or a quick assault forced the enemy elements aside. Nothing would stop Company B. By dawn nine of the 16 Americans and even more Montagnards had

been wounded. The Hatchet Force medic, Sgt. Gary Michael Rose, patched them up and kept them moving.

Not long after sunrise Company B hit an NVA delaying position, and five NVA soldiers, then another 40, hit the company's left flank, supported by mortars and rocket launchers. Company B fought through and called in air strikes. By midday the company's men were walking a ridge a half-mile above Highway 165 when the jungle thinned and they could see the road and hundreds of NVA troops with a dozen trucks alongside. A pair of A-1 Skyraiders destroyed the trucks and scattered the infantry.

The tactically adroit McCarley

Loaded down with ammo and explosives, McCarley's Hatchet Force troops would be almost out of ammo just three days later. (Photo provided by Gene McCarley)

Hatchet Force loads aboard U.S. Marine Corps CH-53s for airlift deep into Laos. (Photo provided by Gene McCarley)

kept off roads and main trails, hurrying along streambeds, small paths, or thinly vegetated ridges. Each time the NVA blocked his unit's way, he pounded them with air strikes and bypassed them.

By now, with more than two dozen men wounded, some seriously, movement was becoming impeded. A CH-53 carrying SOG medics John Padgett and John Browne arrived to extract the worst cases, but before the first casualty was aboard enemy fire surged and the pilot had to climb away. An RPG hit the Sikorsky amidships, but the projectile didn't detonate. The chopper limped 5 miles and sat down, but another arriving CH-53 was also shot down. Finally, a

third helicopter rescued the medics and crews.

By the second night the Hatchet Force men had to get some rest. McCarley had them dig in overlooking the road, on the highest ground he could find. NVA forces probed all night, mostly lobbing RPGs, which were answered by claymores and Spectre gunship fire. Few men slept.

Expecting an NVA attack at dawn, McCarley had his men under way an hour before daylight. It was long and arduous, but day three went like day two, with the advancing SOG company parrying enemy blows, destroying stockpiles, and continuing the march westward.

By the fourth morning, most

Hatchet Force men were so exhausted that they wanted to die; they'd fought their way cross country for 15 miles through thick jungle at an extraordinary pace. That fourth morning they marched another three hours when the point took fire from a few NVA soldiers, who fled into a bunker area. McCarley ordered an attack after softening up the NVA positions with air strikes and small-arms fire. Craig Schmidt and another squad leader, Sgt. Manuel Orozco, got their troops on line and assaulted. The enemy fell back, abandoning a battalion-sized base camp except for two bunkers held by NVA holdouts. While fire kept the enemy heads down, two 'Yards crept forward and rolled grenades to the bunkers.

The base camp was seized, but by now the SOG force wounded had risen to 49—making for nearly 50 percent casualties—and the sole, overstretched medic, Doc Rose, himself wounded twice, could barely keep up with the work. Searching the NVA camp, Company B men discovered four trucks, a 120mm mortar, and 9 tons of rice. Then one of the search parties called Captain McCarley to a large bunker where maps covered the walls and hundreds of pounds of documents were stored in footlockers and pouches. It was a major logistical command center, probably the *binh tram* headquarters that controlled Highway 165. "Pack

The last of McCarley's 126 SOG troopers board Jolly Greens of U.S. Marine Corps Squadron HMH-463. (Photo provided by Gene McCarley)

357

up all the documents," McCarley ordered; the company would carry them out.

By now, four days into the mission, FACs overhead could see enemy units converging on Company B from two directions. Every American had been wounded, and several men had suffered multiple wounds. It was time to get out. To expedite movement McCarley abandoned the jungle for a smooth road and poured on the speed. Then came word that the U.S. Marine CH-53s would be there in 30 minutes.

Despite his fatigue, McCarley fought smart and refused to use the first LZ encountered because enemy gunners on high ground could fire down on the Sikorskys. McCarley's men advanced to another LZ while Covey Rider William "Country" Grimes brought in A-1s led by Air Force Maj. Art Bishop with CBU-30 tear gas bomblets to blind antiaircraft gunners. Then one CH-53 landed and lifted away the most badly wounded and the captured documents. NVA mortars began pounding the LZ but were answered by F-4 Phantoms that swooped low with napalm. Air Force 1st Lt. Tom Stump, who would received a Distinguished Flying Cross for his actions, maneuvered his A-1 beneath low clouds to dump cluster bombs and napalm across swarms of closing enemy soldiers.

McCarley led his two remaining platoons to another LZ where Cobra and Skyraider fire and a sudden landing generated only moderate groundfire. A second Company B platoon climbed into a CH-53 for a clean getaway. Meanwhile, NVA troops by the hundreds were streaming out of the hills and letting loose an almost constant barrage. Down to his last platoon, McCarley boldly advanced to a

third LZ while Cobras and A-1s hit ahead and behind the running SOG men, pounding the NVA with rockets, tear gas, and cluster bombs. With the enemy close behind, the SOG men trotted into the 6-foot-high grass LZ just as the last CH-53 came in. McCarley was the last man to climb aboard.

The extraction had been extraordinary, requiring strikes from 72 U.S. fighters and nearly a half-million pounds of bombs, rockets, and napalm. The SOG men had nothing but praise for the A-1 aviators and Marine pilots who flew repeatedly through heavy fire but never flinched. "Cool, real cool" was how one SOG man described them.

Company B had suffered three Montagnards killed and 33 wounded, along with all 16 Americans being wounded. In three days of heavy fighting Company B had killed 144 NVA soldiers and wounded another 50, with an estimated 288 additional enemy killed by air.

Not only did the diversion succeed, allowing the CIA Hmong force to recapture the strongpoint, but the NVA documents proved a virtual bonanza. The U.S. command's most senior intelligence officer called them "the most significant collateral intelligence on the [Ho Chi Minh Trail] since the beginning of the war." Chief SOG Sadler reported, "[Major General] Potts and Abrams told me they didn't appreciate the full implications of [the Trail system] until all those documents came back."

Two weeks later, the U.S. Marine CH-53 and Cobra aircrews flew to Kontum to celebrate with Company B. They didn't have to buy a drink all night.

Left: BEFORE AND AFTER. Operation Tailwind commander, Capt. Eugene McCarley, aboard U.S. Marine Corps CH-53 en route to Laos. (Photo provided by Gene McCarley)

Inset: WELCOME BACK. Four days later, exhausted and twice wounded, McCarley is welcomed back by old friend Sfc. Wesley McCaslin. (Photo provided by Ted Wicorek)

Top: The last U.S. Marine Corps Jolly Green lifts off from Dak To. Two would be shot down, but miraculously no crewmen were killed. (Photo provided by Gene McCarley)

Bottom: GOING IN! Aboard U.S. Marine Corps CH-53 en route to the LZ, Gary Michael Rose (center) and Captain McCarley (right) camouflage faces. (Photo provided by Gene McCarley)

Top: Six of the 12 Marine Corps Cobra gunships that flew more than 100 sorties for Tailwind on strip alert at Dak To. (Photo provided by Gene McCarley)

Bottom: Air Force pilot 1st Lt. Tom Stump beside his Skyraider. He was awarded a Distinguished Flying Cross for his spectacular flying, which allowed extraction of outnumbered Hatchet Force. (Photo provided by Tom Stump)

Hatchet Force NCO Sgt. Dave Young during a lull in the fighting along Highway 165 in Laos. (Photo provided by Gene McCarley)

Top: Air Force Maj. Art Bishop, who braved heavy groundfire to drop CS gas bomblets that held off swarms of NVA at McCarley's extraction LZ. (Photo provided by Art Bishop)

Bottom: NVA hootch in *binh tram* overrun by Company B. Rear echelon NVA troops put up a weak fight and suffered about 50 KIA. (Photo provided by Gene McCarley)

Top: While one platoon defends against counterattack, McCarley's men hastily search captured *binh tram*, discovering the most important documents ever brought out of Laos. (Photo provided by Gene McCarley)

Bottom: Cheerful despite his wounds, Montagnard medic Koch limps from the helipad with satchels of captured documents. (Photo provided by Gene McCarley)

Top: Sp5c. Craig Schmidt (center) proudly holds captured booty—Ho Chi Minh's portrait displayed until that morning at a *binh tram* on Highway 165 in Laos. His Tailwind soldiers are Sgt. Manuel Orozco (left) and S. Sgt. Donald Boudreau. (Photo provided by Gene McCarley)

Bottom: TAILWIND PARTY. A week after the last shots were fired, Company-B Americans and Montagnards welcome U.S. Marine aircrews for steaks and drinks. (Photo provided by Craig Schmidt)

Thirteen of the 16 Hatchet Force men on Operation Tailwind. Every one of them was wounded, some several times. (Photo provided by Gene McCarley)

HATCHET FORCE MEN ON OPERATION TAILWIND

Capt. Eugene C. McCarley

1st Sgt. Morris Adair

Sgt. Gary Michael Rose

1st Lt. Pete Landon

1st Lt. Robert Van Buskirk

Sfc. Jim Brevelle

Sfc. Bernard Bright

S. Sgt. Donald Boudreau

Sgt. Michael Hagen

Sp5c. Jim Lucas

Sfc. Denver Minton

Sgt. Manuel Orozco

S. Sgt. Keith Plancich

S. Sgt. William Scherer

Sp5c. Craig Schmidt

Sgt. Dave Young

Left: SOG veterans with current Secretary of Defense William Cohen, who rebutted the Cable News Network allegations on Tailwind. Left to right: Chief SOG John Sadler, Eugene McCarley, Chief SOG Jack Singlaub, Secretary Cohen, Medic Gary Michael Rose, Special Forces Association representative Rudy Gresham, Bobby Pinkerton, and John Plaster. (Photo provided by Department of Defense)

Below: Shoulder tab for CCC's Company B of the Hatchet Force. (Photo provided by Harry Pugh)

THE TAILWIND AFFAIR

IN JUNE 1998 CABLE NEWS NETWORK (CNN) BROADCAST a report worldwide alleging that Operation Tailwind had been a far more sinister mission than depicted here. According to the broadcast and an accompanying article for *Time* magazine, coauthored by CNN reporter Peter Arnett and producer April Oliver, Tailwind's purpose actually had been to kill U.S. defectors in Laos, using sarin nerve gas.

The charges were preposterous, an affront not just to the Tailwind men, but to all SOG men killed and wounded while attempting to rescue U.S. POWs and MIAs. Indeed, the NCO club at the Kontum base, from which Tailwind had been launched, was named for Hatchet Force NCO Fred "Huckleberry" Lewis, killed along with Charlie Vessels in Operation Crimson Tide, the bloody 1966 attempt to rescue a U.S. POW, Capt. Carl Jackson.

After the CNN broadcast many SOG veterans—along with the Special Operations and the Special Forces Associations—launched a nationwide campaign to persuade the media that the charges were false. Secretary of Defense William Cohen and Joint Chiefs of Staff Chairman Gen. Hugh Shelton—a Green Beret Vietnam veteran—oversaw a thorough investigation of the CNN/*Time* charges. What followed was the most dramatic media turnaround in history. *Time* magazine apologized, and CNN retracted the story. Three CNN employees lost their jobs, including the story producer, April Oliver; while the reporter, Peter Arnett, did not have his contract renewed when it expired later. And, at last, the Defense Department began to consider SOG for its long-deserved Presidential Unit Citation, along with an upgrading to an award of the Medal of Honor for Tailwind medic Gary Rose and to the Distinguished Service Cross for the Tailwind commander, Capt. Eugene McCarley.

TAILWIND'S GALLANT MEDIC

THE MOST SELFLESS, COURAGEOUS MAN AMONG THEM, Tailwind veterans agree, was the young Special Forces medic, Sgt. Gary "Mike" Rose, who alone treated some 49 casualties, despite being wounded three times himself.

Throughout those four seemingly endless days, Mike Rose was everywhere, hustling to keep men alive, helping to carry the worst cases himself, charging through enemy fire to treat fallen Montagnards or Americans, even sheltering the wounded with his own body to protect them during NVA bombardments.

Below left: Twice wounded, his shirt torn off, Tailwind medic Gary Michael Rose is walked from the helipad by S. Sgt. Bill Spurgeon (left) and Charles Thomas. (Photo provided by Ted Wicorek)

While others slept Doc Rose worked; while others ate Doc Rose worked. He never complained; he just saved lives. Eventually the wounded count rose to 49 men—almost half the Hatchet Force—but that sorely overworked medic never paused for a second. He was an inspiration to all those around him.

After the operation, Sergeant Rose was recommended for the Medal of Honor, but it was downgraded to the Distinguished Service Cross, which was presented to him by Gen. Creighton Abrams in 1971. However, in 1999 Secretary of Defense William Cohen, with the urging of the Tailwind commander, Captain McCarley, called for a review of the recommendation. Should it be approved, Mike Rose's Medal of Honor would be the eleventh awarded to a SOG member.

Below right: Gen. Creighton Abrams, commander of U.S. forces in Vietnam, presents the Distinguished Service Cross to Gary Michael Rose while CCC commander Lt. Col. Serafino Scalise watches. (Photo provided by Ted Wicorek)

PART SEVEN

OTHER FRONTS IN THE SECRET WARS

Chapter Eighteen

Bright Light Rescues

Since SOG was the only U.S. military organization operating secretly throughout Southeast Asia—with its own aircraft, raiding forces, recon units and naval arm—the U.S. Joint Chiefs appointed SOG the primary agency for tracking and rescuing POWs and evadees and retrieving downed airmen after normal Search and Rescue efforts had ended. This rescue program was code-named Bright Light.

To coordinate with outside agencies this effort required its own cover, the Joint Personnel Recovery Center, a supposed MACV staff section. Bright Light's first chief, Col. Harry "Heinie" Aderholt, one of the U.S. Air Force's most experienced special operations officers, had had previous classified tours on loan to the CIA, including heading a top-secret airlift to Tibetan guerrillas in the 1950s. Aderholt proposed recruiting a North Vietnamese guerrilla force to man enclaves west of Hanoi where U.S. flyers could bail out into friendly hands. Washington policymakers turned this down, as they did a SOG proposal for guerrilla-held bailout areas in nearby Laos. The U.S. ambassador to Laos so adamantly opposed SOG operations that available records indicate not one POW rescue mission's being approved beyond SOG's normal 20-kilometer limit in Laos despite many reports of POWs.

This cage had held U.S. POWs but was hastily evacuated before the rescue attempt. (Photo provided by Department of Defense)

SOG still did what it could to enhance the survival of downed aircrews. For example, recon man Bob Howard explored Laotian valleys on the North Vietnamese border to find passes through the rugged terrain for evadees to escape into Laos. And SOG developed airdroppable survival kits.

EARLY BRIGHT LIGHTS

Bright Light missions became some of SOG's hairiest operations. The first Bright Light into North Vietnam, led by the legendary recon One-Zero Dick Meadows, went after a downed U.S. Navy pilot, Lt. Dean Woods, deep in North Vietnam's heartland, halfway between Vinh and Hanoi. Riding Navy Sea King helicopters from the USS *Intrepid*, RT Iowa was inserted about 800 yards from Lieutenant Woods, but the NVA had just captured him.

Meadows attempted to kidnap an NVA officer—leading to a short gunfight and three enemy KIA—then it was time to be extracted. Hit by gunfire, RT Iowa's helicopter had to ditch near a destroyer, but every man made it out.

That same day in Saigon a Vietcong defector told U.S. interrogators that his Mekong Delta camp held an American POW. The name "Jackson" sounded familiar. Air Force Capt. Carl Jackson had been MIA since his C-123 had been downed southwest of Saigon in June 1965.

SOG prepared a company-sized Hatchet Force rescue, Operation Crimson Tide, led by Capt. Hartmut "Mecky" Schuler under mission commander Capt. Frank Jaks. After repeated delays, finally this force was launched from a staging base in the Mekong Delta, but there had been almost no briefing and only fragments

Top: Meadows' Sea King helicopter limped out to sea but had to ditch beside a destroyer similar to the one shown here. (Photo provided by U.S. Navy)

Left: Meadows' North Vietnam Bright Light.

Above: M. Sgt. Dick Meadows (left) and RT Iowa. (Photo provided by Charlie Norton)

CHINA

HANOI

LAOS

DOWNED
PILOT

VINH

DMZ

**MEADOWS
NORTH VIET NAM
"BRIGHT LIGHT"**

The bodies of two U.S. fliers recovered by a Bright Light team and lashed to poles to be carried to an LZ. This was a dangerous, physically demanding job. (Photo provided by Bryon Loucks)

of intelligence. Jaks and Schuler felt uneasy about it.

As the SOG men landed, hellacious fire erupted—a massive ambush set by two Vietcong battalions! One Hatchet Force platoon took the brunt of the fire, with almost all its Nungs killed or wounded and both its Green Beret leaders, Sfcs. Charles Vessels and Fred "Huckleberry" Lewis, killed. It was a bloody price paid by good men who'd done their all for Captain Jackson.

One week later SOG scored its first Bright Light success. An F-105 Thunderchief pilot had bailed out of his crippled aircraft over southern Laos in an area infested with NVA

forces, and SOG Hueys had reached him in the nick of time. "When he got in that helicopter, I'll tell you, he was one happy fella," SOG medic Luke Nance said.

The F-105 pilot was the first of dozens of airmen extracted by SOG—but few aviators had any idea that top-secret SOG teams stood ready to retrieve them from Laos and North Vietnam.

BRIGHT LIGHT TEAMS

SOG eventually kept recon teams on strip alert a week at a time on Bright Light duty, packed and ready to go 24 hours a day, so that as quickly as a Jolly Green helicopter or a C-130 could pick them up, the teams could go on a rescue mission. While on Bright Light duty, One-Zeros "went heavy" with all 12 team members and their heaviest weapons—M60 machine guns and 60mm mortars—along with plenty of ammo, extra first aid gear, rappeling harnesses, and helicopter extraction rigs. The concept was to strike swiftly with great firepower, get the downed airman or evadee, and get out.

These rescue missions were consistently dangerous, putting teams into areas bristling with antiaircraft guns or, sometimes, a well-prepared enemy lying in ambush. Bright Light missions in North Vietnam always were the worst, given the sophistication of enemy defenses, which at times included SAMs and MiGs. Several times, Bright Light rescues were aborted when a downed pilot was cryptically able to warn that he already was in enemy hands.

In-country Bright Lights were no less dramatic. In July 1969, a communist defector told debriefers that he knew of an NVA hospital near Chu Lai where a black GI,

Sp4c. Larry Aiken, was being held. On 10 July 1969 an Allied force raided it just as the NVA forces fled, after hacking the young soldier's head with a machete—Larry Aiken was still barely alive but died 10 days later. It was the closest SOG had come to liberating an American POW.

SEAL RESCUE ATTEMPTS

U.S. Navy SEALs and South Vietnamese Sea Commandos attempted a series of POW rescues for SOG in the Mekong Delta. Paddling small rubber boats, SOG's SEAL-led Sea Commandos slipped ashore from the USS *Washtenaw County* on 8 November 1971 in search of U.S. Army S. Sgt. Gerasimo Arroyo-Baez. Disguised as Vietcong, the Sea Commandos made it to the outskirts of the camp and kidnapped a VC sentry, who mistook them for fellow VC. Although the VC captive agreed to go back and assist in Arroyo-Baez's release, he vanished. The Communists did return Arroyo-Baez's remains to the United States in 1985 but offered no explanation for his death.

On another occasion, the SEALs hit a camp that was claimed to hold two Americans. The raiders found "partially cooked meals and miscellaneous equipment," a SOG report discloses. When they swept another nearby camp, they reported, "Warm rice indicated that the camp had been vacated only 2–3 hours before."

Despite good planning and aggressive execution, the SEALs did not recover a single American, although they liberated 49 South Vietnamese soldiers.

FRUSTRATIONS

"It was very frustrating," Chief SOG Col. John Sadler said, "because it got to the point that you knew [POWs] had been there by [the] writing on the wall and knots on the ropes."

SOG even offered ransoms for POWs—$5,000 apiece to any NVA soldier or VC who could deliver a living American. SOG Capt. Fred Caristo met several times with an alleged VC POW camp commander, offering him $25,000 cash if he brought out five Americans, but it was only an elaborate scam by the alleged camp commander. Other SOG negotiators offered a VC camp commander more than $100,000 for 21 U.S. POWs, but nothing came of that, either.

In a few instances SOG purchased American bodies, which at least gave families the comfort of knowing what had happened to a loved one, so there was a degree of mercy in this. And on a score of Bright Light missions, SOG teams brought out pilots' bodies, so all was not for nothing.

But assessing the overall effort generates some troubling statistics: during the entire war, SOG raids liberated 492 ARVN troopers but not one living American. In hundreds of cases SOG anticipated finding Americans, only to learn they'd been moved just before the raid. The failures were chalked up to bad luck and the enemy's practice of frequently moving POWs. There was, however, more to it: North Vietnamese intelligence had a mole in SOG headquarters in Saigon, an unscrupulous South Vietnamese officer who secretly spied for Hanoi.

But the mole could not compromise the war's greatest Bright Light mission: the Son Tay raid was planned and prepared far away from this traitor's eyes in the United States. This story of great courage and skill is told in the following chapter.

Above: Unit patch for Capt. Mecky Schuler's Hatchet Force company. (Photo provided by Scott Kilpatrick)

Top right: Capt. Frank Jaks and the Vietcong defector whose information led to Operation Crimson Tide. (Photo provided by Frank Jaks)

Bottom: Air Force Capt. Carl Jackson, missing since his C-123 was downed in 1965, was the focus of Operation Crimson Tide. He remains missing. (Photo provided by the Jackson family)

Above: Sfc. Fred Lewis was known as "Huckleberry" because of his preference for a straw hat. J.D. Bath said of Lewis, "He had a country way about him." Huckleberry and Charlie Vessels and almost all their Nungs were massacred on Crimson Tide. (Photo provided by Frank Jaks)

Top left: Crimson Tide Hatchet Force commander, Capt. Mecky Schuler (in cab). (Photo provided by Frank Jaks)

Operation Crimson Tide

Saigon ★

Camp Location

Top: Captain Schuler's Nungs at Kontum airfield await a C-130 for the flight to the Mekong Delta. One-third of them would be dead by nightfall. (Photo provided by Mecky Schuler)

Bottom: Body bags are brought in after Operation Crimson Tide. One entire platoon was massacred; the dead included Sfcs. Charles Vessels and Fred Lewis. (Photo provided by Mecky Schuler)

Top: Bright Lights in North Vietnam and near Mu Ghia Pass ran the risk of SAMs and MiGs. These two North Vietnamese MiGs were photographed from the ground by a SOG recon team. (Photo provided by J.D. Callahan)

Bottom: Recon team Bright Light gear packed and ready to go at a moment's notice, at Dak To launch site. (Photo provided by Newell Bernard)

Top: Stocks for holding POWs in a Vietcong camp. (Photo provided by U.S. Army)

Bottom: SOG air-dropped millions of pamphlets over Laos and Cambodia offering rewards for U.S. POWs. Despite contacts from shadowy middlemen, no ransom was ever paid. (Photo provided by U.S. Air Force)

Top: The body of a missing GI is recovered after SOG negotiated and paid a reward. One American family can find closure. (Photo provided by Bill Kendall)

Bottom: A rescue chopper with a Bright Light team arrives at a Kingbee crash site but finds no sign of life. (Photo provided by Mike Buckland)

ONE BRIGHT LIGHT

WHEN A RECON TEAM WAS ON BRIGHT LIGHT duty anything could happen—one minute you're eating C-rations, the next you're in a rappeling rig, grabbing a CAR-15, and hustling for the cranking Hueys. A typical case was on 15 April 1970.

RT Montana with Mike Sheppard, Joe Sample, and Dennis Neal was at SOG's Dak To launch site when word came that a Huey had been shot down on the border 30 miles away. Four U.S. aviators were running for their lives.

RT Montana's first of two rescue Hueys took heavy fire as it settled into an LZ near the pilots. Gunfire sprayed the helicopter, wounding Joe Sample, Dennis Neal, two Montagnards, and all but one of the Huey crewmen. Still, the RT members grabbed the two downed airmen, shot two NVA soldiers beside the helicopter, and lifted away. Orbiting low overhead in the second rescue bird, Sheppard and three 'Yards fired in support as their comrades cleared the LZ. But the lead Huey had been badly damaged and, unable to reach Dak To, made an emergency landing at Dak Seang Special Forces camp—but that camp was under enemy attack. Both Hueys took more hits as they landed. Sheppard dashed through heavy fire to help the wounded lead pilot get to cover and then returned to lift his teammate, Sgt. Dennis Neal, and lay him on the ground. Neal opened his eyes, spoke once, and died. Then Sheppard carried Joe Sample to cover. Despite enemy fire, Sheppard loaded the wounded on two more Hueys and then administered first aid while en route to Dak To. Sheppard, Sample, and Neal were awarded Silver Stars, the latter posthumously.

It all had happened in less than one hour.

RT Arizona on Bright Light duty at Dak To (rear, left to right): Khek, Sgt. Kyle Dean, Kai, 1st Lt. Jim Young, Oi, Lon. (Front) Mui, Brea, Prea, Sgt. Mike Wilson, Ninh, and Thu. (Photo provided by Kyle Dean)

Above: U.S. Navy SEAL Barry Enoch during a raid in the Mekong Delta. SOG employed SEALs on numerous POW rescue attempts in the Delta, but, as elsewhere, the results were always negative. (Photo provided by Barry Enoch)

Left: A Kingbee pilot circles a downed wing mate, in readiness for a Bright Light mission. (Photo provided by Neil Terrell)

SOG'S LONGEST BRIGHT LIGHT

FOR 10 MONTHS IN 1968, SOG RAN REPEATED Bright Light missions along the Cambodian border, attempting to liberate three Americans kidnapped during the Tet Offensive. Michael Benge, a 37-year-old agricultural adviser; Betty Ann Olsen, 30, a nurse working with Montagnard lepers; and Henry Blood, 53, a Bible translator, had been seized near Ban Me Thuot and led away.

The first Bright Light, staged two weeks after their capture, involved three companies from the 173rd Airborne Brigade and five SOG teams. Only one team, led by Larry "Six Pack" White and Grant Bollenback, made contact with the NVA. Despite heavy fire, White dashed forward to grab a fistful of papers from a dead NVA soldier; the documents later disclosed that Benge, Olsen, and Blood were alive. Forced back by numerically superior forces, White's team members had no idea they had been so close that the American captives had heard their gunfire.

The prisoners were chained together and fed a starvation diet. A month later Benge contracted malaria; then Betty Olsen caught dengue fever. The North Vietnamese refused to treat them.

SOG was still on the captives' trail, launching another raid on 7 April, using a CIA-affiliated Phoenix Program platoon, and found an abandoned camp and evidence that the three Americans had been there only two days earlier. In mid-May intelligence reported that Blood, Benge, and Olsen were 35 miles from Ban Me Thuot. SOG sent in a Phoenix Program team that ran into an enemy company and barely broke free. Two more SOG teams were inserted, but again the party with the captives had moved on.

That summer Henry Blood died of pneumonia, and Benge and Olsen developed scurvy, their gums bleeding and open sores covering their limbs. In late November SOG inserted another team that found the enemy camp, just after the NVA force had left. Betty Ann Olsen grew weaker, and when she lagged, NVA escorts knocked her down and dragged her along. Finally, she simply could not move, and she died. Eventually Michael Benge was brought into Cambodia and up the Ho Chi Minh Trail into North Vietnam. He was released in 1973.

Civilian agricultural advisor Mike Benge sipping rice wine shortly before his capture by the NVA. (Photo provided by Mike Benge)

384

Top: S. Sgt. Larry White, whose recon team came closest to liberating the kidnapped Americans. (Photo provided by Larry White)

Bottom left: Betty Ann Olsen, a civilian nurse, was working with Montagnard lepers when she was taken captive by the NVA. While in captivity, she died of malnutrition and lack of medical care. (Photo provided by Department of Defense)

Bottom right: Bible translator Henry Blood was held captive with Benge and Olsen. He died of pneumonia. (Photo provided by Department of Defense)

Above left: M. Sgt. Sebastian "Tony" DeLuca, noncommissioned officer in charge of SOG's POW rescue program. (Photo provided by Jay Veith)

Above right: Floral arrangement and portrait of Sebastian DeLuca at SOG memorial ceremony in Saigon. (Photo provided by Jay Veith)

THE TRAGEDY OF SEBASTIAN DELUCA

M. SGT. SEBASTIAN "TONY" DELUCA, a former CCS recon man, understood the plight of POWs as few men ever would. As the noncommissioned officer in charge of SOG's OPS-80, he had planned many rescue missions. "He used to come down and talk to me about this thing, that he just couldn't pull anything off," said Lt. Col. Mike Radke, a SOG staff officer. DeLuca knew of POW camps outside SOG's area of operations in Laos and Cambodia, but nothing was being done about them.

One night in June 1971, DeLuca told CCS recon One-Zero Frank Burkhart about an NVA defector who'd identified a camp holding 12 U.S. prisoners in Cambodia, confirmed by aerial photos. The defector had passed a polygraph test, but Washington would not allow a rescue mission. Then DeLuca confided that he'd been working on something else using his own intelligence. The next morning DeLuca took a Thai Air flight to Bangkok, carrying along his collection of gold chains worth thousands of dollars. In Bangkok he met a mysterious Laotian woman with connections to certain middlemen in Laos. "And the last time anyone saw him," a SOG staff officer said, "he was walking into Laos by himself, to go out there and try to find prisoners."

A few weeks later SOG Capt. Jim Butler found DeLuca's bullet-riddled body and brought it back to Thailand. It is now known that the Green Beret was murdered by Royal Laotian soldiers—soldiers of a supposed U.S. ally. All DeLuca's gold, of course, had disappeared. "I feel so much compassion for the man because the whole idea of leaving these guys in there was so foreign to him," said Burkhart. "I'm not going to say he broke, but he just decided to go in and take care of it himself." Sebastian DeLuca was presented no posthumous award for valor, for his was an unauthorized rescue mission conducted while absent without leave.

SOG'S COMBAT RECON PLATOONS

WITH MOST OF ITS COMBAT UNITS having been withdrawn from Vietnam by 1971, the U.S. military lost most of its ability to rescue downed pilots anywhere in the country. To perform this mission, as well as to be ready to rescue POWs, SOG proposed the creation of two special raider companies, reduced by MACV to two platoons and designated Combat Recon Platoons One and Two, or CRP-1 and CRP-2. The U.S. Joint Chiefs approved the concept in May, as did General Abrams in June 1971, "to be effective only as long as MACSOG maintained an operational capability"—an important qualifier, because SOG's forces were also was being gradually disbanded.

CRP-1 was based at Danang and CRP-2 at Kontum. Each CRP contained three recon teams combined as a platoon. CRP-2 consisted of RT California under Donald Davidson and RT Hawaii under Les Dover, along with Larry Kramer's RT West Virginia, all led by Sfc. Donald "Ranger" Melvin.

The CRPs assumed POW rescue responsibilities throughout Southeast Asia but could do no more than U.S. policy allowed. On 24 February 1972, *Los Angeles Times* correspondent George McArthur warned that MACV was about to disband the CRPs of SOG, "its last cloak and dagger outfit specifically honed to fight its way in and out of prisoner camps," which "had stirred heated words within the headquarters of U.S. Gen. Creighton Abrams."

McArthur's exposé made no difference: in its haste to reduce U.S. personnel by 25 slots, MACV disbanded CRP-1 and -2, the last Bright Light elements left in Southeast Asia. There was no longer any unit to go after U.S. POWs or airmen downed behind enemy lines.

Above: Patch for CCN's CRP-1. (Photo provided by Scott Kilpatrick)

Left: Capt. Jim Storter, CCC Recon Company commander, trains with CRP-2 in the Central Highlands of South Vietnam. (Photo provided by Jim Storter)

TOM NORRIS AND THE RESCUE OF BAT-21

ON EASTER SUNDAY 1972, four days into the largest NVA offensive of the war, a SAM missile downed Bat-21, an RB-66 electronic-warfare plane, just below the DMZ. Only one crewman, U.S. Air Force Lt. Col. Iceal Gene Hambleton, 53, parachuted to safety.

Landing beside the Mien Giang River, Hambleton found himself in the middle of a multidivision NVA force, with SAMs, antiaircraft guns, tanks, artillery, and thousands of troops. During an attempt to extract him, heavy fire downed two choppers and drove other aircraft away; one Huey crew was lost. The next day enemy fire downed a FAC above Bat-21, so now there were two pilots to rescue, Hambleton and Lt. Mark Clark, who landed nearby.

As many as 90 air strikes per day, with everything from A-1s to B-52s, supported attempts to rescue the two pilots. Then an HH-53 Jolly Green went in, but NVA guns knocked it down, killing all six aboard. The next day, heavy gunfire knocked down another FAC, whose two crewmen became MIA. Having lost 11 airmen killed or missing, with two more captured and five aircraft lost, the Bat-21 rescue was given to SOG, which dispatched U.S. Marine Corps Lt. Col. Andrew Anderson to the scene. Any air approach was suicide, he concluded, so Anderson sent for a five-man SOG Sea Commando team and their advisor, SOG SEAL Lt. Tom Norris.

Lieutenant Clark was radioed and told to wait until dark and then to inflate his survival vest and float downstream to where Lieutenant Norris and the Sea Commandos—disguised as Communists in black pajamas—would be waiting. An NVA patrol caused Norris to lie low and let Lieutenant Clark float past, but eventually his team reached Clark and brought him out.

Exhausted after 10 days without food or rest—and having lost 45 pounds—Lieutenant Colonel Hambleton crawled a mile to reach the river but collapsed and lay beside it, unable to go on. Tom Norris would have to go get him.

Only one Vietnamese, Petty Officer Nguyen Van Kiet, volunteered to accompany Norris the following night. In pitch darkness they boarded a small

A map of the action that earned Tom Norris a Medal of Honor.

sampan and, disguised as fishermen, paddled quietly upriver. In the foggy darkness they accidentally went all the way to a bridge where NVA tanks and troops were crossing and had to turn back. Finally they found Hambleton hiding under brush at the river bank, delirious. They hid him in the sampan and paddled away, several times coasting past NVA sentries.

Just before dawn an enemy soldier waved and shouted, ordering them to land, but they pretended not to hear him. By dawn they were almost safely away when a heavy machine gun opened up; they took cover in high reeds and called in A-1s. They then directed a set of Phantoms to cover their final run-in by water. They landed safely, and just as Hambleton was being carried away a CBS News reporter arrived and asked Norris, "I bet you wouldn't do that again?" The SOG SEAL's eyes flashed. "An American was down in enemy territory," he said. "Of course, I'd do it again."

Lt. Tom Norris received SOG's only SEAL Medal of Honor, presented by President Gerald Ford. His courageous subordinate, Sea Commando Nguyen Van Kiet, was awarded the Navy Cross, the only Vietnamese to receive so high a U.S. award.

Above left: PO Nguyen Van Kiet, SOG Sea Commando who accompanied Norris on the Bat-21 rescue. For his actions, Nguyen was awarded the Navy Cross—no other Vietnamese received so high a U.S. decoration. (Photo provided by Nguyen Van Kiet)

Above: Lt. Col. Iceal Gene Hambleton, a crewman aboard RB-66, Bat-21. (Photo provided by U.S. Air Force)

Above: Lt. Tom Norris receives the Medal of Honor from President Gerald Ford. (Photo provided by National Archives)

Rigth: SOG SEAL Lt. Tom Norris, who led the Bat-21 rescue. (Photo provided by National Archives)

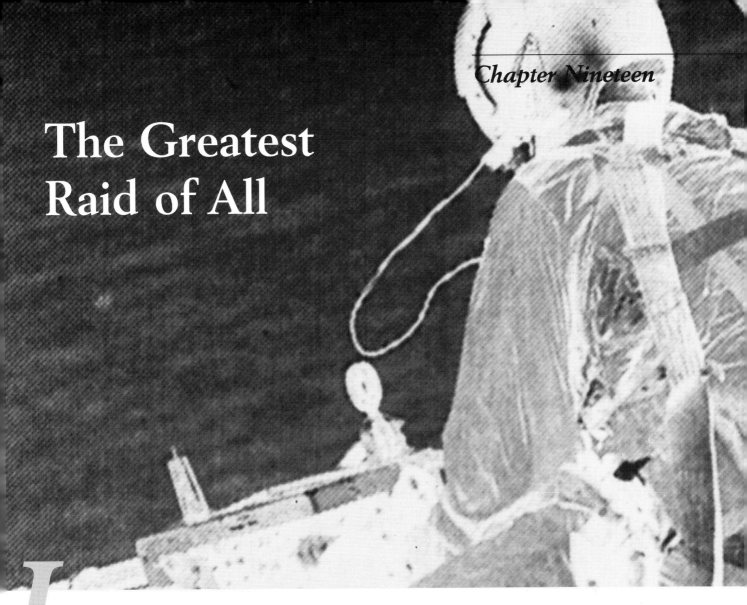

The Greatest Raid of All

Chapter Nineteen

I

In mid-1970, former Chief SOG Donald "Headhunter" Blackburn—now the Pentagon-based brigadier general overseeing worldwide U.S. special operations—was told by U.S. Air Force Brig. Gen. James Allen that a group of POWs in North Vietnam had secretly requested a rescue. Blackburn pondered hard and long. Hanoi was ignoring the Geneva Convention, and dozens of POWs had been tortured and killed or had died of sickness and abuse.

Because of the 1968 bombing halt not one U.S. bomb had hit the North in 19 months—resulting in such laxness there, Blackburn told the chairman of the U.S. Joint Chiefs, Gen. Earl Wheeler, that a rescue mission at a prison camp called Son Tay was worth attempting. General Wheeler concurred.

TARGET: SON TAY

Just 23 miles west of Hanoi, Son Tay Prison sat in a river bend surrounded by rice paddies. The walled compound was 125 feet by 175 feet, overseen by three guard towers. The prison's 57 guards lived in a barracks 100 feet away. The outer perimeter had trenches on the north and south, barbed wire on the east, and a river on the west. Intelligence warned that "the guards' instructions were to shoot the prisoners if any commotion started."

Son Tay raiders after one of their 172 rehearsals. (Photo provided by U.S. Air Force)

The closest outside forces were 100 NVA soldiers at a nearby arms plant; across a river footbridge was Son Tay's citadel with an NVA company-sized garrison. Labeled a "secondary school," one-fourth of a mile south of the prison lay another compound that vaguely resembled the real prison. The greatest dangers were 3 1/2 miles south at Son Tay military base, which housed an estimated 21,000 NVA soldiers, and at Phuc Yen airbase, 16 miles way, where MiGs were on strip alert.

SELECTION AND TRAINING

U.S. Air Force Brig. Gen. Leroy Manor was appointed the mission commander, with former SOG Shining Brass chief Col. Arthur "Bull" Simons as his deputy. Blackburn chose Lt. Col. Elliot "Bud" Sydnor as ground force commander. Leading the 14-man team that would crash-land in the prison was former SOG One-Zero Dick Meadows.

Aircrews included the U.S. Air Force's top Jolly Green, A-1, and C-130 flyers. For instance, Lt. Col. Herbert Zehnder had set a world record flying an HH-3 helicopter nonstop to the Paris Air Show and flew Jolly Greens in Vietnam, while Maj. Frederic Donahue had 131 combat missions in Jolly Greens. Not one aviator was less than the best.

The Special Forces selectees were veterans of such tough units as SOG, the Mike Forces, and Project Delta—only five of the 56 Green Beret volunteers had not seen combat. Training at Eglin Air Force Base, Florida, the Green Berets were told nothing of their target and were denied any visitors or mail. Their primary trainer was seasoned gunfighter Dick Meadows.

Aircrew training focused on night

operations, especially low-level flying. To eliminate two guard towers, Brigadier General Manor had an HH-53 pass between two mock towers and let rip with hand-fired 6,000-round-per-minute miniguns that *vaporized* the towers—that should do it! And to help the C-130 guide planes find their way, the CIA provided secret FLIR systems, which converted heat patterns into a visible TV image.

By the time they were deployed to Thailand in mid-November, the rescue team members had rehearsed their raid 172 times. "We wanted to be able to lose two of anything and still get our people out," U.S. Air Force planner Maj. Larry Ropka said.

PRESIDENTIAL APPROVAL

On 18 November 1970 U.S. Joint Chiefs of Staff Chairman Admiral Thomas Moorer and Brigadier General Blackburn briefed President Nixon, National Security Adivsor Henry Kissinger, and Secretary of Defense Melvin Laird. "I don't know any man that can sit in this job that could say 'no' to this attempt," Nixon said. Weighing heavily on the president's mind was the knowledge that 11 more POWs had died in captivity.

That night a vacillating intelligence analyst told Blackburn that the POWs likely had been moved. Afflicted by uncertainty, Blackburn told Admiral Moorer, "I recommend we go because we'll never have the opportunity again. Second, nothing is being done about our prisoners over there, and they're being treated pretty abominably. And it would demonstrate to them that their [Hanoi's] backyard isn't too damned safe." Later Bull Simons would add, "Given one chance in ten that we could take one prisoner out of there, it was worth trying." Were the POWs still at

Col. Arthur "Bull" Simons discloses the mission to the raiders in Thailand to "thunderous applause."(Photo provided by JFK Special Warfare Museum)

team rode on mattresses to cushion the impact when their helicopter crash-landed. Two HH-53s carried the other raiders—Bull Simons and 21 men as an outer perimeter to defend against reaction forces, and Lt. Col. Sydnor and 20 Green Berets to insert just outside the prison to support Meadows' assault team.

In the Tonkin Gulf the carriers *Oriskany*, *Hancock*, and *Ranger* readied a diversionary raid with 59 planes dumping harmless flares. At 1:23 A.M. the planes were launched, and all along the coast of North Vietnam anxious radar operators waved supervisors to their glowing screens—formations of Yankee planes were approaching at low level! But the alarm didn't reach a distant radar site over a sleepy Laotian valley. When its maintenance crew cut power for 10 minutes' calibration, the raiders slipped unseen into North Vietnam. Their treetop-level procession rushed past antiaircraft belts that didn't even know they were there. Then an eerie glow was seen in the distance—the diversion was under way over Haiphong, with U.S. jets whooshing past and dropping flares.

Six miles out the raiders removed windows to poke out their CAR-15s. The lead C-130 guide bird rose to 1,500 feet as its trailing choppers fanned out. At 2:17 A.M., a sleepy prison guard heard something—a dull hum?—coming from the west. He and another guard stood in their towers, craning their necks. Both turned their heads to the sound of a big plane flashing by and then a million-candle-power flare popped overhead, ruining the guards' night vision just as an HH-53 lumbered over the camp wall and minigunners S. Sgts. James Rogers and Angus Sowell *atomized* the guard towers. Seconds later Meadows' HH-3 slammed into the prison, and as quick

Son Tay? The raiders were about to find out.

SHOWTIME

That evening Bull Simons addressed the raiders in a hangar in Thailand. "We are going to rescue 70 American prisoners of war, maybe more, from a camp called Son Tay," he announced. "This is something American prisoners have a right to expect from their fellow soldiers. The target is 23 miles west of Hanoi." The applause was deafening.

At dusk the raiders took off, refueled in the dark, and then split into two formations, each led by a C-130 guide bird. Meadows' 14-man assault

Son Tay Prison photographed at low level by a pilotless drone. (Photo provided by U.S. Air Force)

as it hit, Meadows' men were gunning down astonished NVA guards.

But Bull Simons' HH-53 was mistakenly put down short of the prison, at the look-alike "secondary school" to the south. His 21 men rushed the wall and streamed inside, but the "secondary school" came alive with dozens of enemy soldiers. Capt. Udo Walthar's team killed several men running from a doorway and then burst in and sprayed 25 awakening soldiers. Sfc. Leroy Carlson popped an M79 round into each window of another building while John Jakovenko ran belt after belt through his M60 machine gun.

Meanwhile, Meadows' men had burst into the nearest POW barracks

as he announced on a megaphone, "We're Americans. Keep your heads down. We're Americans. This is a rescue. We're here to get you out. Keep your heads down."

By then a C-130 was over Son Tay city with two crewmen wildly tossing Nightingale firefight simulators. Then the A-1s roared over at 300 feet, and Maj. Edwin Rhein, Jr., perfectly bombed the citadel footbridge, cutting off the threat from across the river. Meanwhile, Bud Sydnor's force had landed outside the prison and eliminated 20 guards fleeing their barracks. M. Sgt. Herman Spencer's demo team blew a hole in the prison wall and dashed in, linking

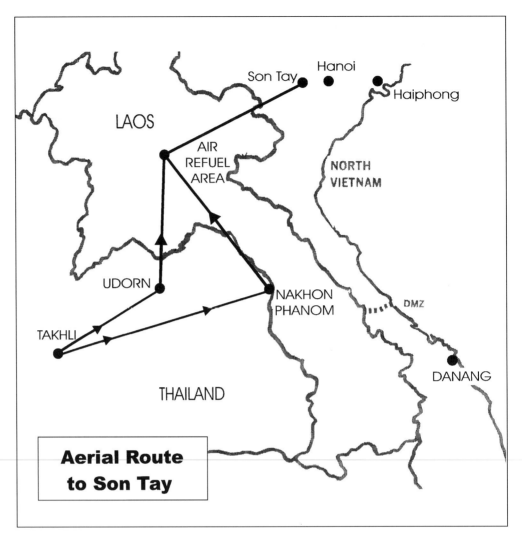

**Aerial Route
to Son Tay**

up with Meadows' men. Already, M. Sgt. Tom Kemmer's team had surprised five NVA soldiers who'd been manning the prison gate. "[We] just greased them all," Ken McMullin said.

After assaulting the wrong camp, Bull Simons' element reboarded an HH-53 and landed at the proper place outside the prison. But who were the 100 armed men they'd killed? Larger than Vietnamese, they may have been Russian or Chinese. It remains a mystery to this day.

There were no POWs at Son Tay. Meadows' men discovered cement sacks and new cell-door fittings: apparently the NVA had moved the POWs in order to refurbish the prison. But there still were

plenty of NVA troops around. An NCO with a "duckbilled" shotgun killed three running enemy soldiers. Two raiders wearing night vision goggles shot three of the enemy creeping through the dark. Then, as a convoy of six NVA vehicles rolled into view from the south, Sfc. Tyrone Adderly took careful aim with a LAW antitank rocket and drilled the lead truck perfectly. The other trucks and troops were hit by the A-1 Skyraiders.

At last the HH-53s were back, and 27 minutes after landing, the raiders were gone, weaving miraculously through a barrage of SAMs to disappear into the darkness from whence they'd come. Debriefers later determined that the raiders had killed at least 43 enemy soldiers at the prison, while Sfc. Joseph Murray had taken a bullet wound in the thigh and Air Force T. Sgt. Leroy Wright had broken an ankle. It was later learned that the POWs had been transferred earlier to Dong Hoi Prison Camp, only 14 miles away.

Even though no U.S. POWs were rescued, the raid was hardly a wasted effort. Fearful of such a repeated attempt, the North Vietnamese closed every outlying POW camp within 48 hours and rushed the pris-

oners into Hanoi. Solitary confinement and systematic torture were ended, food was improved, and POWs received such a spiritual boost that it sustained them through their final two years of captivity. When debriefers interviewed returning POWs in 1973 they were told, "Without exception, those who were prisoners at the time of that raid, and there were no exceptions to this, said that raid was the greatest single thing that happened in all those years for their morale."

U.S. hand-controlled miniguns vaporized Son Tay's guard towers. (Photo provided by U.S. Air Force)

Top: Brig. Gen. Donald Blackburn, former Chief SOG, conceived the Son Tay raid. (Photo provided by U.S. Army)

Bottom: Capt. Dick Meadows (with the megaphone) and Lt. Col. Elliot "Bud" Sydnor (center) at Son Tay Prison mock-up. (Photo provided by U.S. Air Force)

MOCK-UPS AND MODELS

As the Son Tay raiders perfected their respective tasks, full-scale dress rehearsals began, using a mock-up of Son Tay Prison constructed from target cloth and 2 x 4s that could be dismantled when Soviet spy satellites flew past twice a day. The fake walled compound, 125 feet wide and 175 feet long, was patrolled by 15 guard role players, with three times that many guards in a mock-up barracks 100 feet away. In daylight and later at night, the entire force rehearsed the raid some 172 times.

For even more realism, the National Photographic Interpretation Center built an incredibly detailed tabletop model of Son Tay Prison, code-named "Barbara," which one officer found "an absolutely splendid piece of workmanship." The raiders took turns examining "Barbara" through a special optical prism that gave the perspective of a 5-foot, 10-inch man, allowing the Green Berets to "see" the prison exactly as they'd find it during the raid. The model even had adjustable lights to simulate a quarter-moon and flares. Visitors to Ft. Bragg today can see "Barbara" displayed at the JFK Special Warfare Center Museum, housed in the Arthur "Bull" Simons Memorial Building.

Above: S. Sgt. Ken McMullin in front of cloth-and-lumber Son Tay Prison mock-up. (Photo provided by U.S. Air Force)

Left: "Barbara," the tabletop prison model. (Photo provided by JFK Special Warfare Museum)

U.S. Air Force Jolly Green helicopter over Laos being refueled in midair by a C-130. (Photo provided by U.S. Air Force)

Top: Son Tay raider Green Berets with a satchel charge for breaching a wall at the prison camp. (Photo provided by JFK Special Warfare Museum)

Bottom: Raiders aboard a U.S. Air Force HH-53 Jolly Green Giant. (Photo provided by JFK Special Warfare Museum)

SPECIAL WEAPONS AT SON TAY

ALL SON TAY RAIDERS HONED THEIR shooting skills in twice-daily shooting drills, eventually firing 10,000 rounds apiece in training, so that they quickly could eliminate the NVA guard force. U. S. Army shooting experts thought the best rifleman might achieve 35 percent hits at night, but that wasn't enough for Bull Simons. In a gun magazine ad, he had found the $36 Swedish-designed Singlepoint Nite Sight. Instead of a see-through scope, the Singlepoint's tube offered a red-dot aiming point with which the shooter kept both eyes open. Lacking proper mounts, the raiders taped the Singlepoints to their CAR-15s and achieved more than 90 percent low-light hits.

Another challenge was quickly cleaning out the guard force billets. Even the fastest firing assault rifles and submachine guns might require several magazines and a half-minute, possibly allowing some NVA troops to shoot at defenseless POWs. To meet this need, the CIA supplied two 12-gauge "duckbill" shotguns using a special choke that flattened the pattern into a deadly horizontal spread. Developed at the U.S. Navy's China Lake weapons facility, it could fire nine double-odd buckshot rounds in four seconds, each containing 15 pellets the size of 9mm slugs—*a total of 135 projectiles, more projectiles than four M16 magazines*—meaning that the CIA shotgun could clean out a whole room faster than an NVA guard could grab his AK.

Above left: This CIA-supplied "duckbill" shotgun's horizontal buckshot pattern proved a devastating close-range weapon during the Son Tay raid. (Photo provided by U.S. Air Force)

Above right: RT Illinois One-Zero Ben Thompson's CAR-15 sports a Singlepoint Nite Sight. (Photo provided by John Plaster)

U.S. Air Force HH-3 Jolly Green Giant and
a pair of A-1 Skyraiders. (Photo provided by
U.S. Air Force)

Another view of the helicopter wreckage that
was demolished by Dick Meadows' demo
charge. (Photo provided by DRV)

Top: An empty cell at Son Tay. Note the repairs under way on the window bars. (Photo provided by JFK Museum)

Bottom: The wreckage of the raiders' HH-3 in Son Tay Prison. Note the tree trunks that were hacked down by the rotor blade. (Photo provided by DRV)

Destroyed "secondary school" building that was assaulted by Simons' men when they landed in the wrong compound. (Photo provided by DRV)

Secretary of Defense Melvin Laird decorates Son Tay raiders at Ft. Bragg. (Photo provided by U.S. Army)

"SUCH MAGNIFICENT MEN"

QUITE FITTINGLY, THE SON TAY RAIDERS were honored publicly for risking their lives to go into the heartland of North Vietnam to rescue U.S. POWs. When presenting awards to visiting Son Tay raiders at the White House, President Nixon told the nation:

> *What these men have done is a message that the prisoners of war have not been forgotten, and that we will continue to do everything we can to attempt to bring them back home. We can all be thankful that America has produced such magnificent men.*

Receiving awards at the White House are (left to right) Brigadier General Manor, Air Force T. Sgt. Leroy Wright, Sfc. Tyrone Adderly, and Col. "Bull" Simons. (Photo provided by Department of Defense)

Chapter Twenty

SOG in the Defense

As an intelligence-gathering special-operations unit, SOG's only defensive role was protecting its own bases and launch sites. Still, the forward location of SOG bases, the value these sites represented to the NVA, and the enemy's ability to attack by surprise even in rear areas drew SOG into some of the deadliest defensive fights of the war.

SOG's largest defensive mission, by far, was holding FOB-3 at Khe Sanh during the 1968 siege. So preoccupied were these 50 Green Berets and 500 Montagnards that their recon teams and Hatchet Forces suspended cross-border operations and, like their neighboring 6,000-strong U.S. Marine 26th Regiment, dug in for a long, serious fight.

The Khe Sanh defenders withstood up to 1,500 rounds of incoming artillery and rockets per day, much of it fired from concealed positions on Co Roc Mountain, a 3-mile-wide cliff just across the border in Laos. Meanwhile U.S. Air Force B-52s carpet-bombed danger-close to hit enemy trenches inching toward Khe Sanh's barbed-wire perimeter. By mid-January, more than 20,000 troops of the NVA 320th, 304th, and 325th Divisions encircled the base. In those hazardous hills above Khe Sanh prowled recon men from SOG's FOB-1 at Phu Bai, who tapped landlines, uncovered targets for air strikes, and emplaced sensors.

Since the NVA did not launch an all-out ground assault, SOG's casualties at Khe Sanh fell one at a time to incoming artillery. On SOG's darkest day there, 15 April 1968, three men ran from a bunker to aid wounded comrades, when more incoming rounds fell and killed them—Sp5cs. Charles Corry and Daniel Sandoval and Sgt. Dennis Thorpe.

Five miles west of Khe Sanh, on the Laotian border, sat Lang Vei Special Forces camp. Despite SOG's repeated warnings that recon teams had found evidence that the NVA was massing tanks nearby in Laos, MACV Headquarters in Saigon refused to entertain the possibility of an armored attack. Just after midnight of 7 February, 11 NVA PT-76 tanks and 500 infantrymen broke through the wire and overran Lang Vei. A handful of Special Forces holdouts locked themselves in the camp's command bunker while a tank spun its tracks on their sandbagged roof to dig them out.

By sunrise at Khe Sanh, the FOB-3 commander, Maj. George Quamo, and M. Sgt. Charles "Skip" Minnicks

had assembled a dozen SOG recon Americans and 30 'Yards and Nungs, and then flew aboard U.S. Marine choppers to rescue the survivors at Lang Vei. Running bunker to bunker, the SOG men carried away U.S. survivors and as many Montagnard wounded as they could. As the rescue force lifted away, RT Alabama One-Zero John Allen saw an American dash onto the airstrip waving his arms, but the helicopter was not allowed to go back. The abandoned Green Beret, Dennis Thompson, survived five years of enemy captivity. Of the 24 Special Forces troopers defending Lang Vei, 10 were killed or missing; Major Quamo's SOG men brought out 14 Americans, all but one wounded. Of the 11 tanks that had rolled into Lang Vei, seven were destroyed, with two more probables and 250 North Vietnamese dead.

After the siege Major Quamo left Khe Sanh aboard a SOG plane, which disappeared in bad weather. His remains were recovered in 1974.

Aerial view of Khe Sanh. (Photo provided by Bob Donoghue)

DEFENSE AT KHAM DUC

After Lang Vei's fall, not another Special Forces border camp remained in all of I Corps, the northern quarter of South Vietnam, except for Kham Duc, some 75 miles to the south, from which SOG had launched its first 1965 recon missions into Laos. Although bad weather often closed its airfield, Kham Duc was SOG's only launch site within range of Laotian Highway 165.

Intent on eliminating Kham Duc, a reinforced NVA regiment assaulted the camp's sprawling perimeter on 10 May 1968, instigating a catastrophic three-day battle that drew in a U.S. Marine artillery battery and an American Division infantry battalion, along with several Special Forces Mike Force companies. SOG's small launch-site detachment made a good show of itself: Silver Stars were later awarded to the young launch officer, 1st Lt. Jim McLeroy, and to Sfc. Marion Windley.

But Kham Duc could not be held, and SOG teams henceforth could recon only infrequently along Laotian Highway 165 by inserting from 21st Special Operations Squadron Jolly Greens based at Nakhon Phanom, Thailand.

RADIO RELAY SITES

SOG's most continually vulnerable outposts were its radio relay sites, tiny mountain peak enclaves deep behind enemy lines, occupied for months—such as in-country sites Klondike and Sugarloaf—or even held for years, as in the cases of Leghorn and Outpost Hickory.

Leghorn, located on a nearly vertical precipice about 10 miles inside southern Laos, was first occupied on 15 January 1967 by a recon team led by 1st Lt. George K. Sisler, whose later actions led to a posthumous Medal of Honor. Rising more than 1,000 feet above the jungled valleys beneath it, Leghorn's radios could relay messages from recon teams to SOG bases in South Vietnam and offered a perfect location for National Security Agency (NSA) Polaris II radio intercept gear.

Leghorn was occupied continuously for five years, with a security detachment eventually replacing the recon teams. The NVA occasionally lobbed a few mortar shells, but Leghorn was so narrow that the rounds fell harmlessly short or long. During Bernard Newell's tour on Leghorn, a baboon family's night antics—sounding exactly like NVA soldiers climbing in the dark—led to a hunt and a Montagnard barbecue. When Eugene McCarley brought up a half-dozen geese to serve as low-tech, honking sensors of NVA night movement, there was another Montagnard barbecue.

Actress Martha Raye, a great supporter of Special Forces, was smuggled to Leghorn in 1970 to sing

Heavily sandbagged and ringed by wire and mines by 1970, Leghorn offered formidable protection. (Photo provided by Frank Greco)

Resupply Huey approaches Leghorn, SOG's secret mountaintop radio site in Laos. (Photo provided by Newell "Woody" Bernard)

and kiss each Green Beret. She never disclosed one word of her unauthorized visit.

Situated in the same way as Leghorn was the CCN radio relay site, Outpost Hickory, that sat on Hill 950, a mountain peak overlooking Khe Sanh. Initially a U.S. Marine commo site, Hickory was abandoned after the Khe Sanh siege. It was reoccupied by CCN Hatchet Force Company A's 1st Platoon led by Sfcs. Francis Attebery, Ivan Bomark, and James Martin, and S. Sgt. Francisco Olivarez in November 1969. Hickory operated much like Leghorn, as both a radio relay site and NSA monitoring station. But unlike Leghorn, Hickory became the target for an all-out NVA assault in June 1971 (see

"Jon Cavaiani Fights for Hickory," page 430).

SAPPERS!

Sappers were NVA commandos who specialized in night raids against U.S. installations in South Vietnam. Sappers typically struck in squads or platoons, but at 3 A.M. on 23 August 1968, an entire 100-man sapper company waded from Danang's crashing surf into the darkened compound that housed SOG's CCN.

The sappers went undetected until their first charge demolished a billet with such force that men in adjacent buildings were thrown from their bunks. One U.S. NCO awoke just as a sapper put an AK to his

Dead NVA sapper at CCN.
Note the unexploded 40mm
round (left) that may have killed
him but failed to arm. (Photo
provided by Chuck Pfeifer)

head—he shoved the barrel aside as it fired and blew off his little finger. Ignoring the pain, he threw the sapper across the room, seized his own CAR-15, and shot the man dead. Another sapper team tossed a satchel charge inside the CCN commo bunker, killing three Americans. More sappers launched a frontal attack through CCN's landward side.

Capt. Ed Lesesne didn't even have a weapon when he saw an AK slug hit an officer in the bunk below. A lieutenant jumped up and ran out the door only to be shot by a hidden sapper. "They rolled a grenade in," he recalled, "but it didn't go off."

Sfc. Pat Watkins, Jr., rolled from his bunk at the sound of grenades bouncing in his barracks hallway.

Taking a .45 automatic pistol, Watkins shot an NVA sapper who was igniting a satchel charge. Meanwhile, a U.S. lieutenant was shot as he was going out a door; he courageously shouted warnings to his comrades that two sappers had the doorway covered, certainly saving several lives.

A few sappers went up in smoke, shot down with lit demo charges in their hands. Capt. Charles Pfeifer killed a score of sappers with a virtual barrage of hand grenades. As dawn glowed, CCN men formed skirmish lines and advanced methodically through the compound, clearing each room and each crawl space to root out enemy holdouts. They found sappers' bodies in ones and twos every-

413

where. The last two NVA troopers were found crouching in the surf; they refused to surrender and were shot dead.

Some 38 of the enemy were killed and nine captured—all wounded. Sixteen Special Forces officers and NCOs died that night, the greatest single-day loss of Green Berets in the entire history of Special Forces. The dead included many fine soldiers, including Sgt. Maj. Richard Pegram, Jr., who'd gone in with the Lang Vei rescue force five months earlier; and S. Sgt. Talmadge Alphin, Jr., who'd narrowly escaped death at Kham Duc. Also killed were 16 Nungs, Montagnards, and Vietnamese. In 1995 former Vietcong Gen. Dham Duc Nam, who'd commanded the Danang area in 1968, told visiting SOG veteran Chuck

Pfeifer that, absolutely, the sapper attack had been calculated to disrupt SOG operations and thereby relieve pressure on the Ho Chi Minh Trail.

A smaller sapper attack hit CCC on 1 April 1970, when perhaps 15 NVA sappers crept through a waste-filled latrine ditch to demolish the tactical operations center and commander's quarters. All the sappers escaped, and although they had killed about 10 Montagnards, not a single American was even wounded. The sapper raid coincided with a major NVA attack on Dak Pek Special Forces camp and, 12 days later, an attack on Dak Seang. RT Vermont, led by Franklin "Doug" Miller, tracked the sappers but never caught up with them. Despite the sapper attack's success, it had no effect on CCC operations—fresh teams were being inserted the following day.

SAPPER ATTACK CASUALTIES

The 16 men killed in the 23 August 1968 CCN sapper attack make up the greatest loss of Green Berets in a single incident since the 1952 founding of Special Forces. They were as follows:

1st Lt. Paul Potter
Sgt. Maj. Richard Pegram, Jr.
M. Sgt. Charles Norris
M. Sgt. Rolf Rickmers
M. Sgt. Gilbert Secor
Sfc. Tadeusz Kepczuk
Sfc. Donald Kerns
Sfc. Harold Voorheis
Sfc. Albert Walter
Sfc. Donald Welch
S. Sgt. Howard Varni
Sgt. Talmadge Alphin
Sgt. James Kickliter
Sgt. Robert Uyesaka
Sp4c. Anthony Santana
Pfc. William Bric III

Inset: A string of exploding bombs from B-52s hits NVA trenches on Khe Sanh perimeter. (Photo provided by Bob Donoghue)

A-1 Skyraider drops napalm on NVA trench at the edge of SOG's FOB-3, Khe Sanh. (Photo provided by Bob Donoghue)

Co Roc Mountain and its prominent cliffs, just across the Laotian border from Khe Sanh. (Photo provided George Gaspard)

Top: A trail of B-52 bombs detonate, their blasts walking the edge of Khe Sanh. (Photo provided by Bob Donoghue)

Above: Thousands of B-52 Arc Lights prevented NVA forces from massing and assaulting the sprawling U.S. Marine Corps and SOG base. (Photo provided by Bob Donoghue)

Top: Napalm canister bursts on SOG base perimeter at Khe Sanh, 1968. (Photo provided by Bob Donoghue)

Bottom: What looks like a rising storm is a B-52 strike just beyond Khe Sanh's wire, close enough to throw debris (center) into the SOG compound. (Photo provided by Hammond Salley)

Top: North Vietnamese 122mm rocket hits U.S. Marine Corps fuel dump at Khe Sanh. The besieged base took thousands of rounds daily. (Photo provided by Hammond Salley)

Bottom: SOG recon team ventures through the devastation outside Khe Sanh near the end of the siege. (Photo provided by Hammond Salley)

Top: RT Colorado One-Zero Paul Douglas (left) with teammate Fred Crane. On 21 February 1968 Douglas was killed by incoming artillery fire at Khe Sanh. (Photo provided by Fred Crane)

Bottom: LANG VEI THE DAY AFTER. Destroyed NVA tank beside collapsed command bunker in which the final hold-outs were rescued by SOG force. (Photo provided by Shelby Stanton)

U-17 Crash Site
AT 905 927

Top: S. Sgt. Dennis Thompson ran onto Lang Vei airstrip as SOG rescuers flew away and then was captured by the NVA. (Photo provided by Department of Defense)

Above: Personal effects of Maj. George Quamo recovered with his body in 1974. (Photo provided by Larry White)

Top left: Gutted Camp Lang Vei with three knocked-out tanks (in circles). (Photo provided by Shelby Stanton)

Bottom: Soviet-built PT-76 tank. (Photo provided by John Plaster)

Top: Results of the baboon hunt at Leghorn. (Photo provided by Newell "Woody" Bernard)

Bottom: Resupply helicopter at Leghorn. (Photo provided by Newell "Woody" Bernard)

Top: Leghorn Peak (center) dominated all approaches. The NVA never mounted a serious attack. (Photo provided by Mike Sheppard)

Above left: Lt. George Sisler observes the NVA from Leghorn, which he founded, 15 January 1967. Lieutenant Sisler later received the Medal of Honor posthumously. (Photo provided by Jane Sisler)

Above right: Huey helicopter on the helipad at Leghorn radio relay site, 1967. (Photo provided by Merritte Wilson)

Enemy operations order for sapper attack on CCN captured during the attack. (Photo provided by Chuck Pfeifer)

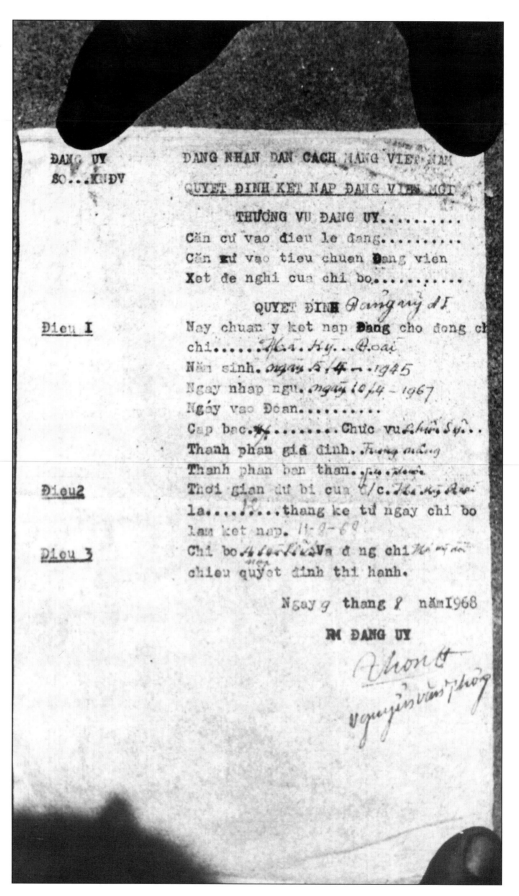

Top: Dead enemy commando and a demolished recon team room behind him. (Photo provided by Robert Parks)

Bottom: CCN compound was located at the base of Marble Mountain, on the edge of Danang. NVA sappers reached the base by wading through the ocean. (Photo provided by George Gaspard)

Inset: NVA sapper's basket of grenades. The sapper died before he could throw them. (Photo provided by Chuck Pfeifer)

Right: This sapper died still grasping an armed hand grenade. (Photo provided by Chuck Pfeifer)

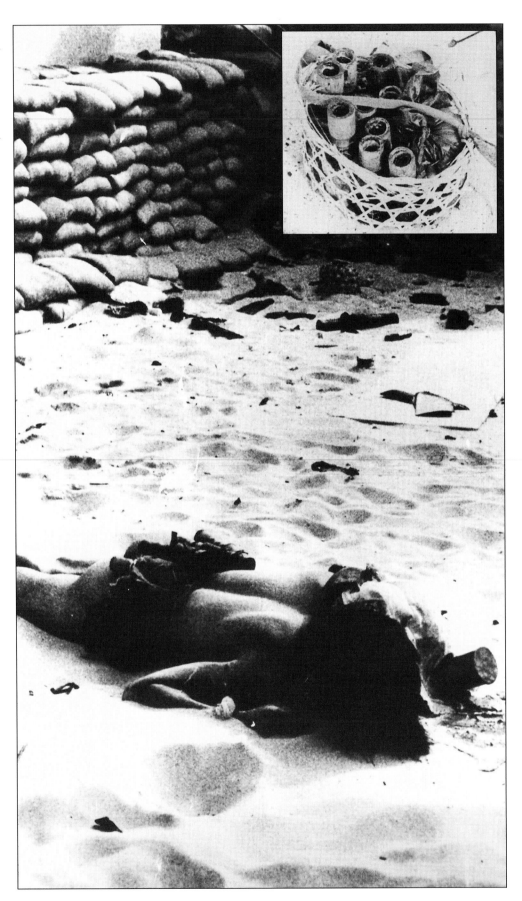

Top: Dead NVA sapper lies amid ruins of building he blew up at CCN. (Photo provided by Chuck Pfeifer)

Bottom: Some sappers carried RPG rockets rigged for throwing by hand. (Photo provided by Chuck Pfeifer)

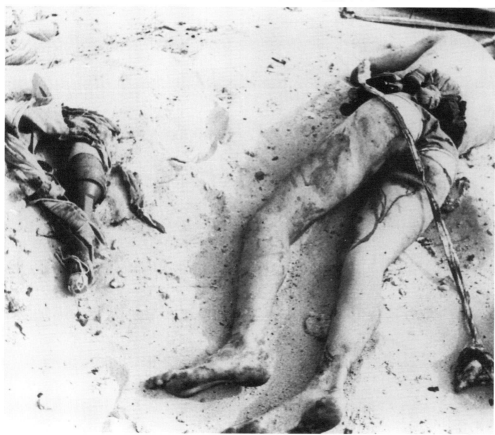

Top: Unexploded enemy satchel charge (center) discovered after sapper attack at CCC, March 1970. (Photo provided by Frank Greco)

Bottom: This NVA bangalore torpedo failed to explode during CCC sapper attack, March 1970. (Photo provided by Frank Greco)

Top: CCC TOC on fire after an NVA sapper attack. (Photo provided by Frank Greco)

Bottom: After the 1970 sapper attack, CCC beefed up its defenses to include this Jeep-mounted mini-gun, fired here by recon man Terry Sorsby. (Photo provided by Terry Sorsby)

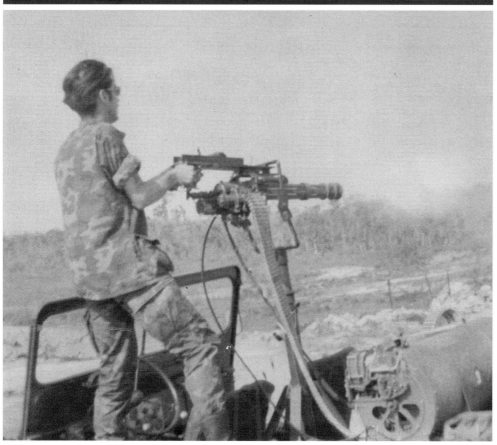

JON CAVAIANI FIGHTS FOR HICKORY

By June 1971 CCN's Outpost Hickory radio relay site, just north of the abandoned Khe Sanh airstrip, was the final allied presence in northwest South Vietnam. Commanded by S. Sgt. Jon Cavaiani and his assistant, Sgt. John Jones, the tiny site was held by 67 indigenous and 27 U.S. soldiers, including sensor readers and a squad from L Company, 75th Rangers.

At sunrise on 4 June, Cavaiani spotted Chinese claymore mines in the wire and began machine gunning them, but NVA soldiers detonated more mines, which wounded several men, including John Jones. Then NVA troops opened fire and loosed a mortar and RPG barrage, wounding more men.

A U.S. Army sensor reader, Walter Millsap, climbed into Cavaiani's bunker and took over his .50-caliber machine gun, so that Cavaiani could redistribute ammo and secure the wounded. When an RPG round hit the bunker, Millsap ignored his own wounds, dragged the gun back, and resumed firing, knocking out five NVA machine guns. With Millsap's supporting fire, Cavaiani carried a wounded captain to safety. Then another barrage shook Hickory and wounded more men; Cavaiani called for an evacuation, which would take several relays.

Below: S. Sgt. Jon Cavaiani at SOG's "One-Zero" school. (Photo provided by Jim Shorten)

Below right: Sensor reader Walter Millsap fought ferociously on Hickory, earning the Distinguished Service Cross. (Photo provided by Walter Millsap)

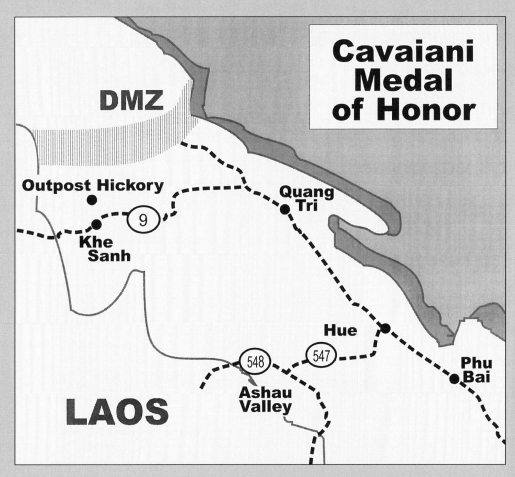

Cavaiani Medal of Honor

DMZ

Outpost Hickory

Quang Tri

Khe Sanh

9

Hue

548 547

Ashau Valley

LAOS

Phu Bai

He put Millsap and most of the defenders on the first lift, but the young Texan climbed off to stay in the fight.

The action had ebbed by 4:30 P.M., when Cavaiani was told that just one more Huey would come in to evacuate seven men—but he had 31 men! Unwilling to abandon his men, Cavaiani forced the thrice-wounded Millsap and six 'Yards onto the Huey, leaving 23 'Yards and ARVN soldiers and John Jones.

Abandoning half of Hickory so that he could hold the most defensible uphill area, Cavaiani shifted three machine guns and then built a firing position for himself atop a bunker. About 7 P.M. the sun sank, and a U.S. Air Force C-119 Stinger gunship arrived. An hour later came the first NVA probes, but the Stinger couldn't fire because of dense fog.

At 8:30 P.M. 15 NVA soldiers rushed into the three intersecting machine guns' fields of fire; by the time they saw the muzzle flashes they were dead. Ten minutes later came another 15 NVA, with the same result—then another 15. By midnight enemy forces had launched eight assaults; by then Cavaiani sensed they were about to launch a mass attack so he began shifting men into Hickory's heaviest bunkers. The NVA forces struck immediately and in the confusion stormed across Hickory. Cavaiani bent over from his position on

Similar to NSA Polaris-II System used on Leghorn and Hickory, this radio intercept gear features frequency-skipping scanners and voice-activated recording. (Photo provided by the National Archives)

top of a bunker and was hit with an AK round in the small of his back. The slug tore into his flesh almost to the shoulder and knocked him to the ground. He crawled into a bunker with John Jones.

NVA troops were going from bunker to bunker, shooting and tossing grenades. Cavaiani pulled his Gerber Mk II fighting knife just as two NVA assailants climbed into the bunker with him and Jones. Cavaiani jammed his dagger into one foe, killing him instantly, while Jones shot the other. Suddenly, a hand grenade bounced in, wounding Jones and all but deafening Cavaiani. Too badly injured to resist, Jones climbed out to surrender; but an AK fired, and Jones tumbled back, dead. An exploding grenade knocked Cavaiani out.

When he groped his way back to consciousness he had to play dead while an NVA soldier prodded his chest with an AK, then set the bunker afire. Hot tar dripped on Cavaiani's face and his pants caught fire, but he dared not move. After the soldier left Cavaiani crawled out, only to have a bullet graze his head and knock him out. Cavaiani awoke when a rummaging NVA soldier almost stepped on him. The American pulled his Gerber knife and slammed it so hard into the enemy's chest that he couldn't extract it.

For 10 days Cavaiani stumbled eastward toward Firebase Fuller, only to be captured within sight of the U.S. base. The North Vietnamese did not admit he was a POW until his release in 1973. For his defense of Hickory, Jon Cavaiani was awarded the Medal of Honor, while the gallant sensor reader, Walter Millsap, was awarded a Distinguished Service Cross.

Capt. Robert Noe firing a .50-caliber machine gun on Hickory, July 1970. (Photo provided by Robert Noe)

Top: Outpost Hickory sat atop a prominent peak (front) overlooking Khe Sanh. (Photo provided by U.S. Army)

Bottom: Outpost Hickory, CCN radio relay site on a precipice overlooking Khe Sanh. (Photo provided by George Gaspard)

Jon Cavaiani at the Vietnam
Veterans Memorial Wall. (Photo
provided by Eldon Bargewell)

THE LAST STAND OF RT KANSAS

IN AUGUST 1971, TWO MONTHS AFTER OUTPOST HICKORY WAS LOST, RT Kansas landed on an old hilltop firebase about 10 kilometers east of there to snatch a prisoner so that U.S. intelligence could learn why masses of NVA had crossed the DMZ along the Cam Lo River valley.

RT Kansas' One-Zero, 1st Lt. Loren "Festus" Hagen, his One-One, Sgt. Tony Andersen, and One-Two, Sgt. Bruce Berg, had a clever plan. They'd land conspicuously, stay overnight, and extract half the team—hiding the rest to ambush any NVA sent up to search the hilltop and to capture one NVA soldier. RT Kansas went in with 14 men, including eight 'Yards and three "straphangers," S. Sgt. Oran Bingham and Sgts. Bill Queen and William Rimondi. Unknowingly, Hagen's men had landed near a secret fuel pipeline laid across the DMZ that would be essential in a few months when NVA armored forces rolled through for the war's largest offensive.

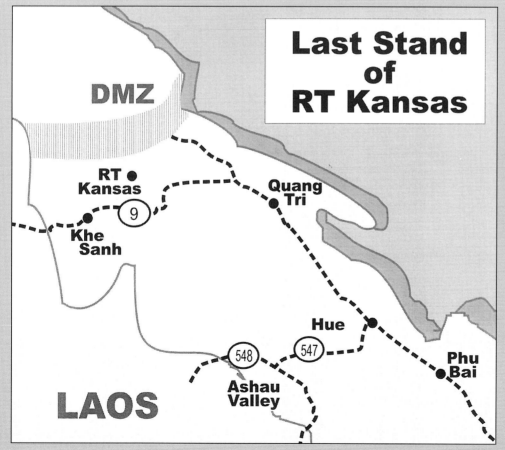

Above: RT Kansas team patch. (Photo provided by Scott Kilpatrick)

Left: The last stand of RT Kansas.

435

From 1:00 A.M. to dawn, a U.S. Air Force Spectre gunship fired for RT Kansas. (Photo provided by U.S. Air Force)

It was quiet until midnight, when NVA elements fired shots around the hillside. At 3 A.M. Hagen's men heard truck tailgates dropping, and just before sunrise it became forebodingly quiet. Chief SOG Sadler later learned that a reinforced regiment had surrounded the hill—2,000 NVA troops versus 14 SOG men! At the Alamo, 188 Americans had stood against 3,000 Mexicans, a ratio of 16 to 1; the 1879 Battle of Rorke's Drift, the most heralded action in British military history, resulting in 11 Victoria Crosses, pitted 140 Brits against 4,000 Zulus, or 28 to 1. RT Kansas was outnumbered 107 to 1.

The battle began with a well-aimed RPG rocket that smashed Bruce Berg's bunker. Suddenly, like a burst dam, the NVA forces were firing 10,000 rounds per second. Despite that tremendous fire, Hagen ran to check Berg, bullets flashing all around him. But he made it hardly a dozen yards. Then Klaus Bingham left a bunker and didn't get 6 feet before a bullet struck him in the head, apparently killing him. One 'Yard jumped up to pull back and fell dead in Tony Andersen's lap.

Top: RT Kansas (left rear): Bruce Berg and Lt. Loren Hagen, plus Montagnards (left to right) Xapet, Ken, Ero, Pahai, and Po. All but two were KIA or MIA. (Photo provided by Tony Andersen)

Bottom: Soviet troops lay a fuel pipeline like the one the NVA was secretly extending into South Vietnam. (Photo provided by Defense Intelligence Agency)

Andersen dashed over the hill to look for Hagen and saw 100 of the enemy almost at the top! He ran back for his M60 machine gun, fired one belt at NVA soldiers on his own slope, then sped to the other and ran belt after belt at the enemy. Covey arrived and called for fighters. Meanwhile members of RT Kansas were heaving grenades to airburst above the NVA attackers until there were no more grenades. A North Vietnamese grenade exploded beside Andersen's M60—he grabbed a CAR-15 and then tossed back a grenade that went off in front of him. Shrapnel hit him, and then a bullet slammed into his elbow.

The perimeter was pinched almost in half when Andersen grabbed his last two 'Yards, circled below the nearest NVA soldiers, and reached his surviving teammates. Bingham was dead, and Bill Queen was wounded. Only Rimondi wasn't hit yet. They sat back to back to make their last stand.

NVA troops were rolling over the crest of the hill like a tidal wave, their firing AKs blending into one never-ending burst. Precise Cobra gunship fire stacked the NVA up in front of them; then the assault turned, and the NVA

S. Sgt. Oran Bingham, Jr., fought and died on the hilltop. (Photo provided by Eldon Bargewell)

RT Kansas One-Zero Lt. Loren Hagen received the Medal of Honor posthumously. (Photo provided by Tony Andersen)

fled for cover, and the Hueys had arrived. With Rimondi's help, Andersen got several teammates' bodies aboard the first Huey and helped the wounded and others aboard the second. A Bright Light mission commanded by Noel Gast with Jimmy Reeves, Sam "Injun" Adams, and the CCN commander, Lt. Col. Donnie Bellfi, recovered Lieutenant Hagen's body and those of several 'Yards, but they did not find Bruce Berg.

Killed along with Hagen and Bingham were six 'Yards, while Berg was presumed dead. Rimondi, Queen, Andersen, and the other 'Yards had been wounded. The U.S. Air Force later determined that 185 NVA soldiers had all been killed and probably three times that many had been wounded. Hagen's family received the U.S. Army's final Vietnam War Medal of Honor. Tony Andersen and Bill Queen were awarded Distinguished Service Crosses, while Rimondi, Berg, and Bingham received Silver Stars.

SOG SUPPORT TO LAM SON 719

IN EARLY 1971, SOG LAID ON AN ELABORATE diversionary effort to support Lam Son 719, the invasion of Laos by the ARVN. Initially, SOG Blackbirds dropped dummy parachutists with firecrackers in seven areas west of Khe Sanh; then U.S. teams faked inserts at another four points. Atop Co Roc Mountain, just west of Khe Sanh, SOG inserted three recon teams and two Hatchet Force platoons; they were extracted when U.S. policy changed and Americans were no longer permitted in Laos after 7 February 1971.

An inflatable paratrooper dummy similar to those dropped over Laos by Blackbirds. (Photo provided by John Plaster)

On 8 February the ARVN invaded, rolling west from Khe Sanh along Highway 9. While the ARVN advanced into Laos, SOG's Naval Advisory Detachment staged its first Nasty boat raids above the DMZ in 27 months. On the night of 11 February, three Nastys sank a junk, a trawler, and a 100-ton coastal steamer and damaged two Soviet-made submarine chasers. On 19 February came the war's greatest Nasty surface action when four Nastys sank a 60-foot patrol boat and heavily damaged a 130-foot Shanghai II fast attack craft and a Swatow gunboat. When the North Vietnamese navy attempted to intercept them, the SOG crews disabled one PT boat and sank a Shanghai II. Only one SOG Vietnamese crewman was killed in the engagement.

On 18 February, the first of six U.S. recon teams was inserted into the Ashau Valley to tie down enemy forces and gather intelligence for when the ARVN exited Laos along Highway 922. Making contact shortly after landing, RT Intruder was coming out on strings when heavy fire knocked down a Huey, from which hung Capt. Ronald "Doc" Watson and Sgt. Allen Lloyd. The only survivor, Sfc. Sammy Hernandez, miraculously fell through the jungle canopy when his rope was cut.

RT Habu, led by Cliff Newman and Billy Waugh, went after the bodies of Watson and Allen and the Huey crew and had to rappel down a cliff to reach the crash site. Although the recon team members found Watson's and Lloyd's bodies, a reinforced NVA compa-

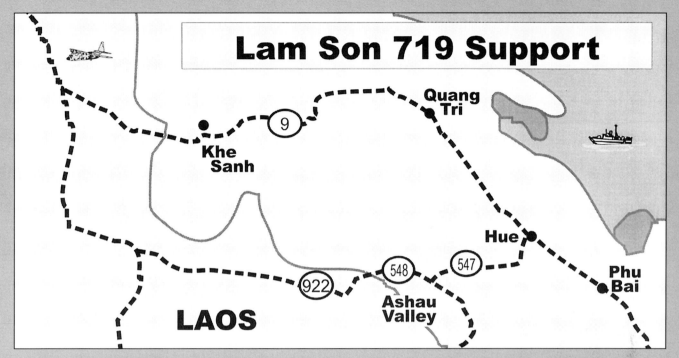

Lam Son 719 Support

ny pinned RT Habu against a sheer drop and likely would have overrun it except that the team, with half its men wounded, left behind the bodies and escaped by jumping over the cliff. The bodies were never recovered.

RT Python, led by Capt. Jim Butler with S. Sgt. Leslie Chapman as One-One, occupied the abandoned Firebase Thor to block the NVA-controlled Highway 548. The first night RT Python was probed and took occasional mortar rounds; all night they watched flashlights and vehicle headlights on the valley floor. The team suffered two wounded. Just after dark on the next night, the NVA shelled the team's hilltop with mortars and recoilless rifles. Finally, two Hueys narrowly snatched away RT Python before the NVA force swarmed over the hill. Butler's men were credited with killing 42 of the enemy and directing air strikes that killed an additional 300. Les Chapman was awarded the Distinguished Service Cross.

Another SOG team in the Ashau occupied a small peak and used a mortar and recoilless rifle to pin NVA trucks and troops along Highway 548 and direct U.S. Air Force gunships night after night. Along with two other teams, they interdicted the road for 21 days, destroying 15 NVA trucks and inflicting numerous casualties at a cost of two Americans and four 'Yards slightly wounded.

Although SOG's diversions killed a considerable number of NVA, the diversions had limited effect because the invasion became a bogged-down, bloody debacle, with ARVN units cut off and annihilated piecemeal, never making it to the Ashau Valley.

SOG C-130s dropped dummies (upper left), blocked the Ashau Valley roads with recon teams (center), and raided North Vietnamese waters with Nasty boats (right).

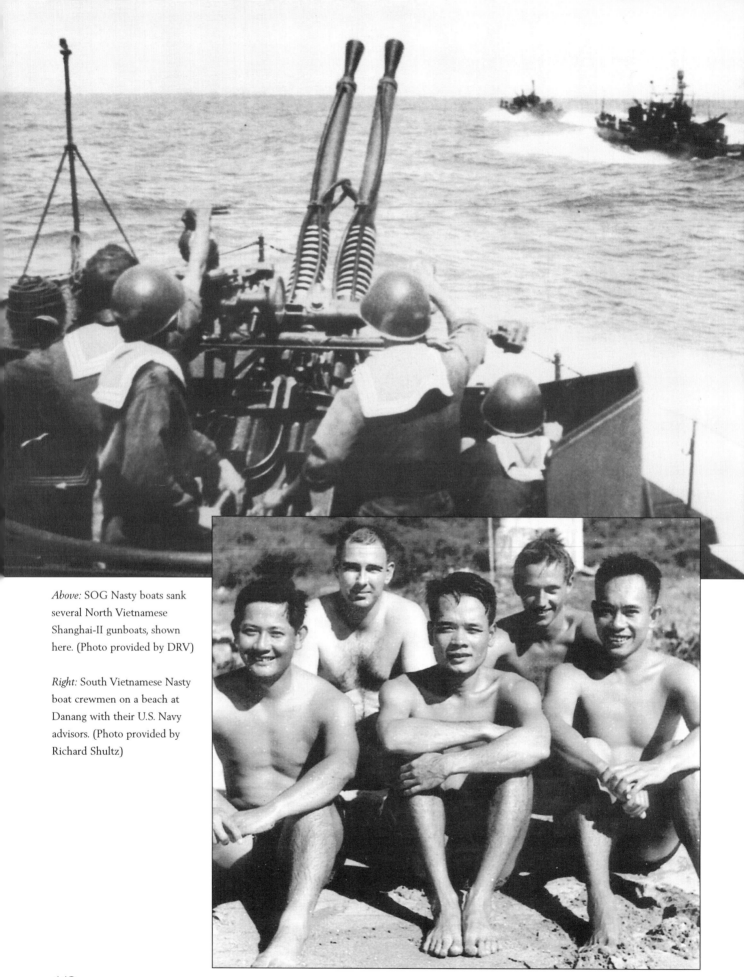

Above: SOG Nasty boats sank several North Vietnamese Shanghai-II gunboats, shown here. (Photo provided by DRV)

Right: South Vietnamese Nasty boat crewmen on a beach at Danang with their U.S. Navy advisors. (Photo provided by Richard Shultz)

Top: This NVA sapper carried handmade grenades fashioned from C-ration cans and wooden handles. (Photo provided by Chuck Pfeifer)

Bottom: This NVA had been tossing RPG rounds specially rigged for throwing by hand. (Photo provided by Robert Parks)

Chapter Twenty-One

SOG's Darkest Programs

S SOG's most closely held, most sensitive operations were those involving agent teams and "black" propaganda. Begun under the CIA and turned over to SOG in 1964, the Long-Term Agent Teams in North Vietnam always had been subject to suspicion because of hints their agents had been captured and "turned" by Hanoi's Ministry of Security. The questions came to a head on 1 April 1968, when President Johnson suspended bombing of the North, which also stopped resupply flights by SOG Blackbirds. Before he appealed the decision, Chief SOG Jack Singlaub first had to determine which teams—Remus, Easy, Tourbillon, Red Dragon, Eagle, Hadley, Romeo, and Singleton Agent Ares—were free and worth the physical danger and political fight to retrieve them.

One by one, a panel of CIA and military intelligence experts reviewed each team from its day of landing through 1 April 1968. Every radio message, every resupply drop, every shred of related intelligence was scrutinized. After two months of analysis the panel unanimously agreed that all were under enemy control. By 1968, the CIA and SOG had trained and fielded 54 Long-Term Agent Teams in North Vietnam with 342 men—and all of them had been lost.

SOG decided it was time for "payback." One "turned" team was told to prepare for a resupply drop—instead, the North Vietnamese Ministry

Top: FREE-LANCE PSYOPS. Some recon men inserted their own psychological warfare items—such as this card that was published untraceably in Thailand—and left them on NVA bodies. (Photo provided by John Plaster)

Bottom: SOG "calling card" designed to be left by recon teams behind enemy lines. (Photo provided by Richard Shultz)

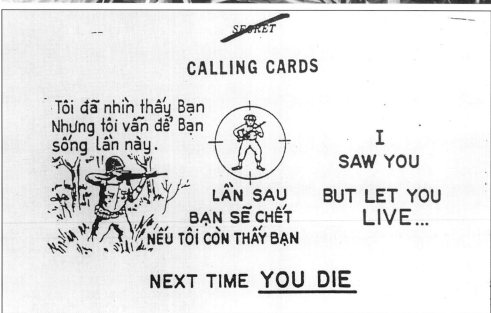

CALLING CARDS

Tôi đã nhìn thấy Bạn
Nhưng tôi vẫn để Bạn
sống Lần này.

LẦN SAU
BẠN SẼ CHẾT
NẾU TÔI CÒN THẤY BẠN

I
SAW YOU
BUT LET YOU
LIVE...

NEXT TIME YOU DIE

of Security troops posing as the team were bombed. Blackbirds flew a number of resupply missions, but their bundles contained payback packages of cleverly booby-trapped radios and equipment. Eventually, the enemy did not even pick up the bundles.

AGENT DECEPTION PROGRAMS

To replace the defunct agent network, SOG combined real and imaginary assets "to exploit Hanoi's almost paranoid fear of any perceived threat to their control of the population." The new effort was Projects Oodles, Borden, and Urgency.

Project Borden agents were NVA prisoners purposely selected because they were untrustworthy, but allowed to believe that they'd fooled the Americans. "Our general feeling," explained Chief SOG Steve Cavanaugh, "was that these people were not loyal to us, would not be loyal to us, that they were opportunists, and that the minute they got on the ground they would immediately double on us." Each Borden "ringer" was groomed through weeks of training to absorb information from chats with his pseudo-teammates—agent identities, code names, and plans—to believe he was joining a large network of agents. As quickly as he landed, the

Borden agent would dash away to turn in his comrades and their local co-conspirators and, certainly, to confuse enemy counterintelligence officers.

Project Oodles was a network of 18 nonexistent "phantom teams," supposedly running loose in North Vietnam. Simulated messages were transmitted, identical to those sent to real teams, along with aerial supply drops. The only Blackbird lost over North Vietnam disappeared while resupplying Oodles phantom team Mikado in extreme northwest North Vietnam.

Paradise Island

The maritime element of SOG's agent deception program, Project Urgency, used SOG Nasty boats to kidnap North Vietnamese fishermen, hold them for two weeks, and then return them to North Vietnam—but in such a way that they appeared to be newly trained agents. The most zealous Communists were incriminated by money, secret-ink chemicals, and false messages hidden in their clothes. No amount of explanation

could talk a suspect out of such a fix.

Actually, Project Urgency overlapped SOG's most elaborate deception program, Project Humidor, which for years had been kidnapping North Vietnamese fishermen, whisking them away by Nasty boat—so that the high speed would confuse their ability to estimate distance—to Cu Lao Cham Island, south of the 17th Parallel, near Danang. The operation on Cu Lao Cham—"Paradise Island" to the Americans—was designed to fool the fishermen into believing they were at a hidden enclave on North Vietnam's mainland and liberated by their hosts, the Sons of the Sword Patriot League.

For two weeks the fishermen would do nothing but eat, talk about the old days, and learn the league's liberation program. Their hosts would boast of other enclaves, hidden camps in the hills, and their own clandestine radio stations that broadcast almost every day. Before going home, the fishermen were given names of league contacts and told how to receive instructions by the clandes-

SOG's Paradise Island fishing village, shown here, so perfectly resembled North Vietnam that kidnapped fishermen couldn't tell the difference. (Photo provided by Richard Shultz)

This AK, destroyed by an Eldest Son round, was recovered by U.S. troops. (Photo provided by Hammond Salley)

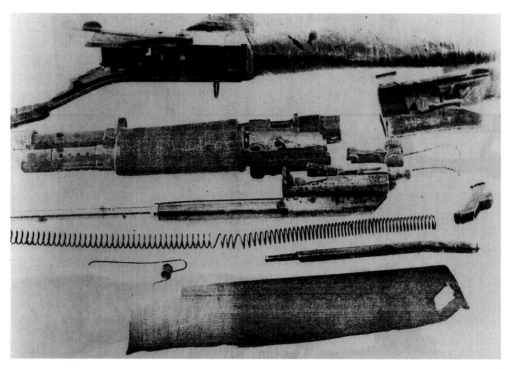

tine radio broadcasts. To make the program credible to enemy counterintelligence officers, SOG also had Short-Term Roadwatch and Target Acquisition (STRATA) teams plant league leaflets along North Vietnamese roads and trails, plus had First Flight C-123s airdrop resupply bundles to phantom resistance units. By 1967, SOG's secret island was processing 27 kidnapped fishermen each month, any one of whom—or all—might return as sincere spies or saboteurs.

Project Eldest Son

Paradise Island had been hatched in SOG's den of the devious, the Psychological Studies Branch, the only U.S. element in Southeast Asia practicing those darkest of deceptive arts, *black propaganda*—vile, bold lies that are falsely attributed. One of the branch's efforts blossomed into the war's deadliest deception, Project Eldest Son, in which SOG inserted sabotaged AK and mortar ammunition into the enemy supply system. When fired, Eldest Son ammo

exploded, killing or wounding NVA soldiers and—for psychological effect—undermining faith in their Chinese Communist allies who'd provided this "defective" ordnance.

Recon teams often carried a few Eldest Son rounds, usually as loose AK cartridges or a single round in an otherwise full AK magazine, to be left on bodies of ambushed enemy soldiers, the least detectable means of insertion. Sometimes whole AK ammo cans and cases of 82mm mortar ammo were slipped into NVA caches, while special teams even built false caches. One such team was lost west of Khe Sanh on 30 November 1968 when a 37mm antiaircraft round hit a Kingbee, apparently detonating cases of Eldest Son mortar ammo. Missing were Maj. Samuel Toomey, Lt. Raymond Stacks, and S. Sgts. Klaus Scholz, Arthur Bader, Richard Fitts, Michael Mein, and Gary LaBohn.

But proof of Eldest Son's effectiveness rolled in. On 6 June 1968, U.S. 1st Infantry Division soldiers came upon a shattered AK-47 "found beside the body of an NVA soldier" who'd died while firing at the Americans. Paratroopers of the 101st Airborne Division found a dead NVA soldier grasping his exploded rifle. U.S. 25th Infantry Division soldiers discovered a whole North Vietnamese mortar battery destroyed, with dead gunners sprawled around four peeled-back tubes. The enemy actually concluded that the ammo was exploding due to manufacturing problems, not sabotage, and this created all sorts of logistical problems.

The Forger's Art

SOG forged many documents to confuse and manipulate the enemy. To help SOG accomplish these frauds, the CIA maintained special catalogs of North Vietnamese and Vietcong officials' signatures, letter formats, and bureaucratic jargon. Through its CIA connections, SOG was able to insinuate forgeries directly into the enemy's distribution channels.

In at least one case, the U.S. media reported the contents of false documents, unaware this was SOG's handiwork. In 1971 the South Vietnamese government gave U.S. reporters what it honestly thought were enemy documents claiming

that floods had so devastated the North that North Vietnamese Defense Minister Vo Nguyen Giap had ordered thousands of troops back home. SOG had planted this forgery to raise anxiety among NVA soldiers and encourage a "go home" movement. Although Hanoi hollered long and hard, the U.S. press never realized this was a SOG forgery.

SOG operated several forgery programs, the largest being "Poison Pen Letters," which incriminated North Vietnamese officials by inventing evidence of espionage and disloyalty. Drawn up in Saigon, poison pen letters were posted to North Vietnam from Hong Kong and countries as far away as Africa. Mere suspicion was enough to lock up almost anyone who was liable to confess and incriminate others after interrogation.

Similar forged letters, under the code name Soap Chips, were planted in Cambodia and Laos by U.S.-led recon teams. Planted by hand on NVA bodies or left beside heavily used trails, the letters were folded over and over as if they had been read and reread. One ingenious forgery was a "Happy Tet" card that SOG teams inserted by the dozen in Laos. Signed by Truong Chinh, a high

Below: Counterfeit enemy currency planted to falsely incriminate and confuse NVA counterintelligence.

Bottom: Counterfeit NVA chit planted in Laos to drain the enemy's tiny PX system. It did. (Photo provided by Mike Duggan)

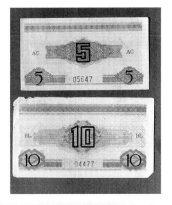

North Vietnamese official, and coming well before the Party Central Committee had announced Ho Chi Minh's successor, the cards seemed a usurper's attempt to wrest power for himself. Truong Chinh never did become premier.

SOG also wreaked havoc by counterfeiting North Vietnamese money, although U.S. policy limited its use to intelligence and psychological purposes rather than destroying Hanoi's economy. U.S. recon teams frequently inserted "Benson Silk," counterfeit NVA occupation money that drained the enemy's tiny PX system in Laos and Cambodia. Other counterfeit money was planted to confuse the enemy and make it appear that some NVA were traitors secretly working for the Americans.

Black Radio

SOG operated several "black radio" stations, such as its own version of Radio Hanoi that twisted Hanoi's policies and confused audiences, plus a number of clandestine stations claiming to be run by resistance groups in North Vietnam. These black radio broadcasts targeted North Vietnamese civilians and soldiers, not the officials who knew full well that the broadcasts were fraudulent.

To mimic North Vietnamese

radio stations, SOG used "surfing," which meant transmitting alongside a real station's frequency to capture listeners who mistakenly thought they'd tuned to the real one. Or there was "hitchhiking," which was to come up on the same frequency as a real station was signing off and using its call sign. To increase effectiveness, SOG acquired a U.S. Navy EC-121 aircraft to broadcast black radio programs from off the North Vietnam coast, confusing enemy RDF operations and overwhelming local station signals.

To make up for a shortage of radios in enemy hands, SOG even manufactured its own CIA-designed radios, code-named Peanuts. On the Peanuts radio dial the real Radio Hanoi would be lost in preplanned static, but right there, clear as a bell, was SOG's Radio Hanoi. Thousands of Peanuts radios were inserted by U.S. recon teams, air-dropped by Blackbirds, and floated ashore by Nasty boat crews.

Even though the results of black propaganda remain immeasurable, Hanoi verified their effectiveness at the Paris peace talks in May 1968: Hanoi's negotiators insisted on a precondition that the United States halt its black psyops programs, especially that despicable "Sons of the Sword Patriot League."

SOG's U.S. Navy EC-121 flew with a civilian paint scheme and broadcast black radio off North Vietnam's coast. (Photo provided by U.S. Navy)

SSPL MEMBERSHIP CARD

MẶT·TRẬN GƯƠM·THIÊNG ÁI QUỐC   Sớ 1109/CMT/NB
XỨ ỦY NAM·BỘ

CHỨNG MINH THƯ

XỨ ỦY MẶT·TRẬN GƯƠM·THIÊNG ÁI·QUỐC NAM·BỘ
Chứng nhận : Người mang giấy này là đồng chí
có bí số ...... , cấp bậc Cán bộ Quân sự nống cốt
của Xứ Ủy Nam Bộ có nhiệm vụ liên lạc, phát triển
và sinh hoạt với các Tổ Tỉnh trên toàn Xứ.
Yêu cầu các Bộ phận triệt để giúp dỡ đồng chí
mọi phương diện để hoàn thành nhiệm vụ.

.... tháng ...... năm 1971
TM. BCH. XỨ ỦY NAM·BỘ
UỶ VIÊN THƯỜNG VỤ

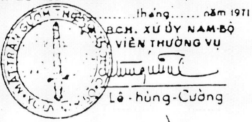

Lê·hùng·Cường

The SSPL Southern Committee   Nbr 1109/CMT/NB

IDENTITY CARD

The SSPL Southern Committee Certify: The bearer is a member
having the secret number .... grade hardcore military cadre of
the SSPL Southern Committee entrusted with the mission to take
relations, develop and coordinate activities with diverse secret cells
in the whole Southern region. The strict assistance on all aspects
from our agencies to him will be warmly welcomed.

Date 1971
FOR THE SSPL SOUTHERN
EXECUTIVE COMMITTEE
MEMBER FOR CURRENT AFFAIRS

As part of a deception program, SOG published Sons of the Sword Patriot League membership cards for planting on enemy bodies. (Photo provided by Richard Shultz)

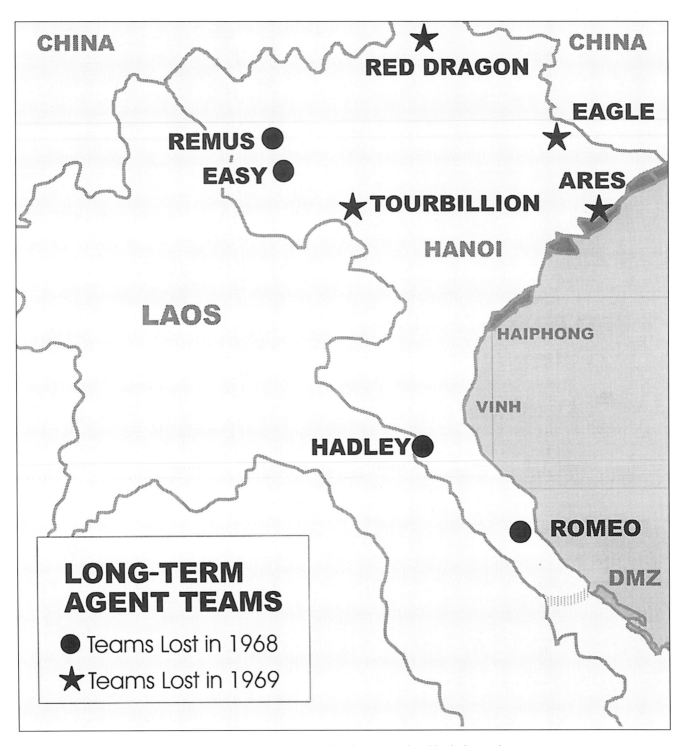

A 1968 review found that all eight teams were under enemy control, but four were "played back" for another year.

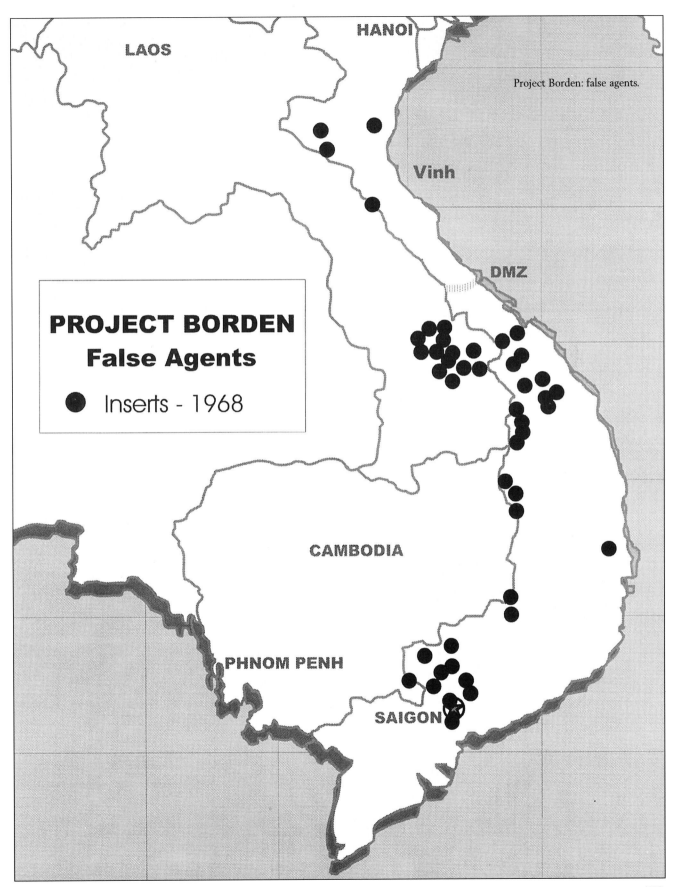

Project Borden: false agents.

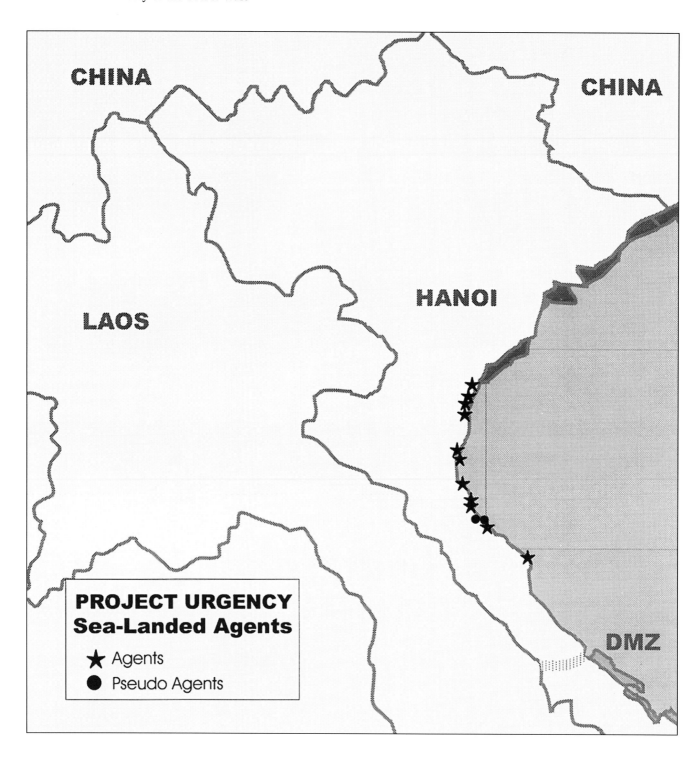

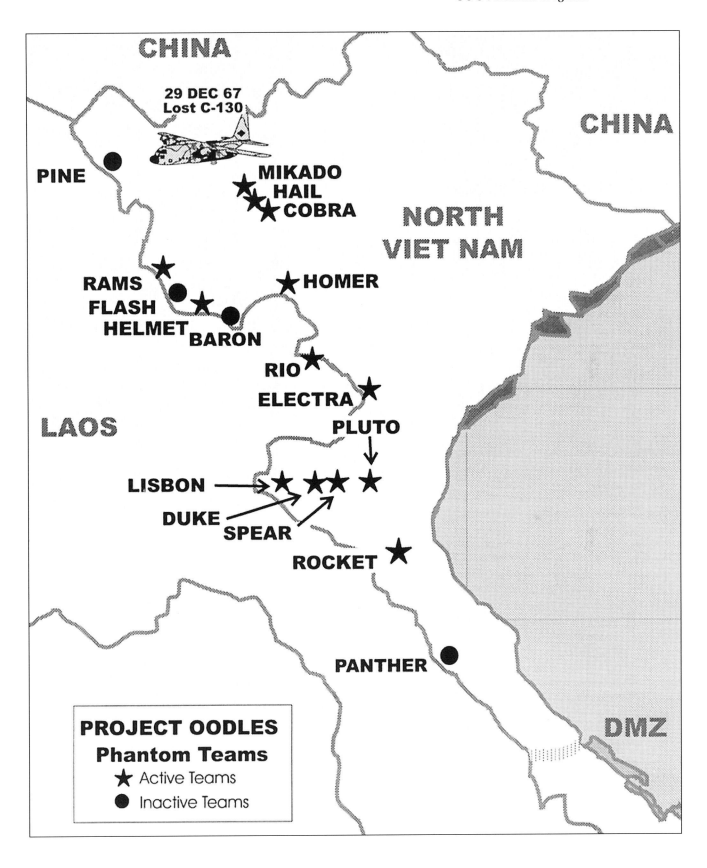

29 DEC 67
Lost C-130

CHINA

CHINA

PINE

MIKADO
HAIL
COBRA

NORTH
VIET NAM

RAMS
FLASH
HELMET
BARON

HOMER

RIO
ELECTRA

PLUTO

LAOS

LISBON

DUKE

SPEAR

ROCKET

PANTHER

DMZ

PROJECT OODLES
Phantom Teams
★ Active Teams
● Inactive Teams

Above: Paradise Island deception succeeded because kidnapped fishermen traveled so fast on Nasty boats that they thought they were still north of the DMZ. (Photo provided by Batservice Holding A/S)

Right: Artist's version of a Nasty boat inviting fishermen to come along. (Photo provided by W.T. "Red" Cannon)

LET US WIN YOUR HEARTS AND MINDS OR WE'LL BLOW YOUR ASS OUT OF THE WATER!

Top: SOG brochures explained how to use an air-dropped Peanuts radio. (Photo provided by Hammond Salley)

Bottom: Two versions of SOG's Peanuts radios. (Photo provided by John Plaster)

SAU KHI THÁO GIÁY KÉO CHUNG-QUANH HỘP XONG, BẠN HÃY MỞ
NẮP RA. BẠN SẼ THẤY CÓ MỘT MÁY RA-DÔ VÀ 2 CỤC PIN.

4

Top: This exploded AK rifle, which killed its shooter, was recovered by U.S. 1st Infantry Division soldiers. (Photo provided by Hammond Salley)

Bottom: This three-round case of Chinese 82mm mortar ammo was another form of Eldest Son sabotaged ordnance. (Photo provided by Gene McCarley)

Chúc mừng năm mới

Miền Bắc thi đua tăng năng suất với tinh thần mới.
Miền Nam thi đua diệt Mỹ dành nhiều thắng lợi mới.
Quyết phát huy cao độ ưu thế tất thắng của chiến lược
chiến tranh nhân dân với những nỗ lực mới.
Trường kỳ kháng chiến nhất định thắng lợi.

Trường-Chinh

be delayed because of improper identification. Where forms do not have a separate block, the SS number will be entered in the same block as the service number, officials say.

● *Enemy Has 2d Chance to Kill*

U.S. officials are again warning troops in Vietnam about the dangers of using captured enemy weapons. Numerous incidents have caused injury and sometimes death to the operators of enemy weapons, the Combined Materiel Exploitation Center in Vietnam says.

It reports "analyses of damaged enemy weapons have revealed that possible defective metallurgy in many cases leads to fatigue cracks in the firing surfaces which cause the weapons to explode." Faulty enemy ammo is also causing problems, so don't give Charlie a second chance to kill, CMEC says.

● *Flame Round Potential Improves*

OBVIOUSLY encouraged about the potential of factory-filled flame rounds, the Army has started tests of large caliber, rocket-launched flame rounds fired from a gun tube. "The range achieved was many hundreds of meters," the Army claims. As reported earlier, a new flame weapon, the XM-191 multi-short portable flame weapon systems, is being sent to Vietnam. The 27-pound weapon fires factory-

Top: Forged "Happy Tet" card designed to undermine the chances of Truong Chinh's becoming Hanoi's new premier. (Photo provided by Richard Shultz)

Left: Forged order from North Vietnamese high command signed by Defense Minister Vo Nguyen Giap authorized leaves for NVA soldiers to come home and help families during severe flooding in 1971. (Photo provided by Richard Shultz)

Above: This notice appeared in the *Army Times* tabloid, 1969, unwittingly disseminating a warning about Project Eldest Son. (Photo provided by Hammond Salley)

459

Top: S. Sgts. Richard Fitts (left), Gary La Bohn, and Arthur Bader, Jr., were aboard a Kingbee shot down over Laos 30 November 1968 while inserting Eldest Son ammo. Also lost were Maj. Samuel Toomey, Capt. Raymond Stacks, S. Sgt. Michael Mein, and S. Sgt. Klaus Scholz. (Photo provided by Bobby Evans)

Bottom: Some Eldest Son ammo was cleverly inserted into "Chinese sardine cans" and resealed by CIA with no signs of tampering. (Photo provided by John Plaster)

STRATA TEAMS

To produce intelligence from North Vietnam that was more reliable and responsive than Long-Term Agent Teams, SOG instituted the Short-Term Roadwatch and Target Acquisition (STRATA) team program in late 1967. The all-Vietnamese STRATA teams spent just a week or two per operation, too short a time for the enemy to capture and play the teams back. They operated as deep as 150 miles north of the DMZ.

STRATA operations focused upon the road network leading toward the Mu Ghia, Ban Karai, and Ban Raving Passes, which emptied into the Ho Chi Minh Trail. STRATA recruits received training similar to that of the long-term agents, then were based at Monkey Mountain in Danang. To confuse enemy analysts, the 14 STRATA teams were variously numbered Teams 90 through 122.

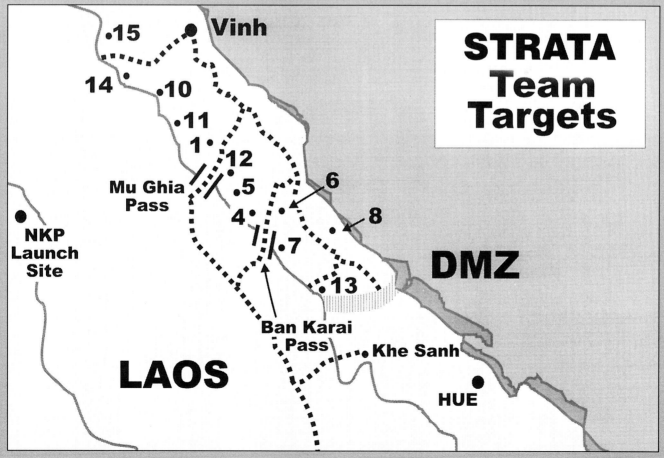

STRATA teams were launched from Nakhon Phanom Airbase in Thailand. After changing into NVA uniforms, the STRATA men climbed into 21st SOS "Pony" helicopters, then took a half-hour flight across the narrow 65-mile neck of Laos to reach North Vietnam. The program ended on 15 October 1968, when President Johnson extended his North Vietnam bombing halt all the way south to the DMZ.

From their first insertion until their final extraction 13 months later, STRATA teams penetrated North Vietnam 26 times. Even though hardly a returned man was wounded, STRATA lost 26 men MIA—including two entire teams—because bad weather often delayed even emergency extractions an average of five days and made any contact with the enemy lethal. Approximately one-quarter of STRATA's 102 troops were lost.

U.S. Air Force 21st Special Operations Squadron HH-3 inserts STRATA Team 93 deep inside North Vietnam at Target 4. (Photo provided by George Gaspard)

TREACHEROUS TRAITOR: AGENT FRANÇOIS

"Agent François" (in checkered shirt) was identified from this photo standing beside then Maj. George Gaspard, circa 1968. (Photo provided by George Gaspard)

MANY SOG AMERICANS, VIETNAMESE, MONTAGNARDS, AND NUNGS went to their deaths or captivity due to enemy moles who'd penetrated SOG headquarters in Saigon, the South Vietnamese Joint General Staff, and even the office of South Vietnam's president. During the war, several of these moles were unmasked and prosecuted, but for SOG men there was always a lingering doubt that the most important mole was still in position. It was a doubt based on some hard realities.

From the earliest CIA agent insertions in North Vietnam, teams often were apprehended upon landing—Hanoi's Ministry of Security *had* to have known they were coming. After the 1968 bombing halt, when SOG ceased sending teams into the North and enemy security concerns shifted to the Ho Chi Minh Trail, American-led recon teams also began encountering NVA troops that seemed to have been waiting for them. Two of the war's most critical Hatchet Force operations—the raid on the Trail headquarters in Laos and the raid on COSVN headquarters in Cambodia—immediately followed B-52 strikes, but the raids turned into *ambushes* in which many SOG men died. Twice, just before HALO jumps, the NSA intercepted NVA radio messages alerting enemy forces to the jumps—complete with grid coordinates! And how was it possible that SOG Bright Light rescues liberated nearly 500 South Vietnamese POWs, but not one single American? Bright Light teams often found that Americans had been there, but had been moved only hours before the raid. Why?

Late in the war, a low-ranking South Vietnamese enlisted man serving at SOG headquarters had failed a polygraph test, but he lacked enough access to have compromised so many key operations over so many years. Most SOG men believed there was a much deeper mole who held higher rank. They were right.

Long after the war, analyst Sedgewick Tourison reported to SOG Maj. George Gaspard that Vietnam's communist newspapers and TV had hailed a "hero" identified only as Agent François, who had helped the Ministry of Security thwart many U.S. spy operations. He was cited as a senior South Vietnamese officer working in SOG headquarters. Looking through Gaspard's extensive SOG photo collection, Tourison found the face that matched the shadowy Agent François he'd seen on TV in Hanoi—it was the major who'd run the Long-Term Agent program, then worked elsewhere at SOG headquarters. In fact, Gaspard recalled, the Vietnamese officer had told him he'd begun his intelligence career working with French intelligence—the Deuxième Bureau—in the French–Indochina War.

Perhaps today François is a hero in his land, but to the wartime friends and allies he betrayed—Americans and indigenous—he is the most despicable of traitors.

Afterword

SOG's greatest achievement was saving the lives of so many U.S. soldiers, marines, airmen, and sailors based in South Vietnam, who unknowingly benefited from the valuable intelligence that SOG RTs and Hatchet Forces brought back from the Laotian Ho Chi Minh Trail corridor and the Cambodian sanctuaries. From tracing the first roads that could not be seen from the air in 1965 to uncovering targets outside besieged Khe Sanh for B-52 bombers to pinpointing enemy base camps in Cambodia for the 1970 incursion to documenting the enormous NVA buildup before 1972's Easter offensive, SOG provided timely and often crucial intelligence.

Lives were saved, too, because SOG extracted a bloody toll from the enemy when RTs and Hatchet Forces either directly attacked enemy forces and supplies or called in U.S. air strikes to prevent the enemy assets from reaching the battlefields of South Vietnam. By such direct action, SOG forces killed thousands of NVA soldiers and destroyed thousands of tons of enemy supplies and munitions. And yet more lives were saved due to the sophisticated threat that SOG posed to enemy rear areas—the Hanoi high command was compelled to add layer after layer of defensive forces, eventually committing up to 60,000 troops as rear-area security—against which SOG rarely fielded more than 50 U.S. Special Forces soldiers at one time. Thus SOG's investment of less than a company-sized U.S. force tied down the equivalent of four-plus divisions in Laos and Cambodia, an economy of force unparalleled in U.S. history, perhaps without precedent in world military history. Had these additional NVA forces been in South Vietnam, the result could only have been significantly higher U.S. casualties.

THE COST

To achieve this, SOG's all-volunteer Special Forces elements suffered casualties not comparable with those of any other U.S. units of the Vietnam War. Particularly telling is the high percentage of SOG Green Berets missing in action—163 were killed in action, and an additional 80 were reported missing, a ratio magnitudes higher than that for other U.S. ground combat units. Equally telling is that not a single one of SOG's cross-border MIA Green Berets ever turned up as a POW. The lone Special Forces recon man to survive enemy imprisonment, S. Sgt. Carroll

Flora, captured in 1968, was allowed to live, many Special Forces men believe, because he'd been seized not in Laos or Cambodia, but inside South Vietnam's Ashau Valley. About 20 of SOG's cross-border MIAs' remains have been recovered, mostly near downed aircraft.

Beyond these KIAs and MIAs, SOG RT and Hatchet Force men incurred wound rates bordering on the universal, especially in 1968, 1969, and 1970. During Operation Tailwind, for example, virtually all Hatchet Force Americans were wounded, some of them more than once. In 1968, SOG combat personnel were awarded more Purple Hearts for wounds than there were slots in RTs and Hatchet Force units.

We cannot even estimate the substantial casualties among SOG's indigenous troops—the Montagnards, Nungs, Cambodians, and Vietnamese—because records simply do not exist. All the captured Long-Term Agent Team members were

SOLE RETURNEE. The only SOG recon man to return from captivity was Sfc. Carroll Flora (left, front), who was captured in South Vietnam's Ashau Valley in 1968. He is shown here at the release ceremony in 1973. (Photo provided by Larry Wright, U.S. Army)

SOG DISTINGUISHED SERVICE CROSS RECIPIENTS

Some 23 SOG recon and Hatchet Force men were awarded the Distinguished Service Cross (DSC), the nation's second highest award for U.S. Army personnel. Some had been considered for the Medal of Honor, and, perhaps, had the Awards Board fully understood where they were and the terrible odds before them, they would have received that pale blue ribbon. We cannot say. Nor can we even imagine the incredible acts of bravery performed by the recon men of those teams that vanished or fought to the last man—for example, RT Arizona was surrounded and its members called an airstrike on themselves, yet not one of its three missing Green Berets received any kind of valor award whatsoever. At least in the cases below, the United States of America conferred official recognition to some very brave, deserving men.

Date of Incident	SOG DSC Recipients
30 Dec. 1966	1st Lt. Frederick J. Caristo
21 Jan. 1967	Sfc. Morris G. Worley
21 Feb. 1967	Sfc. Domingo R. Borja (MIA)
30 Mar. 1967	Sfc. Gerald V. Grant
31 Mar. 1967	Sfc. Billy D. Evans
8 Nov. 1967	M. Sgt. Bruce R. Baxter (KIA)
4 Jan. 1968	Sfc. Paul H. Villarosa (KIA)
17 Jan. 1968	Sfc. Gilbert L. Hamilton (KIA 15 days later)
21 Jan. 1968	M. Sgt. Steven W. Comerford
22 Mar. 1968	Sfc. Linwood D. Martin (KIA)
27 Mar. 1968	S. Sgt. Johnny C. Calhoun (MIA)
20 May 1968	M. Sgt. Robert D. Plato (KIA)
31 Oct. 1968	Sgt. Timothy W. Clough
17 July 1969	Sgt. Michael D. Buchanan
17 July 1969	Sgt. James N. Pruitt
14 Aug. 1970	Sfc. Antonio J. Coehlo, Jr.
10 Sept. 1970	S. Sgt. Gary Michael Rose
29 Nov. 1970	Sgt. Edward C. Ziobrun
18 Feb. 1971	S. Sgt. Leslie A. Chapman
21 Apr. 1971	Sgt. Richard A. Hendrick
7 Aug. 1971	S. Sgt. Anthony C. Andersen
7 Aug. 1971	S. Sgt. William R. Queen
27 Sept. 1971	S. Sgt. Eldon A. Bargewell

Below: Ken Bowra in 1971. Bowra was One-Zero of RT Cobra, CCN, as a first lieutenant. (Photo provided by Ken Bowra)

believed to have been executed until the mid-1980s, when Hanoi surprised U.S. intelligence by releasing hundreds of former team members along with indigenous soldiers who'd been captured with U.S. RTs in Laos. Some of these prisoners had rotted for 20 years in the dankest prisons of Southeast Asia; after their plight became publicized on the CBS program *60 Minutes*, Congress authorized a lump-sum $50,000 pension to each. Unfortunately, no pension was authorized for the handful of SOG Montagnards who survived years in "reeducation" camps or those who survived a two-year overland escape to Thailand, during which 90 percent of their companions died.

A few other SOG indigenous veterans have made it to the United States, including several Kingbee pilots. Prominent among these courageous aviators is Maj. Nguyen Quy An, who lost both arms while rescuing SOG men from his burning H-34 in 1970. Twenty-six years later, in San Jose, California, Major An raised his right prosthetic device to take his oath of U.S. citizenship, an occasion he called "a great day," a sentiment shared by the SOG men who know him. An equally proud Vietnamese veteran is Kiet Van Nguyen, the Sea Commando who along with SEAL Medal of Honor recipient Tom Norris rescued the downed Bat-21 crewman, Lt. Col. Iceal Hambleton. In October 1998, the U.S. Navy welcomed Nguyen and Norris at the dedication of a new headquarters for Naval Special Warfare Group Two at Norfolk, Virginia. The new building commemorates their valorous deeds.

Nearly 1,000 Montagnards gathered at a picnic site in North Carolina to celebrate the Fourth of July, 1999, with many of their old Special Forces comrades. After an American-style barbecue and ceremonial sips of rice wine, each Montagnard veteran was given a Special Forces certificate of appreciation, signed and presented by Ft. Bragg's JFK Special Warfare Center commander, Maj. Gen. Ken Bowra, former One-Zero of RT Cobra. "I personally owe my life to my Bru team," Gen. Bowra said. "To me this was a most special day, a day to say thanks to our old friends and their families and to reflect on those who gave their lives for all of us, for Special Forces, for this great Army and our Nation." For most of the Montagnards, it was the first time their combat service had ever been recognized.

Ken Bowra in 1999. A two-star major general, Bowra now commands the JFK Special Warfare Center and School at Ft. Bragg, North Carolina. (Photo provided by U.S. Army)

REMEMBERING SOG'S FALLEN

Even though they've been little noticed, SOG's missing and killed Americans have also been recognized. The largest memorial by far is the USNS *Sisler*, a mammoth ship large enough to transport an entire armored brigade, launched in February 1998 and named for SOG's first posthumous Medal of Honor recipient, 1st Lt. George "Ken" Sisler.

The name of each SOG Green Beret killed or missing is displayed in the Court of Honor outside U.S. Army Special Operations Command Headquarters (USARSOC) at Ft. Bragg, North Carolina. The court is visible from the office of USARSOC's three-star commander, Lt. Gen. William Tangney—the one-time launch officer at CCS who inserted and extracted teams from Cambodia. Only 20 paces from the memorial wall is a larger-than-life statue of Dick Meadows, a larger-than-life SOG Green Beret. That statue will be joined on the 29th anniversary of the Son Tay raid by a larger-than-life statue of Col. Arthur "Bull" Simons, who commanded Meadows in SOG and on the raid.

"Bull" Simons is remembered also by the Ft. Bragg building a mile away that bears his name and houses the JFK Special Warfare Museum. Across the street from the Simons Building stands the JFK Center Headquarters, in which portraits of nine SOG Medal of Honor recipients line the halls, and here the commanding general is Maj. Gen. Ken Bowra. Only a block away is Zabitosky Road, named for the RT Maine One-Zero who earned SOG's second Medal of Honor, and not far away runs Kedenburg Street, named for posthumous Medal of Honor recipient John Kedenburg.

Nearby Son Tay Street honors the Son Tay raiders.

Another recon One-Zero who made general is Eldon Bargewell, the current commander of all U.S. Special Operations Forces in Europe. It was during Bargewell's tour as the Delta Force commander that SOG HALO team leader Cliff Newman made good on his promise to the dying Walt Shumate—to scatter his ashes during a HALO jump over the Delta compound.

At the Pentagon in Washington, a display of MIA names includes many SOG men. Not far from that display is the office of U.S. Air Force Gen. Ralph "Ed" Eberhart, a one-time first lieutenant Covey FAC who piloted his little O-2 Skymaster in support of SOG teams. Today a four-star general, he holds the number two position in the entire U.S. Air Force.

The names of SOG MIAs are not far from retired Col. Robert Rheault, either. The former commander of the 5th Special Forces Group, Rheault today directs the sailing school at Hurricane Island Outward Bound on the coast of Maine, where the students sail a skiff donated by the family and friends of SOG's final Laos MIA, David Mixter.

Visitors driving onto Hurlburt Field, Florida, on the Gulf Coast near Pensacola, will notice just to the right

Lt. Gen. William Tangney today heads the U.S. Army Special Operations Command. As a captain at CCS, he inserted and extracted RTs behind NVA lines in Cambodia. (Photo provided by U.S. Army)

Top: Sailing Scow 13 was donated to Hurricane Island Outward Bound School by the family and friends of SOG's final Laos MIA, David Mixter. Former 5th Special Forces Group commander Col. Bob Rheault currently directs the school. (Photo provided by Bob Rheault)

Bottom: SOG HALO team leader Cliff Newman (left) and Walter Shumate, who became the Delta Force founding sergeant major. After Shumate passed away in 1993, Newman skydived over the Delta Force compound to fulfill Shumate's last request: to have his ashes scattered there. (Photo provided by Cliff Newman)

of the main gate an impressive display of aircraft flown by the U.S. Air Force Air Commandos, including an A-1 Skyraider, O-2 Cessna Skymaster, HH-3 Jolly Green Giant, and AC-130 Spectre. Nestled among these impressive craft stand a half-dozen memorials to crewmen; the brick and bronze memorial closest to the gate recalls the lost men of Stray Goose Crew S-01, the SOG C-130 Blackbird that vanished over North Vietnam.

But SOG's ultimate memorial is not cut in stone or cast in bronze—it is the living flesh and blood of hundreds, perhaps thousands, of American Vietnam veterans, alive today to see their children and grandchildren because three decades ago men they never met, and a unit they never heard of, secretly fought in support of them.

1970: 1st Lt. Ralph "Ed" Eberhardt examines the wing damage on his O-2 Covey FAC plane. While flying for SOG Eberhardt was awarded a Distinguished Flying Cross and 13 Air Medals. (Photo provided by Mike Cryer)

Inset: Today, Eberhardt is a four-star general and the newly appointed commander of Combat Air Command, responsible for all U.S. Air Force fighter and bomber units. (Photo provided by U.S. Air Force)

Former CCN Hatchet Force company commander Chuck Pfeifer meets with former North Vietnamese Defense Minister Gen. Vo Nguyen Giap in Hanoi, 1995. During the Khe Sanh siege CCN teams hunted Giap in Laos, and a meeting then would not have been so cordial. (Photo provided by Chuck Pfiefer)

Above: SOG veterans were instrumental in the founding of Delta Force and the creation of U.S. Special Operations Command.

Top: Capt. Chuck Pfeifer belatedly receives the Silver Star for courageously repelling NVA commandos in the 1968 CCN sapper attack. Presented in 1999 at West Point by his 1965 classmate and current superintendent, Lt. Gen. Daniel Christman, the award was delayed 31 years because the paperwork had been misplaced. (Photo provided by USMA, West Point)

Bottom: 1999 HALO Reunion. SOG HALO veterans assemble for a jump in North Carolina. Back, left to right: Ben Dennis, John Trantanella, Montagnard Tak, Billy Waugh, Cliff Newman, Charles Wesley, Bob Castillo, Sammy Hernandez. Front, left to right: Mel Hill, J.D. Bath, Jesse Campbell. (Photo provided by Billy Waugh)

Inset: 1969, S. Sgt. Eldon Bargewell, RT Michigan One-Zero, with Montagnard teammates Contua and Lang. Twice wounded and awarded a Distinguished Service Cross, Bargewell served a phenomenal three years in recon. (Photo provided by Eldon Bargewell)

By 1999 Bargewell had spent more than a decade in Delta Force, which he commanded, and had gone on to receive a general's star and command of U.S. Special Operations in Europe. (Photo provided by U.S. Army)

Top: In 1969, Sp5c. Sam Helland (American in the rear, right) dyed his normally flaxen hair so he'd appear less distinctly a Caucasian, a slight edge for close-quarters gunfights with the NVA. His RT Wyoming teammates are (rear, left to right) One-Zero Ralph Rodd, One-One Al Lamp, One-Two Helland. (Middle Row) One-Three Joe Paris, Kip, Choy, Chow, and Phoi. (Sitting) Doc, Poi, and two unidentified Montagnards. The veteran SOG recon man left the Green Berets to attend college. Afterward, Helland was commissioned as a U.S. Marine Corps officer.

Bottom: By 1999, 30 years later, the old SOG Green Beret gunfighter was a U.S. Marine Corps brigadier general serving in the Kosovo campaign as the Albanian-based Deputy Commander of Joint Task Force Shining Hope, which housed and fed thousands of desperate Kosovo refugees. Brigadier General Helland (second from left) and a French two-star general (right), here with United Arab Emirate Officers at a refugee camp near Kukes, Albania, which held more than 10,000 Kosovo Albanians. It's a very small world: during the same Kosovo campaign, the overall commander of European-based Special Operations Forces was former recon One-Zero Eldon Bargewell, also now a brigadier general.

Above: Memorial to SOG's lost "Stray Goose" Blackbird crew, at Hurlburt Field, Florida, dedicated in July 1998. (Photo provided by John Plaster)

Top right: This rest stop on I-90 just north of Rockford, Illinois, memorializes two state natives who were MIA in SOG: 1st Lt. Jerry Pool and Sfc. Alan Boyer. (Photo provided by Steve Keever)

Bottom: The 10th Special Forces Group headquarters building at Ft. Carson, Colorado, Thorne Hall, named for SOG's first MIA, Capt. Larry Thorne. (Photo provided by John Plaster)

Top left: Ft. Bragg's Court of Honor, beside the U.S. Army Special Operations Command headquarters, memorializes all lost Green Berets, including SOG's MIAs and KIAs, each with a separate brass plate. (Photo provided by John Plaster)

Top right: This magnificent statue of legendary SOG Green Beret Dick Meadows was dedicated at the Court of Honor in June 1997. (Photo provided by John Plaster)

Left: Ft. Bragg's JFK Special Warfare Museum is housed in Simons Hall. It is named for Col. Arthur "Bull" Simons, who oversaw the Son Tay raid and commanded SOG RT and Hatchet Force operations. (Photo provided by John Plaster)

477

The launch of USNS *Sisler*, named for SOG's first Medal of Honor recipient, Lt. George "Ken" Sisler. The February 1998 San Diego ceremony was attended by his widow, sons, teammates, and SOG veterans. (Photo provided by John Plaster)

FULL RED LAUNCH

Street names at Ft. Bragg memorialize SOG Medal of Honor recipients John Kedenburg and Fred Zabitosky and the Son Tay raiders. (Photos provided by John Plaster)

Top: Flag and flowers left at "The Wall" in Washington before the inscribed name of MIA David Davidson (upper right). (Photo provided by the Davidson family)

Middle: NOT FORGOTTEN. RT Florida One-Zero Ken Worthley, killed in August 1969, is memorialized as the namesake of Ken Worthley Chapter, Special Forces Association, gathered here with his family at his gravesite in Sherburne, Minnesota. (Photo provided by Jeff Arnold)

Bottom: Special Forces Association Chapter XX holds a graveside memorial service for KIA SOG Lt. Greg Harrigan while his family and friends watch on Memorial Day 1994. Young Harrigan was killed in the April 1969 COSVN raid in which "Mad Dog" Shriver became MIA. (Photo provided by John Murphy)

Glossary

A-1 Skyraider: Korean War-vintage, propeller-driven fighter-bomber, a SOG favorite because of its heavy payload, long loiter time, and precision ordnance delivery.

Arc Light: Code name for a B-52 strike. Arc Lights were planned in multiples of cells of three planes each.

ARVN (Army of the Republic of Vietnam): South Vietnamese Army.

BDA (bomb damage assessment): Post-strike ground reconnaissance of a B-52 target, conducted by SOG recon teams.

binh tram: Literally, a "commo-liaison site." North Vietnamese complexes along the Ho Chi Minh Trail, with autonomous engineer, transport, antiaircraft, supply, and security units.

black propaganda: Purposeful lies and deceptions intended to confuse the enemy or cast him in the worst possible light.

Blackbirds: Unofficial term for the black U.S. Air Force C-130s in SOG's 90th Special Operations Squadron.

Bra: Especially dangerous NVA base area in southern Laos, called The Bra because Highway 96 crossed a double-curved river there.

Bright Light: SOG code name for POW and evadee rescue attempts behind enemy lines.

C&C (Command and Control): Danang field headquarters for SOG's U.S.-led cross-border operations. Also a generic term for these operations.

CAR-15: Submachine gun version of M16 rifle, with folding stock and shortened barrel. A SOG recon man's favorite weapon.

CCC (Command and Control Central): SOG base at Kontum, South Vietnam, for U.S.-led SOG missions into northern Cambodia and southern Laos. Also called FOB-2.

CCN (Command and Control North): SOG base at Danang near Marble Mountain, with outlying FOBs at Khe Sanh, Phu Bai, Kham Duc, and Kontum. CCN men operated mostly in Laos and the DMZ.

CCS (Command and Control South): SOG base at Ban Me Thuot, for U.S.-led missions into central Cambodia.

Chief SOG: Official title for the SOG commander.

CISO (Counterinsurgency Support Office): Okinawa-based office that handled covert logistic duties after the CIA transferred its covert programs to SOG.

COSVN (Central Office for South Vietnam): Field headquarters for the Vietcong's political wing, the National Liberation Front (NLF), located 2 miles inside Cambodia, northwest of Saigon.

Covey: Call sign for U.S. Air Force Forward Air Control (FAC) units at Danang and Pleiku that directly supported SOG cross-border missions.

Covey Rider: Long-time Special Forces recon man who flew with U.S. Air Force FACs to help direct air strikes, insert and extract SOG teams, and monitor the Ho Chi Minh Trail corridor.

DMZ (demilitarized zone): A 14-mile-strip straddling the 17th Parallel in which neither North nor South Vietnam was to place military forces.

DSC (Distinguished Service Cross): U.S. Army award immediately lower in precedence to the Medal of Honor, equivalent to the Navy Cross and Air Force Cross.

FAC (forward air controller): U.S. Air Force pilot flying a small airplane such as the Cessna O-1 Bird Dog and tasked to find and mark bombing targets and to control air strikes.

5th Special Forces Group: Official headquarters for all Green Berets in South Vietnam, although SOG's Green Berets actually took their orders from Saigon and the Pentagon.

1st Flight Detachment: Ostensibly a U.S. Air Force unit, the First Flight's SOG C-123 transports often were flown by Chinese Nationalist pilots so, if they were downed over North Vietnam and captured, U.S. involvement could be plausibly denied.

1st Special Forces Group: The Okinawa-based 1st Group provided support and personnel to SOG; the 1st Shining Brass recon men were 1st Group volunteers.

Fishhook: Major NVA base area in southeast Cambodia that typically housed two or three enemy divisions. One of SOG's most dangerous cross-border targets.

FLIR (forward-looking infrared): Top-secret night-viewing devices.

FOB (forward operating base): Permanent SOG camp where Special Forces and mercenary troops were housed and trained.

Fulton Recovery System: A clandestine extraction system using a gas-filled balloon to suspend a cable, which the yoke installed on a C-130 Blackbird's nose could snare, snatching a man from the ground and then winching him inside. Nicknamed "Skyhook."

Green Hornets: Code name for a U.S. Air Force Huey unit, the 20th Special Operations Squadron, which flew SOG missions in Cambodia.

HALO (High Altitude, Low Opening): Military skydiving.

Hatchet Force: Code name for SOG platoons and companies.

Ho Chi Minh Trail: A camouflaged highway network in the jungled southeastern Laos corridor occupied by the NVA after 1959, across which flowed supplies and soldiers for the war in South Vietnam.

immediate action drill (IA drill): A series of planned, practiced actions a recon team executed to break contact with numerically superior enemy forces.

JACK (Joint Advisory Commission, Korea): The CIA-affiliated Korean War unit that conducted covert special operations.

Jolly Green Giant: Originally the Sikorsky HH-3 helicopter. When the larger but similar-looking HH-53 was introduced, it was dubbed the Super Jolly Green Giant.

Kingbee: Code name for South Vietnamese Air Force (VNAF) H-34 helicopters that supported SOG cross-border operations.

Leghorn: SOG radio relay and NSA signal intercept site atop a pinnacle in southern Laos.

Long-Term Agent Teams: CIA- and SOG-recruited North Vietnamese refugees, trained then infiltrated back into the North, for long-term intelligence missions.

McGuire rig: A large swing seat attached to a rope, lowered from a helicopter hovering above the treetops, for emergency extraction of SOG recon men. Also called "strings." See STABO rig

Montagnards: South Vietnamese hill tribesmen related ethnically to Polynesians. Heavily recruited as mercenaries for SOG and other Special Forces units. Called 'Yards by Americans.

Nasty-class PTF: CIA-acquired, Norwegian-built gunboats SOG used for hit-and-run raids against North Vietnam's coastline.

Nightingale device: A CIA-developed diversionary device whose continuing explosions sounded like a firefight.

NKP (Nakhon Phanom Royal Thai Air Force Base): SOG launch site for operations into Laos and North Vietnam, beginning in 1967.

NSA (National Security Agency): U.S. organization responsible for intercepting enemy signals and code breaking.

Nungs: South Vietnamese tribesmen of Chinese origin, renowned for their fighting qualities. Employed as mercenaries by SOG.

NVA: North Vietnamese Army.

One-One: Code name for a U.S. Special Forces SOG recon team assistant team leader.

One-Two: Code name for a U.S. Special Forces SOG recon team radio operator.

One-Zero: Code name for a U.S. Special Forces SOG recon team leader.

OSS (Office of Strategic Services): America's World War II precursor to the CIA responsible for espionage, sabotage, and covert operations. The OSS was the model for SOG.

Outpost Hickory: SOG radio relay and NSA signal intercept site, located on a precipice northeast of abandoned Khe Sanh base.

Parrot's Beak: A Cambodian salient just northwest of Saigon, across which the NVA sometimes infiltrated units, especially during the 1968 Tet Offensive.

Prairie Fire: SOG code name for Laotian operations area. Replaced Shining Brass in 1967.

Project Delta: Special Forces recon unit that operated inside South Vietnam, assigned to 5th Special Forces Group.

Project Eldest Son: A SOG black propaganda project that inserted booby-trapped Chinese ammunition into NVA stockpiles.

PTF (Patrol Type, Fast): See Nasty-class PTF.

RT (recon team): A SOG recon team typically consisted of three U.S. Special Forces men and nine Nungs or Montagnards. To minimize detection, however, most One-Zeros took only six or eight men on each operation.

Sons of the Sword of the Patriot League: False North Vietnamese resistance organization created by SOG to divert and confuse enemy counterintelligence.

SACSA (Special Assistant for Counterinsurgency and Special Activities): Pentagon element in the Office of the Joint Chiefs that oversaw and coordinated SOG activities with the White House, State Department, and CIA.

Sea Commandos: South Vietnamese counterparts to U.S. Navy SEALs.

Shining Brass: SOG code name for Laotian operations area. See Prairie Fire.

Sihanoukville: Cambodia's major seaport, through which entire shiploads of military supplies were smuggled for the NVA.

Skyhook: See Fulton Recovery System.

SOE (Special Operations Executive): Clandestine British World War II unit that conducted sabotage, espionage, and special operations in Occupied Europe.

SOG (Studies and Observations Group): The Vietnam War's covert special warfare unit, essentially the OSS of Southeast Asia.

Spectre: Heavily armed gunship version of U.S. Air Force C-130 transport plane.

STABO rig: An emergency extraction rig using special web gear that converts to a harness for attaching to a rope lowered through the treetops from a hovering helicopter. Also called "strings."

sterile: Unmarked or untraceable, usually referring to weapons or aircraft employed in covert operations.

STRATA (Short-Term Roadwatch and Target Acquisition Teams): Vietnamese-led recon teams that SOG inserted in the panhandle of North Vietnam to monitor supply routes, usually for 10 to 20 days per mission. No U.S. personnel accompanied these teams.

strings: SOG slang for McGuire and STABO rigs.

Trinh Sat: North Vietnam's secret intelligence service.

VC (Vietcong): Military units of indigenous South Vietnamese Communists. Almost ceased to exist after the 1968 Tet offensive.

Vietminh: Communist military forces in the French-Indochina War, 1946-54.

'Yard: American slang for Montagnard tribesman.

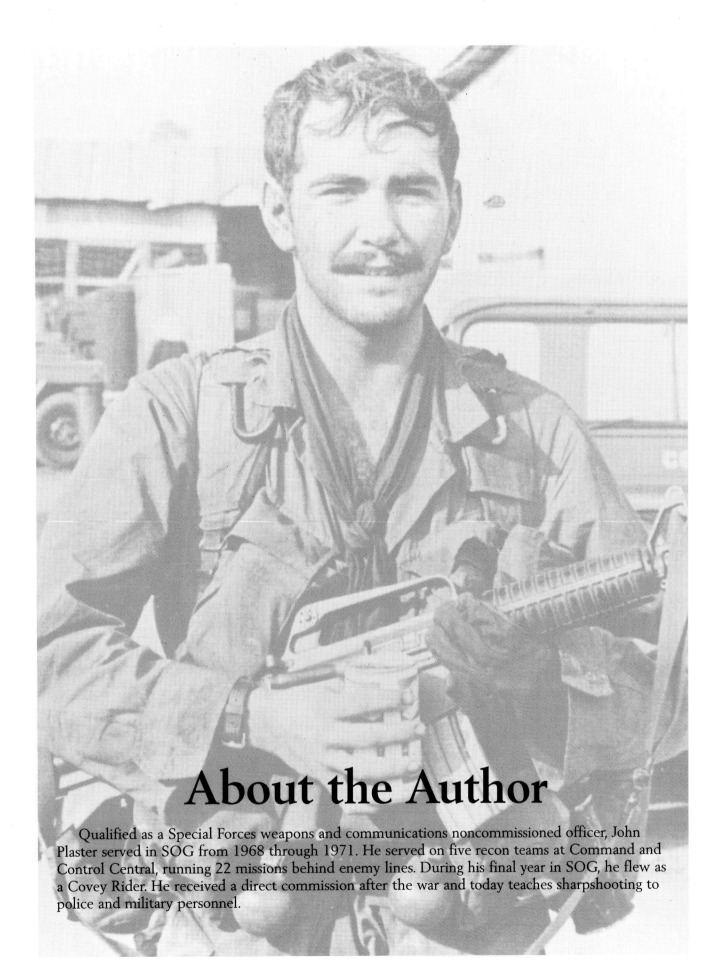

About the Author

Qualified as a Special Forces weapons and communications noncommissioned officer, John Plaster served in SOG from 1968 through 1971. He served on five recon teams at Command and Control Central, running 22 missions behind enemy lines. During his final year in SOG, he flew as a Covey Rider. He received a direct commission after the war and today teaches sharpshooting to police and military personnel.